THE KEY ISSUES LECTURE SERIES
is made possible through a grant from
International Telephone and Telegraph Corporation

This series of lectures and dialogues
took place on successive days
in Los Angeles and San Francisco, California

Accounting for Multinational Enterprises

Edited by

Dhia D. AlHashim   James W. Robertson
California State University, Northridge

With a foreword by
Harold S. Geneen

Bobbs-Merrill Educational Publishing
Indianapolis

The Bobbs-Merrill Company, Inc.
4300 West 62nd Street
Indianapolis, Indiana 46268

First Edition
First Printing 1978
Library of Congress Cataloging in Publication Data
Main entry under title:

Accounting for multinational enterprises.

(The Key issues lecture series)
"This series of lectures and dialogues took place on successive days in Los
Angeles and San Francisco."
1. International business enterprises—Accounting—Addresses, essays,
lectures. I. AlHashim, Dhia D. II. Robertson, James W., 1933-
HE5657.A259   657'.95   77-13732

Contents

Preface

James W. Robertson

Dean, School of Business Administration and Economics
California State University, Northridge

In the recent history of the accounting profession, the practitioner and the academician have often found themselves working in parallel channels.

However, with the increasing pressure from government agencies, watchdog consumer groups, and general public speculation on business ethics, these two "houses" of accounting need to freely exchange views on a key area—the varied and demanding accounting practices surrounding the multinational enterprise.

Through the Key Issues Lecture Series, the independent strengths of the academicians and the practitioners emerged through formal presentation in Los Angeles and in San Francisco. Speakers included respected academicians from the nation's top universities, professionals from leading international accounting firms, and ranking members of pertinent government agencies.

The end result provided participants and audience alike with a greater understanding of the complexities and challenges facing the accounting profession in its relationship with multinational corporations.

This series of presentations brought several unique elements to the Key Issues Lecture Series, which is funded through the generosity of the International Telephone and Telegraph Company. For the first time:

1. A specific, technical area, i.e., accounting, was highlighted rather than the broader issues previously presented.
2. Professional certification was granted to the CPAs in attendance since the lectures satisfied Rule 87 of the California State Board of Accountancy which requires that a practicing Certified Public Accountant or Public Accountant obtain 80 hours of acceptable continuing education in each two-year period beginning January 1, 1975, in order to obtain renewal of his or her certificate.
3. Due to the quality and wide appeal of the program, among accounting and financial professions throughout the state, each session was presented twice—on Wednesdays in Los Angeles and on Thursdays in San Francisco. This back-to-back format enabled more than 1,500 persons to benefit from the series.

A special word of thanks must be made to Dr. Dhia AlHashim, professor of accounting at Northridge, who was personally responsible for contacting and involving the excellent speakers for the program. In addition, his paper was presented in the Keynote session and he has coedited these proceedings. Appropriate recognition must be given to the directors and the staffs of the Bureau of Business Research and Services and of the Word Processing Center for the School of Business Administration and Economics, particularly Professor Robert Kiddoo, Mrs. Sonja Marchand, and Mrs. Pat Sullivan.

Let me also express my appreciation to the international accounting firms represented in the series, especially to the national, Los Angeles and San Francisco offices without whose support the program would not have been possible.

Finally, I wish to thank ITT again for their sponsorship. My personal involvement in this project has been most rewarding. It has also been extensive enough to be held accountable for whatever weakness may be present.

Foreword

Harold S. Geneen

Chairman and Chief Executive
International Telephone and Telegraph Corporation

International corporations face a multitude of problems arising from the complexity of their operations, differences in accounting practices, and the growing volume of regulations and reports required by international bodies.

It is obvious that the business environment in foreign countries requires a more adaptive treatment than is necessary in any single national area. A strict adherence to U. S. historical accounting rules would hardly be acceptable and would certainly be less useful to the Brazilians than would a reasonable approach to the recognition of protracted inflation. The requirements of France's uniform accounting plan are different from the demands placed upon companies practicing in the accounting environment of the United Kingdom.

It is inevitable that different business mores will bring forth varying patterns of accounting emphasis. Although unsecured short-term business credit is extensively used in the mature Western economies, such a financing approach is less emphasized in South America and certain parts of Asia. In those economies credit is much more formally stipulated and business operations can be seriously curtailed if such formal documentation is not forthcoming from the purchaser.

Obviously, the managers of foreign profit centers would be considered negligent if they failed to abide by their current laws, or if they failed to take advantage, where appropriate, of situations that are permissible and advantageous in their environment. Of course, the regulatory environment must be considered as distinct in each operating nation. Such regulation concerns employment practices, pricing policies, and tax computations. In total these regulations constitute a massive pattern of legal constraint and require constant attention to reconciling the allowable circumstances in the domestic and in the foreign communities.

Business transactions are usually conducted in the national currencies at the points of operation. These currencies must eventually be converted or "translated" into the terms of the single currency representing the consolidated reporting entity. The currency translation process produces many anomalies which are difficult to comprehend without a specific exposure to the detailed calculations. When these foreign currency problems are superimposed upon the normal difficulties of an inflationary economic world, the economic meaning of the data contained in annual reports loses a degree of credibility.

I believe that the solutions to accounting and monetary complexities and the resolution of the other legal problems of international life are going to be among the most difficult tasks facing the multinational enterprise during the 1980s. Both Dean James Robertson and Dr. Dhia AlHashim are to be commended for organizing this unique series.

We are all indebted to the fourteen distinguished speakers who took turns at the rostrum on successive days in Los Angeles and San Francisco.

ONE

International Dimensions of Accounting

An analysis of the challenges facing the international accounting community in its response to the growing complexities and volume of accounting reports crossing national borders.

Dhia D. AlHashim

*Associate Professor
and Program Coordinator
California State University,
Northridge*

Robert I. Jones

*Co-Chairman
Arthur Andersen & Co.*

Dr. AlHashim holds a B.B.A. degree from University of Baghdad, an M.B.A. degree from University of California at Los Angeles, and a Ph.D. degree from University of Missouri at Columbia. He has authored numerous papers, articles, and books on national and international accounting.

Mr. Jones holds a B.S. degree from Northwestern University. He is responsible for operations in the western United States, Canada, the Pacific Basin, the Middle East, Asia, and Scandinavia. He represents his firm in internationally oriented councils and associations.

International Dimensions of Accounting

Dhia D. AlHashim

Professor of Accounting
Director of Center for International Accounting Studies
California State University, Northridge

Over the last decade and a half, the serious attention always paid to international problems of accounting has increased steadily. This attention has come from the professional accounting, business, and finance communities as a matter of real-world necessity. During this period, the investment of United States companies abroad more than doubled and total sales abroad more than tripled. As a result of this growth, American investors are faced with the problem of understanding foreign financial statements.

Accounting reports prepared on the bases of different national accounting standards and kept in many different national currencies need to be adjusted, translated, and consolidated. These reports must be prepared to satisfy the needs of the owners, the needs of the regulators of various governments, and the needs of international agencies. The flow of accounting reports across national borders generates the imperative need for an international dimension in accounting.

Michael N. Chetkovich, managing partner of Haskins & Sells and chairman of American Institute of Certified Public Accounts (AICPA) states: "Accounting is the language of business and if it is to serve the needs of interna-

3

tional business enterprises it must become an international language through more uniform standards of accounting and reporting."[1]

The purposes of this paper are to bring into focus the variety of accounting practices throughout the world and to emphasize the need for an international dimension in accounting.

DIFFERENCES IN ACCOUNTING PRACTICES

It has been suggested by many scholars that in order to create an international comparability of accounting reports, a worldwide harmonization of accounting standards must exist. To answer this need, three models for accounting standardization are identified and discussed in the literature: (1) *the absolute uniformity model,* which describes a situation in which there is one set of accounting methods and reports regardless of differences in circumstances or user needs; (2) *the circumstantial uniformity model,* which describes a situation in which different accounting methods and standards can be used for different economic facts under different circumstances; and (3) *the purposive uniformity model,* which considers the uses of accounting information as determinants of appropriate accounting methods and standards.[2] While the first model has the appeal of administrative ease, the model has not fallen upon fertile soil in free-enterprise societies, probably because it is too radical and too inflexible. The second model has been discussed quite extensively in the literature, whereas the third model has not. For example, in 1965 in advice given to the AICPA, its Special Committee on Opinions of the Accounting Principles Board reported the following: "The Board should move toward the reduction of alternative practices in accounting by adopting policies under which it will: (a) Recognize the objective that variations in treatment of accounting items generally should be confined to those justified by substantial differences in factual circumstances."[3]

In making its report to the AICPA, this committee furthermore furnished an example of "substantial differences in factual circumstances": "The field of medicine provides an analogy. The doctor may encounter the same disease in patients, but a variation in treatment is applied where the attending circumstances are different. So also in accounting the circumstances surrounding the application of a given principle may be substantially different. That is what justifies and even necessitates variations."[4] This position seems to be congruent with Securities and Exchange Commission Accounting Series Release

No. 177, "Notice of Adoption of Amendments to Form 10-Q and Regulation S-X Regarding Interim Financial Reporting."[5]

The main difference between the circumstantial and the purposive uniformity models is the fact that the former is flexible with respect to different circumstances, whereas the latter is flexible with respect to both different circumstances and different purposes. Under the purposive uniformity model, different purposes (needs) demand the use of different accounting standards, and different circumstances (sets of facts) demand the use of different accounting procedures, each of which accurately reflects the application of an accounting standard under a specified set of facts. The circumstantial uniformity model, on the other hand, suggests that once different sets of circumstances have been identified—as islands of truth—that appropriate accounting methods and standards would follow *ipso facto* from those circumstances.

Attempts are presently being made to explicate the circumstantial uniformity model[6] but without great success because of the subjectivity needed to define what amounts to artificial sets of factual circumstances. The purposive uniformity model, by contrast, is descriptive of regulatory practice in the United States and underlies accounting in most socialist countries; hence, experience in developing and operating this model is immediately at hand.

It is clear from the above that in talking about harmonization of accounting standards, a person needs to specify the model he is following in order to communicate better with others.

For example, Gerhard G. Mueller considers the environmental forces influencing accounting postulates and standards as the most formidable barriers to international harmonization of accounting standards. According to Mueller, there are four factors which separate one business environment from another.[7] These factors are as follows: (1) states of economic development, (2) stages of business complexity, (3) shades of political persuasion, and (4) reliance on some particular system of law.

This writer agrees with Mueller's position, assuming that Mueller is thinking in terms of *absolute uniformity*. In this paper the author takes the position that differences in the environmental forces demand the use of different accounting systems. Differences in the cultural, social, political, legal, and economic conditions are the determining factors in the selection of accounting postulates and standards as shown in Fig. 1.1. The use of different accounting systems in this case leads to international comparability of accounting information.

Accounting postulates derived from the free-enterprise environment are necessarily different from those derived from other environments, e.g., a centrally controlled economy. Using the deductive approach, accounting standards developed from the first set of postulates should differ from those derived from other sets of postulates. This seems to support the assertion that different accounting standards are derived from different sets of postulates for different cultural, social, legal, political, and economic systems.

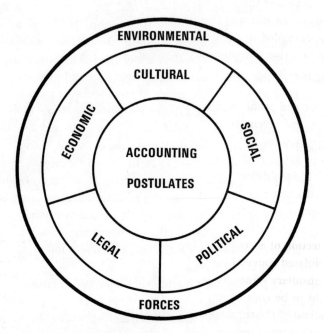

FIG. 1.1 THE ENVIRONMENTAL FORCES INFLUENCING ACCOUNTING POSTULATES

The concept of profit accepted in the U.S. is measured by the excess of revenue over expenses; expenses are measured in terms of historical cost. In Holland, by contrast, expenses are measured in terms of replacement costs. The Dutch emphasis on replacement rather than historical cost is based on the thinking that accounting must make sense first of all from the viewpoint of business economics; from the economic standpoint, profit is measured as the maximum that could be consumed while still leaving the entity as "well off" at the end of the period as it was at the beginning. One way to ensure the integrity of the capital is to match replacement costs against revenues. The premise here seems to be that the real cost of what comes out at the delivery end of a pipeline is the cost of what has to go in at the other end to keep up the supply. Philips N. V. is one of the major Dutch corporations which has been applying the replacement-value concept for almost two decades. The former Chief Internal Auditor of Philips, A. Goudeket, stated that at Philips:

> The application of the replacement value theory is not merely a calculation technique used in preparing the annual statements of the concern. It is integrated in the accounting system of all sections of the concern at every stage. In this way it is ensured that all information for management is compiled in accordance with this principle, and thus the replacement value automatically enters into all management considerations and decisions.[8]

Valuation and profit calculation at Philips are based on replacement value. Fixed assets and inventories are revalued annually on the basis of the changes in the specific price levels. The differences between the replacement values and the original costs of all nonmonetary assets are credited to a "Revaluation Account." If, in addition, monetary assets exceed monetary liabilities, the loss in the purchasing power of the invested capital related to the difference is charged against the revenue of the period.

As mentioned earlier, environmental forces have a great deal of influence on the selection of accounting standards. This would suggest that in preparing consolidated statements of a U.S. parent company and its Dutch subsidiary, the subsidiary's financial statements prepared on the basis of replacement costs ought to be considered. Users of financial statements are interested in the operations of the subsidiary in the foreign environment, and, as such, it is important that the translated statements reflect the differences in the environment which may demand the use of different accounting standards. In translating the Dutch financial statements from the foreign currency to that of the parent company, the current exchange rate should be employed. In other words, rather than translate "as if" the foreign-based operations had been conducted in the parent company's environment, the translation process should be directed toward recognizing operations actually conducted in the foreign environment. To present the foreign-based operations fairly, it is imperative that translation attempt to preserve the relationships in the foreign statements (i.e., financial ratios). This can be done through the use of the current exchange rate method.

Another area in which accounting responses vary a great deal is in the treatment for inflation. Accounting responses to inflation have traditionally varied with the severity of the inflation. In the U.S., there has been no formal accounting recognition given to the decline in value of the dollar. Recently, however, the Financial Accounting Standards Board issued an exposure draft related to price-level accounting.[9] In Brazil, where a degree of inflation substantial enough to invalidate historical costs of assets has been experienced, a series of governmental indexes for adjustment of assets value have been adopted. The Brazilian tax law accepted the principle of accounting for inflation in 1964. The following is an excerpt from the Brazilian government's policy statement on inflation. "The recognition of the importance of the retention and use of capital in the development of Brazil: This principle recognizes, in order to retain capital, its purchasing power must remain intact despite the fact that the country would continue to have heavy rates of inflation in years to come.[10]

The Brazilian government allows the following—

1. Restatement of value of fixed assets, with a credit to a capital account: Depreciation is based on the new value;
2. Recognition of loss in purchasing power on all assets and liabilities other than fixed assets: The loss is charged to income;
3. Savings deposits adjusted quarterly to reflect the decline in the purchasing power: For example, if one assumes a 5% interest rate on a saving deposit of Cr$1,000, and a 35% inflation rate for the period, the saving is increased from Cr$1,000 to Cr$1,350 at the end of the period, and the 5% interest is calculated on the adjusted amount. In order to encourage savings, special tax exemptions are granted for the additional interest earned due to inflationary adjustment.

In preparing consolidated financial statements, it would seem wise for a U.S. parent company to consider the price-level adjusted financial statements of its Brazilian subsidiary given the high rate of inflation in Brazil. This position would be justified on the assumption that the Brazilian statements reflect an important environmental factor, that is, the high rate of inflation in Brazil. In the interest of fair presentation of the operations, therefore, consolidated statements should include price-level adjusted statements of the subsidiary, translated at the current exchange rate.

It can clearly be seen from the foregoing discussion that consolidated statements would be more informative if they were prepared by deliberately making the translation biased toward showing the financial relationships as they stand in the foreign countries. This direction is markedly different from the FASB position of presenting foreign operations "as if" they were conducted in the home country.[11]

The application of price-level accounting can also be seen in other countries, such as Argentina. On July 1, 1975, the accounting profession in Argentina adopted price-level adjusted financial statements. This step was an inevitable response to an inflation rate in Argentina approaching 300%.

The United Kingdom, on the other hand, responded to inflation in a different manner. The government-appointed Inflation Accounting Committee (Sandilands Committee) in its September 1975 report rejected price-level accounting in favor of replacement-cost accounting as the only long-term solution to inflation accounting. The accounting and industrial bodies in the United Kingdom and Ireland have supported the recommendations of this committee with some reservations. The accounting profession has recommended that, in addition to considering replacement costs, the effect of inflation on monetary items should be shown on financial statements. Rules to implement the recommendations of the Sandilands Report are to be developed by the accounting profession following a request by the government and are anticipated to go into effect for the year ending subsequent to December 23, 1978.

In other countries of the world, accounting is thought of as an instrument of national economic policy. For example, in Sweden it is considered good accounting practice to provide for investment fund reserves (up to 40% of profit before tax) in profitable years and then to use these funds in periods when the economy is under stress. Thus, corporations can avoid up to 40% of their annual tax bill through the establishment of these funds. To benefit from these anticyclical investment funds, companies have to deposit 46% of the allocation to the funds in noninterest-bearing accounts in the central bank (Sveriges Riksbank), i.e., about what is actually saved in tax. These funds cannot be used by corporations without the approval of the Labour Market Board. Based on the need of the economy, this Board then decides when and for what purposes these funds can be used. However, after five years of its deposit in the central bank, a company can withdraw 30% of the amount on deposit without the prior approval of the Board. Upon the release of the funds, corporations can take additional tax deductions equal to 10% of the funds released. However, a corporation cannot claim depreciation expense on the asset purchased out of these funds, resulting in an increase in its future taxes.

Accounting practices in socialist countries differ from those in free-enterprise countries, due primarily to the difference in the political, social, cultural, legal, and economic factors. The Egyptian government, for example, acquired control of approximately 80% of the country's economic resources through the nationalization decrees of 1961. The government has taken steps since

Table 1.1
ALNASER COMPANY
CURRENT OPERATIONS ACCOUNT
(For the Year Ended June 30, 1971)

1969-70 Egyptian Pounds	Uniform Account No.	Egyptian Pounds	Egyptian Pounds	
				Value of Production & Services
				Production at selling price:
7,021,300	411	8,518,483		Net sales of finished goods ..
(197,271)	412	382,506		Cost of the difference between beginning and ending finished goods ....
(155,420)	413	(486,329)	8,414,660	Changes in value of the difference between beginning and ending finished goods ....
6,668,609				
16,711	414	(17,386)		Cost of the difference between beginning and ending work in process........
230	416	—		Revenues from others.........
28,757	417	26,364	8,978	Services sold ....
45,698				

Uniform Account No.	1969-70 Egyptian Pounds		Egyptian Pounds	Egyptian Pounds
		Wages		
311	429,201	Monetary wages	452,158	
312&313	100,865	Nonmonetary wages	107,013	559,171
	530,066			
		General Expenditures		
32	4,568,221	Raw materials & supplies used	5,633,766	
33	174,615	Services acquired.........	178,586	
34	179,694	Finished goods purchased for sale.....	—	
	4,922,520			5,812,352
		Current Transferred Expenditures		
3511	363,743	Custom duties.......	371,939	
3514	9,399	Other taxes (e.g., tax on franchises)	4,348	
	373,142			376,287
		Depreciation		
3522	60,181	Bldg., construction & roads ...	76,421	
3523	315,958	Equipment........	347,857	
3524	25,514	Cars ...	26,126	
3525	3,422	Tools	4,988	
3526	3,308	Furniture...	2,793	
3528	—	Deferred revenue expenditure.	32,774	
	408,383			491,959
353	11,639	Rent expense........	9,991	
354	102,316	Difference between assumed rents for depreciable assets and their depreciations....	100,638	
	113,955			110,629

(Table 1.1 con't)

Left page

1969-70 Egyptian Pounds	Uniform Account No.	Egyptian Pounds	Egyptian Pounds	
				Furnished Goods Purchased for Sale
240,455	4181	—		Net sales...............
(31,278)	4182	—		Cost of the difference between beginning and ending finished goods........
(6,053)	4183	—	—	Changes in value of goods purchased for sale on hand......
203,124				
6,917,431			8,423,638	Income from normal operations
				Transferred Revenues
256,121	441	3,903		Interest earned ....
6,437	442	28,106		Rents earned ....
23,091	444	66		Prior years' revenues.......
—	445	413		Fines earned ....
915	446			Other revenues ....
102,316	447	100,638		Difference between assumed rents for depreciable assets and their depreciations
370,609	448	288,843		Difference in interest.......
759,489		421,969		
113,852			1,036,374	Income from normal operations
873,341			1,458,343	

Right page

Uniform Account No.	1969-70 Egyptian Pounds	1969-70 Egyptian Pounds		Egyptian Pounds	Egyptian Pounds
			Interest Expenses		
355	204,277		Local interest.............	197,353	
356	42,360		Foreign interest..........	36,999	
357	370,609	616,976	Difference in interest.......	288,843	523,195
358		(155,420)	Changes in value of finished goods produced on hand....		(486,329)
359		(6,053)	Changes in value of goods purchased for sale on hand....		—
		113,852	Income from normal operations		1,036,374
		6,917,431			8,423,638
			Current Transfers		
361	252		Gifts.....................	20	
362	101		Contributions to others	—	
363	—		Fines.....................	1,969	
365	99,592		Prior years' expenses	32,666	
367	454,819	554,764	Additional allowance for depreciation.............	1,342,591	1,377,246
228	318,577		Profits for the period.......	81,097	
		873,341			1,458,343

that time to establish a uniform system of reporting financial statements for nationalized businesses. This tendency toward accounting uniformity is present in controlled economies, since it is difficult, if not impossible, for a central government to find out which sector of the economy is lagging in efficiency and productivity without comparable accounting information. To help achieve the objectives of the Egyptian National Planning Board, the Uniform Accounting Law of 1966 has been written with unusually explicit detail. In fact, it is more in the nature of an accounting handbook as it traces the movements between accounts, sets norms for accounting classifications, and spells out valuation and reporting methods.

The stated objectives of this uniform system of accounts in Egypt are the following: (a) to facilitate national planning and control; (b) to permit the screening of inefficient enterprises; and (c) to provide information to management. Through the first objective, financial and social accounting are coordinated in order to facilitate the preparation of the Gross National Product and other statistical data used to analyze the economy and to control its direction as illustrated in Tables 1.1 and 1.2. It is of interest to note that the Uniform Accounting Law of 1966 requires enterprises to use replacement-cost accounting in order to maintain the integrity of the invested capital.[12]

The uniform system of accounts, however, is not peculiar to the socialist countries alone. In France, for example, accounting standards and methods used by enterprises are also based on a uniform system of accounts called "Plan Compatible General," which was enacted in 1946. The French plan has been mandatory since 1947 for publicly owned enterprises, for enterprises in which 20% or more of the capital stock is government owned, and for enterprises that receive 10 million francs or more in government aid. Through an amendment in tax law, this uniform system of accounts became mandatory on all enterprises in France in 1970.

The examples delineated above illustrate the influence that environmental factors have had on the accounting standards used by different nations. Users of foreign financial statements, therefore, are obligated to go through a tremendous educational process in order for them to understand and to utilize these statements intelligently.

Table 1.2

ALNASER COMPANY
VALUE-ADDED

1969-70 Egyptian Pounds	Uniform Account No.	*For the Year Ended June 30, 1971* *Value of Production and Services at Selling Price*	*(in thousands pounds)* Budgeted Egyptian Pounds	Actual Egyptian Pounds
		Production at selling price:		
7,021	411	Net sales of finished goods	7,308	8,518
(197)	412	Cost of the difference between beginning and ending finished goods	28	383
(155)	413	Changes in value of finished goods produced on hand......................	2	(486)
17	414	Cost of the difference between beginning and ending work in process	12	(17)
29	417	Services sold	19	26
		Finished goods purchased for sale:		
240	4181	Net sales	...	...
(31)	4182	Cost of the difference between beginning and ending finished goods	...	...
(6)	4183	Changes in value of goods purchased for sale on hand......................	...	...
6,918		Total	7,369	8,424
(180)	34	Less: Finished goods purchased for sale	...	...
6,738		Value of production and services at selling price..........................	7,369	8,424
		Less:		
(364)	3511	Custom duties.............................	(402)	(372)
(9)	3514	Other taxes.............................	(5)	(4)
6,365		Value of production and services at factors of production costs......................	6,962	8,048
		Less:		
(4,568)	32	Raw materials and supplies used	(6,535)	(5,634)
(175)	33	Services acquired	(240)	(178)
(408)	3522–3528	Depreciation	(575)	(492)
1,214		Net value-added at factors of production costs .	(388)	1,744
		Distribution of Value-Added:		
530	311–313	Wages	601	559
114	353–354	Rents	114	111
617	355–357	Interest	916	523
(155)	358	Changes in value of finished goods produced on hand......................	2	(486)
(6)	4183	Changes in value of goods purchased for sale on hand......................	...	...
144		Income from normal operations..............	(2,021)	1,037
1,214			(388)	1,744

EFFORTS TO ESTABLISH INTERNATIONAL ACCOUNTING STANDARDS

Progress toward international accounting standards has been very slow. In order to establish a forum for an exchange of ideas, the First International Congress of Accountants was held in the United States in 1904. Subsequent conferences have been held periodically in different parts of the world, but without any significant accomplishments. However, two significant developments did occur at the Tenth International Congress of Accountants held in Sydney, Australia in 1972—the formation of the International Coordination Committee for the Accountancy Profession (ICCAP) and the International Accounting Standards Committee (IASC). The main objective of ICCAP has been the development of a worldwide accounting profession with common standards. ICCAP is composed of representatives from Australia, Canada, France, India, Japan, Mexico, the Netherlands, the Philippines, the United Kingdom, and the United States. The U.S. representatives are Michael N. Chetkovich of Haskins and Sells, and AICPA President, Wallace E. Olson. In February 1976, ICCAP sent an interim report to ninety-nine professional accounting bodies in sixty-nine countries recommending that it be replaced by a more permanent worldwide organization to be based in New York called the International Federation of Accountants (IFAC). This proposal will be considered by the delegates at the Eleventh International Congress of Accountants to be held in Munich on October 10, 1977. IFAC would work toward the establishment on international standards of auditing, ethics, education and training, leaving the formation of international accounting standards to IASC.

As mentioned earlier, the first step toward the formation of IASC was taken at the Tenth International Congress of Accountants held in Sydney. In June 1973, representatives of professional accounting bodies from nine countries met in London to participate in the establishment of IASC, with Joseph P. Cummings of Peat, Marwick, Mitchell and Co. as the U.S. representative and chairman of the Committee. The membership of this Committee has since increased through the association of professional accounting bodies of other countries. At present (August 1976) the total number of accounting associations participating in IASC is forty-seven.

Although the main objective of IASC is to formulate basic international accounting standards, only three International Accounting Standards have been issued to date by IASC, namely, IAS 1, "Disclosure of Accounting Policies," IAS 2, "Valuation and Presentation of Inventories in the Context of the Historical Cost System," and IAS 3, "Consolidated Financial Statements." Two other standards have been approved by IASC for issue on October 6, 1976, namely, IAS 4, "Depreciation Accounting," and IAS 5, "Information to be Disclosed in Financial Statements." Professional accounting bodies associated with IASC have had the responsibility of introducing these international accounting standards into their respective countries. One way to facilitate the adoption of these standards further is to ask international stock exchanges to require multinational enterprises to employ these standards.

Steps toward the establishment of international accounting standards have also been taken by the European Economic Community (EEC), which was established in the late 1950s to promote full freedom in the movement of goods and labor between member countries. As a by-product of this cooperation, the EEC developed a scheme for harmonization of accounting standards for its members. The uniform system of accounts that resulted is related to the presentation of financial statements for enterprises in the EEC. Directives of the EEC, however, are not mandatory; member countries have discretionary power as to how these directives are to be incorporated into national laws. Since different environments demand the use of different uniform accounting systems, this has proven to be a wise policy.

Other organizations such as the Union Européene des Experts Comptables, Économiques et Financiers (UEC) and the Inter-American Accounting Conference (IACC) have also furthered an interest in international accounting. These organizations have succeeded in generating some interest in the establishment of international accounting standards.

CONCLUSION

While it is recognized that some degree of uniformity in international accounting is desirable, the form that uniformity takes must be based on the purposive uniformity model referred to earlier. This model is differentiated from other models in that it includes purpose within its framework. If there is a change in purpose, an accounting standard more appropriate to the new purpose is called into play. A vernacular description of this model might be the old adage, "The ends justify the means." It can, therefore, be summarized that the understanding of accounting as practiced in other countries and the underlying economic philosophies of these different nations lead to a better appreciation of a specific country's approach to the solution of economic problems and of its own accounting standards and procedures. Thus, the need for an international dimension in accounting should be obvious.

NOTES

1. Michael N. Chetkovich, "International Accounting Cooperation," *Proceedings of the Seminar on Accounting in Economic Growth and Development* (Chapel Hill: University of North Carolina, April 25-27, 1976).

2. For more information on these models, see John W. Buckley and Dhia D. AlHashim, "Four Accounting Control Models and the Concept of Purposive Uniformity" (UCLA: Accounting-Information Research Program, Working Paper 71-2, February 1971).

3. American Institute of Certified Public Accountants, *Report of Special Committee on Opinions of the Accounting Principles Board* (New York: AICPA, Spring 1965), p. 16.

4. *Ibid.*, p. 17.

5. Security and Exchange Commission, *Notice of Adoption of Amendments to Form 10-Q and Regulation S-X Regarding Interim Financial Reporting,* Accounting Series Release No. 177 (Washington, D.C.: SEC, September 10, 1975).

6. For more details, see Gary M. Cadenhead, *Differences in Circumstances: Fact or Fantasy* (UCLA: Accounting-Information Research Program, Working Paper No. 3, January 1969).

7. Gerhard G. Mueller, "Accounting Principles Generally Accepted in the United States Versus Those Generally Accepted Elsewhere," *The International Journal of Accounting Education and Research,* vol. 3, no. 2 (Spring 1968), 92, 93.

8. A. Goudeket, "An Application of Replacement Value Theory," *The Journal of Accountancy,* vol. 110, no. 1 (July 1960), 37-47.

9. Financial Accounting Standards Board, *Exposure Draft: Financial Reporting in Units of General Purchasing Power* (Stamford, Conn.: FASB, December 31, 1974).

10. Arthur Andersen & Co., *The Brazilian Method of Indexing and Accounting for Inflation* (Chicago, Ill.: Arthur Andersen & Co., May 1975), p. 2.

11. Financial Accounting Standards Board, *Accounting for the Translation of Foreign Currency Transactions and Foreign Currency Financial Statements* (Stamford, Conn.: FASB, October 1975).

12. For more information on the Egyptian Uniform Accounting Law of 1966, see Dhia D. AlHashim, "Trends in Third World Accounting," *Proceedings of the Fifty-ninth Anniversary Convention of the American Accounting Association* (Tucson, Arizona: AAA, August 18-20, 1975).

International Dimensions of Accounting

Robert I. Jones

Co-chairman

Arthur Andersen and Co.

In his presentation, Professor AlHashim has provided us with an excellent summary of our profession's present efforts to establish international standards of accounting. He has also given us his own views favoring "the purposive uniformity model," which contemplates a country-by-country approach, considering the uses to which accounting information is put in each country, and which would then be determinate of the appropriate accounting methods and standards for each individual country. He suggests that accounting should be recognized as a by-product of its environment and that different accounting standards for different countries be derived from various sets of postulates for different cultural, social, legal, political, and economic systems. He also suggests that a more meaningful, consolidated presentation is achieved when financial statements are utilized in the consolidation prepared on the same basis as they would be prepared in their respective countries.

Professor AlHashim acknowledges other concepts of approach to the matter in his discussion and cites a number of international organizations committed to achieving progress in this important area.

My comments on the subject will not be in the area of methodology for coping with international accounting standards, since Professor AlHashim has well summarized this for us. Instead, I would like to review what I believe are very fundamental aspects of the world economy which will mandate early progress in establishing international accounting standards.

The overriding fact of the world economy today is that the more developed, mature nations which have developed monetary capital and technology now lack sufficient natural resources to maintain independently their present position, whereas the natural resources necessary to maintain and further develop the world economy are largely concentrated in what are today the less-developed nations of the world. Fortunately for the developed nations, their monetary capital and technology are yet needed to properly develop the natural resources of the lesser-developed nations. This mutual dependence sets the stage for what I believe is the inevitable demand for early progress in international accounting.

Let us now examine the probable economic climate for doing international business in the future and observe how it will be different from the past. First of all, we must recognize that every nation today—whether large or small, developed or developing, militarily strong or weak, aligned or unaligned—asserts its own political and economic independence. To challenge that premise or to seek to impose terms of international finance or trade inconsistent with that asserted national independence would today risk either military consequence or charges of improper and immoral conduct. This newly asserted independence now demands partnership—oftentimes equal or controlling—by the host country, either by its government or by its citizens. In addition, the host country now usually seeks a greater participation in the processing of its own natural resources to broaden its industrial base, to develop its own national technology, and to provide employment for its people. Thus, the oil-producing nations seek to develop a petrochemical industry, and countries like Malaysia and Indonesia, rich in timber, seek to develop an integrated forest products industry. Accordingly, it appears that although nations of the world will continue to be interdependent upon each other, each will seek the maximum economic independence which its circumstances will permit including the broadest processing of its natural resources and the development of a local industrial and distribution capacity to serve its own consumer and industrial markets, as well as export markets. Considering the tremendous potential which yet remains for progress in raising standards of living and industrial development throughout the world, there should be no shortage of opportunity to the business community for the future development of these markets, provided that they effectively adjust to the new environment described.

Since the private sector of the free world must inevitably be the catalyst for developing the world economy in terms of both capital as well as technology, we must now anticipate how this can be attracted. I stress *attracted*. In reality, capital in the vast amounts needed and technology at the level of sophistication required for both production and marketing can only be provided by an organization qualified to function as a multinational enterprise, whether it be in the financial, production, or marketing areas. Thus, companies and organizations with multinational capabilities must continue to be attracted to this task. I continue to stress *attracted* because their involvement in multinational commerce in the future is destined to be carried out with less direct control and perhaps less profit than it has been in the past. Thus the risk-reward evaluation in committing capital and technology will be more critically made in each case by qualified multinational companies, and the investment performance will be more critically monitored—by operating management as well as by *all of the partners* in the business community, whether international bankers and investors, or home or host country participants. Thus, the sound economic evaluation of operating and investment performance by all parties with interest in the multinational development of our world economy would appear to loom as an absolute requirement for the future, thereby creating the basic demand for international accounting standards. This is in sharp contrast to previous periods of international economic development, in which evaluations and monitoring were primarily conducted *within* a multinational company lacking an external accountability on either a country or project basis in most instances.

Doesn't this prospective economic environment for the future suggest to you—as it does to me—that necessity will once again prove to be the mother of invention, and that we can accordingly expect to see some breakthrough with respect to the development of international accounting standards soon? The discussion and debate over alternative approaches will continue, and this will be healthy for the distilling process of upgrading the quality of what is done. In any case, we can be assured that as soon as multinational partnerships increasingly become a way of doing business, international accounting standards will not be far behind. Until it does come, however, we can realistically expect home-country accounting practices to be the principal influence because that is the mental framework in which the business decisions will originally be made and against which performance will still be primarily monitored. An analogy of necessity motivation can be easily found in the evolution of accounting practices to recognize inflation which have been developing around the world. Accounting for inflation has been recognized in each country of the world having an accounting profession for generations, with many advocates for different methodologies to deal with the problem. Yet it has never been adopted in any form until the economic climate of necessity *required* its recognition, namely that inflation reached levels which rendered historical cost useless and that adjustment, or disclosure at a minimum, became necessary for the financial statements to serve a useful purpose. It is still, however, dealt with on a national basis under differing concepts of price-level adjustment, replacement-cost adjustment, et cetera.

With this prospective early demand for progress in international accounting, it appears to me that the accounting profession has a unique opportunity for asserting a leadership role in contributing to the development of the world's future economy, rather than in limiting itself to recording our past. The latter is so typically the role which people would attribute to accountants. I would rather like to make a very strong case for real leadership. AlHashim developed very well the concept of how accounting standards are influenced by the social, political, and economic factors that exist in every country. What I would like to see us do as accountants is just to turn that coin over in order to provide a climate whereby accounting can in turn influence those developments, particularly economic developments.

Certainly a clear international definition of the objectives of financial statements, together with a definition of the postulates on which they should be prepared, would appear to be the keystone on which all procedures should be based. Here, again, much discussion and much debate has occurred over such things as the objectives of financial statements, but no conclusions have been rendered, no actions have been taken up to this point in time. With the proper foundation laid, attention could then be given to the many specific accounting problems which unfortunately still cry out for solution in all countries of the world, such as the following: inflation; business combinations; goodwill; leasing; consolidation and translation of multinational financial statements; determination and use of all types of reserves; income tax allocations; and cost determinations, including content and allocation of overheads. The scope of the above topics in which further progress is needed only illustrates the extent to which the profession in most countries is still struggling, let alone developing approaches which marshall worldwide support for an international standard of practice.

Under these conditions, when the practical need for international standards arises to serve multinational partners as previously described, the vacuum will be filled. In the absence of professional leadership, it will likely be filled by security market regulators overseeing the capital markets in which the funds are raised to finance the specific investments, or by negotiation and agreement between the partners of the home and host countries with respect to standards which will serve their immediate needs. Thus, we may again see the development of a series of procedures and practices having the credentials of "general acceptance" but not the generation of financial statements which would meet the proper test of *fairness* to all users of the financial statements. I shudder just to contemplate the picture of this evolution that will take place in the absence of professional leadership. You can anticipate a two-country or a three-country situation—something which is happening everyday in our practice—when a country processing natural resources is trying to attract capital and technology. When the parties involved in the transaction encounter a problem for which there is no professional standard available for its solution, negotiation between the parties would introduce a solution for that particular problem. If twenty contracts introduce the same solution for the problem encountered, then you have "substantial authoritative support." Soon you have an evolution again which is being built like "topsy"—what I call the false credential of a general acceptance and a substantial authority— but an evolution which fails to meet that basic test of *fairness*. Now, is that the test of fairness that we need to strive for?

In the final analysis, it may be the ability of the accountant to develop procedures and practices which will "square" this basic test of fairness with generally accepted practice, an event which would prove to be an important turning point in how our world economy develops generally and in the role to be played by the private sector particularly. Certainly some of the prevailing attitudes of the less-developed countries toward the more-developed countries and their multinationally operating home-based companies suggest that they presently have some questions about the fairness of local financial statements being a sound basis for taxation, some serious questions about transfer pricing between countries, and other critical questions about international accounting practices.

Much has been said of late—often critically—about the accounting practices of multinational companies as well as their business ethics in conducting business in host countries. From the vantage point of a practicing professional having had considerable exposure to both the accounting as well as ethical practices of multinational companies over many years, I am pleased to state that in my judgment both are of high quality from an overall standpoint. As we all know, unfortunate human error in judgment has occurred in a number of situations involving what is generally termed *sensitive payments*, though the moral responsibility in most cases should be shared by individuals in both the home and host country. The important point is that—speaking generally—

whenever such instances have been made known to top management and boards of directors of multinational companies, appropriate corrective action has been promptly taken. By their corrective action and full disclosure of such exceptions to their general business policies, multinational companies continue to merit the role of leadership which they have historically fulfilled in the development of our world economy. Business ethics, like accounting, badly needs international standards to be adopted by all countries and members of the multinational business community. In the absence of such international standards, both may tend to drift toward the lowest common denominator, and like the economic law governing money, the bad will drive out the good. We in the United States cannot declare a moral (ethical) climate or an accounting standard climate, impose it on U.S. home-based multinational companies, and yet expect it to survive unless the rest of the world joins in subscribing to those same standards of both accounting and ethical conduct. A climate of necessity exists here to motivate us toward finally doing something about establishing standards in both of these important areas.

It is thus incumbent upon multinational companies in their increasingly frequent role as partners, rather than sole proprietors, in developing the world economy to provide leadership also in adopting accounting policies and procedures as well as ethical codes of conduct which will meet the basic tests of fairness to all parties concerned. Thus, they—as well as we in the professional and academic fields—will be conducting their present practices against a philosophy which will be compatible with high international standards when the day comes that they are finally adopted.

Let us now turn briefly to what we can do to hasten the day of establishing international accounting standards. First of all, we must make more effective progress toward establishing sound standards which meet the test of fairness on an individual country basis. Only then can we begin to have real communication and dialogue among countries with any hope of developing international standards. It must be an upward evolution of progress, supplemented as much as possible by input from all disciplines of the business community— industry, law, finance, economics, academia, and so on. Despite the adoption of new organizational concepts for developing accounting standards in the U.S. (FASB), as well as in other countries, progress has been discouragingly slow, so slow that either the organizational concepts or their leadership must be judged inadequate to the job at hand. Accordingly, the profession must initiate whatever corrective action program is necessary to accelerate our progress.

Secondly, we must join with other countries of the world in adopting an organizational vehicle that we are all willing to cloak with authority, subject to the following of appropriate administrative procedures to assure a hearing of all viewpoints. The final result would be to promulgate international accounting standards which serve the needs of international business partners. Several years ago, our firm proposed the establishment of a Council for World Accounting to develop worldwide financial reporting and cost accounting standards and to encourage the use of such standards for international finance within each of the participating countries.

Without going into great detail, council membership would be open to any person throughout the world. It would have a large board of directors consisting of persons of major stature from various disciplines—international bankers, industrialists, lawyers, economists, academicians, and professional accountants. This board would in turn establish from its members a policy committee, workable in size, with a balanced composition from the various disciplines. A managing director would be supported by an adequate, trained multinational staff. There would be provision for an exposure draft procedure, subsequent to the research and the position paper, and before the adoption of a standard. Standards adopted by such a council would, no doubt, be different from those used presently in most countries, and it would be necessary to include explanatory reconciliations between world standards and local national standards. However, if the board members of the council—decision-makers within their own organizations and thought-leaders in their own countries—provide the necessary leadership for the development of the council's pronouncements, there is every reason to hope that a worldwide commonality of accounting and reporting standards can be achieved and the differences between local and worldwide standards would narrow.

As a firm, we believe the concept reflected in our proposed Council for World Accounting is both urgently needed and practical to implement. We hold no pride of authorship, however, and will strongly support any other concept which may be advanced that will offer a superior approach and will marshall the necessary international support for such an objective.

In summary, the world badly needs early tangible progress toward establishing international accounting standards which meet basic tests of fairness to all parties at interest. We should seize the initiative—each within our own area of influence—and practice, and make it happen!

TWO

The Role of the Accounting Profession

in International Business Ethics

A pragmatic and frank discussion of payments made to foreign governments and influential individuals to stimulate international transactions and the effects of the latest IRS and SEC findings in this area.

R. Lee Brummet,
AAA Past President

Willard J. Graham Professor of Business Administration University of North Carolina

Michael N. Chetkovich

AICPA Chairman-Elect & Managing Partner, Haskins & Sells

Dr. Brummet holds a B.Ed. degree from Illinois State University, an M.S. degree from University of Illinois, and a Ph.D. degree from University of Michigan. He has taught throughout the world and has authored numerous papers, articles, and books on various aspects of accounting.

Mr. Chetkovich holds both a B.S. and M.S. degree from University of California-Berkeley. He has authored many papers and articles on national and international accounting. He is the U.S. representative on numerous international committees.

The Role of the Accounting Profession

in International Business Ethics

Willard J. Graham Professor
of Business Administration
University of North Carolina

My subject is sensitive, troublesome, and very challenging, but one I think of utmost importance. I will not attempt a constraining definition of the term *ethics*—a subject of learned works throughout the history of the world. I would only call your attention to the usual use of the word to relate to acceptable human behavior, and suggest that in such a context it may be used to relate to organizational practices that reflect human motives and actions.

The concept and content of the field of ethics are necessarily based on individual value judgments that range across a broad spectrum. But there is, I think, enough concensus among people to justify our consideration of ethical behavior of business executives and of accountants.

The economic and social well-being of the human race is inextricably tied to the performance of its institutions—the wealth-producing organizations—and their performance is inextricably tied to the respect and credibility which they engender within our society. These wealth-producing organizations—these businesses—have been eminently successful in producing goods and services over the past several decades, but recent developments have given cause to consider and perhaps question the long-run viability of our system.

We see at every turn clear evidence of society's decreasing confidence in the business establishment. We hear ever so clearly outspoken criticism of business practices that many of our citizens perceive to be ethically deplorable Increasing popularity of the so-called principle of the "right to know," expansion of mass media, increasing desire of large numbers of our population to be involved, a seeming rebirth of individualism, and return to a kind of moralism have combined to encourage awareness of serious problems within our business establishment. This awareness has brought into being a much broader set of constituencies for all of our institutions. These broad constituencies did not exist even a decade or two ago.

The franchises granted to our corporations by our states are only the legal trappings of the real societal franchises that these corporations depend upon. Businesses are gradually—and sometimes very painfully—becoming aware that their real franchises are societal rights voluntarily granted by all people who are affected by them, and that these rights operating within society are constantly being reviewed, and that they will be renewed or perpetuated only as long as large and varied groups of people choose to tolerate their existence.

Constituencies of business corporations exert their powers as individuals, as pressure groups, as governmental bodies, and in other forms to communicate their views and to exact their toll on business credibility. They are being heard and they will continue to be heard. Their targets include all institutional groups, but particularly those large corporations that control large amounts of resources, and most especially those that operate in many parts of the world. Concerns are heard from highly creditable sources within the United States; with regard to transnational companies, these sources are joined by representatives of the increasingly more powerful third world countries that are banding together to respond to practices which they consider unjust.

This year a group of representatives of seventy-seven developing countries met in Dakar and called for rigorous curbs on what they called "unacceptable practices of the transnational corporations."

We are reminded of claims made against both domestic and international practices such as illegal political contributions, tax dodges and inside deals, bribes and kickbacks into the millions of dollars, systematic destruction of the environment, unjustified waste of irreplacable scarce raw materials, shoddy products and false advertising, and exploitation of employees. While some claims in these areas are exaggerated in some instances, there *is* adequate documentation and even admissions by company executives to establish the credibility of many of the claims and to justify concern for all of us.

It seems reasonable to ask why our business establishment has not put its house in order. Can it not see the writing on the wall? Cannot business executives who are known for their vision of the future and their change-agentry capability adjust to this new environment and lead our institutional establishment into a new era of compatibility with human needs and desires?

These provocative questions should not imply that our large business organizations are not performing a most important economic and social service in their host countries. They provide investment capital, technology, important training and development, stable employment for people in the host countries, tax revenues for local governments, and—most important—products and services for citizens of host countries. Contrary to the popular conception, over 93% of the dollar value of the products made abroad by affiliates and subsidiaries of American corporations are distributed abroad.

But now back to our questions: some insist that the misbehavior attributed to international business executives can be traced to the blinding aspects of the profit motive. Although their contentions may be justified in isolated instances of unscrupulous and unenlightened actions of exploitation usually made possible by a monopoly position, I suggest that this is not the primary answer. The invisible hand suggested by Adam Smith 200 years ago can still perform its function in society. The pursuit of profit in a world competitive environment will cause even our largest corporations to produce goods and services that people desire. It will encourage the economic use of resources, and it will provide tax revenues in host countries where they may be sorely needed. Indeed, although many have tried, no country of the world has succeeded in finding a substitute for the profit motive.

The problem, I suggest, is that some of our business executives have simply not perceived fully the impact of the changing social contact of their companies with society. They have not adequately appreciated the pace of the societal evolution or revolution that has taken place in the past few years. Practices tacitly condoned by society for many decades have become the subject of highly publicized intolerable practices of today. At the same time our international businesses have become so large, and with such far-flung operations, that control of individual behavior of all those representing our business establishment has become much more difficult. Further, in many instances, the defensive flurry of activity to justify, to answer, or to correct questionable practices that have been made public, has overshadowed constructive programs to guarantee ethical behavior throughout highly diversified organizations where reward systems may be clearly tied to short-run profit performance. The crucial long-run need for clear economic and social contribution to host countries and the well-recognized social constraints on short-run profit have not been adequately reflected in international business practices.

Some concerned business executives and others have suggested a general commitment to a code of ethics for business such as exists for most professions. Some businesses are currently in the process of developing such codes. In May 1976, the twenty-four-member Organization for Economic Cooperation and Development approved a code of business conduct including nondiscrimination as well as noninvolvment in illegal political contributions and in improper local politics, or with improper payments to public office holders. While this code has no teeth in it at the present time, legislative action of participating countries *could* provide the teeth and the accounting profession *could* assist in the effecting of its provisions. Yet without the support of such codes, I wholeheartedly agree with Dr. W. M. Blumenthal, the chief executive of Bendix Corporation who said recently:

> —it is entirely possible to be successful in making decisions that are at once motivated by profit considerations and yet responsive to society's larger needs and changes, and, most certainly, it is possible to guide one's decision-making by standards of ethics and morality of a high order—it really does come down to the individual for it is not the corporation that engages in ethical or unethical conduct, it is the individuals within it that do so. A corporation executive who understands the goals of the enterprise and of the people in it, who is willing to accept personal responsibility and who is concerned not only by what is legal but also by what is decent and proper, can look forward to a very high level of satisfaction in his work in a corporate setting.[1]

Now, we are to consider the possible role of the accounting profession in this problem of international business ethics. But, before that, we should at least take a glimpse at the ethical posture of the accounting profession itself. I have not intended to picture international business executives to be either more or less ethical than accountants, or than professors for that matter, but it would seem inexcusable not to make some observations at least about ethical behavior of members of the highly respected accounting profession.

The recent phenomenon of rapidly changing social contracts of institutions with the people they serve has been all pervasive. Clearly it has included the professions, and accounting, as one of them, has not been immune. Members of our profession have been accused, sometimes indicted, and in a few instances, have been ruled against in court for matters that amount to lack of attention to duty, lack of real independence, failure to disclose significant information, and failure to provide relevant financial information. While it may not be clear just which of these kinds of accusations are "ethical" matters, it is clear that the public is expecting the Certified Public Accountant to perform better for the public. The accounting profession is being asked very strongly to improve its performance and to be more socially accountable to society. How is the profession responding?

It appears to me that the profession *is* responding but with a degree of reluctance, with some defensiveness, and thus I think too slowly. On the positive side of the ledger, the profession does have a code of ethics which it respects generally, but more important perhaps is its effort to improve its services to society. The profession is thus far giving strong support to the Financial Accounting Standards Board which is seriously and intelligently—although painfully slowly—reaching some reasoned agreements on accounting standards which should be in the public interest. It is commendable, further, that the working relationships and lines of communication between the Financial Accounting Standards Board and the Securities and Exchange Commission continue to be active and healthy.

A plan for a voluntary quality control review program for Certified Public Accounting firms with SEC practices or with general audit practices has been approved by the board of directors of the American Institute of Certified Public Accountants and will be presented to its Council next month. I believe this program can be successful in assuring the profession and the public, as stated in the plan, "that a high level of competence is maintained and that every practicable effort is being made to prevent substandard performance on the part of practitioners."[2]

With strong support from the American Institute of Certified Public Accountants many states have enacted legislation requiring continued education for Certified Public Accountants as well as increasing the preentry educational requirements for the profession. Also, with credit to the AICPA, the Board on Standards for Programs of Professional Accounting is in the process of finalizing a set of standards that should increase the quality of education for accountants.

The AICPA Committee on Auditing Standards has within the past few months issued a discussion document concerning the role of the auditor in connection with the illegal payments controversy which was primarily related to international business activities. The profession is indeed giving this problem serious attention.

The AICPA, further, has established a Commission on Auditors' Responsibilities headed by Manuel Cohen, previously chairman of the SEC. This Commission is currently completing the first phase of its study which will determine possible extensions of the public auditor's role, as well as clarify his role in terms of what society or the public may legitimately expect. Considerations will definitely include the sensitive payments issue in the international sphere. The profession is cooperating fully with the study of a group appointed by the Securities and Exchange Commission and headed by former Commissioner, A. A. Sommer, to determine what the public wants and needs from financial reports.

Within the past few years the National Association of Accountants has instituted a quality program for the recognition of competence in the field of management accounting. It is hoped that the Institute of Management Accounting which sponsors this program will encourage the development of a code of ethics for its certificate holders. To do so would add significantly to the credibility of their work within the international setting.

At this international level, our profession is making a start on developing a degree of uniformity in accounting standards throughout the world with the work of the International Accounting Standards Committee. And, for the near future, efforts will be made at the International Accounting Congress in Munich in 1977 to establish an International Federation of Accountants.

And finally, and I personally find this most significant, the profession is reflecting its interest in accounting for corporate social performance. Within the next few months, the American Institute of Certified Public Accountants will publish a book prepared by a committee of accountants on the subject of corporate social accounting.

These are but a few of the favorable signs of life of our accounting profession. There are others. But the opposite side of the ledger is not without entries. The need for independence and a clearly perceived primary commitment of the Certified Public Accountant in audit practice to the public, even though the audited company is the source of the audit fee has not been adequately managed. In this connection, I suggest that the use of an outsider nonmanager, nonboard member, stockholder committee is worthy of consideration. Such a committee could be newly designated each year to engage the audit firm and receive its audit report. In any event, if this problem of possible conflict of interest is not adequately resolved by accountants within the next several years, we may well see more and more use of auditors appointed and perhaps paid by government agencies.

I suggest further that all of the favorable developments that I have listed should have been initiated earlier. The profession should have anticipated its needs and those of the public and initiated these programs accordingly, rather than embarking upon them only in response to loud and clear voices that could no longer be ignored.

A great profession is one which does its research and deals with the future. It constantly reviews and anticipates its potentials for service to society. It continually retrains itself to serve in the fullest and most relevant ways. The profession of accounting has not, at this time, achieved such greatness. It continues to cling tenaciously to practices that are crudely based on the questionable assumption of "the economic man" and to the double-entry balancing technique so ingeniously devised in Italy over five centuries ago. The accounting profession needs to define its role in society—not just to determine the purposes of financial statements. It needs to improve its ability to assess performance of organizations along many dimensions—not just to determine standards for financial accounting.

The profession should seriously consider expanding its involvement in the much needed area of compliance audits. As regulations related to corporations operating internationally increase in number and complexity, the need for compliance audits also increases. This is a good example of a newly developing need of society that cries out for response from some profession and I suggest that the profession of accounting is the most logical one.

In view of the exceedingly rapid rate of change in societal expectations, it is my opinion that the accounting profession should initiate a program to chart a strategy that would increase the probability that it will sense its changing opportunities and prepare itself to serve. While continuous updating would be necessary, this strategy for the profession should view its horizon at least to the year 2000. Our current cadre of accounting students in our universities—and they are legion and bright of mind—will be in the prime of their careers at the turn of the century. With contributions from many disciplines a well-thought out, well-documented strategy for our profession could be at least as contributive to accounting education as the possible enactment of educational standards with accreditation procedures.

The accounting profession is involved in two distinct but closely related aspects with regard to ethical behavior. It must itself be highly ethical, behaving in a manner that engenders confidence from the public. And it must define its role in that public to include the encouragement, if not the assurance, of ethical behavior by its clients or business employers, including those involved in international operations. My comments, thus far, have related to both these aspects. Let us now turn more particularly to the latter one relating to the businesses that accountants serve.

Accountants performing their services in the international arena should adopt a broader view and take a greater responsibility for performance measurement, public disclosure, and audit assurances. They should recognize and reflect in their practice the different needs and value structures of people in different countries and their relevance to different performance criteria. The performance of an affiliate of a U.S.-based corporation operating in a Latin American country should hardly be assessed on the same criteria as its operations in the United States. Sales, profits, or earnings per share may not be the primary criteria. Other, perhaps more important, criteria may include items such as the effect on the local balance of payments situation, employment of foreign nationals, degrees of management autonomy, relations with local government representatives, and the local social image.

To assess matters such as these will require measurement skills new to accountants, but these may be the criteria which are critical to success and thus they should be recognized as part of the accountant's job. Carl Madden, the chief economist of the United States Chamber of Commerce, has offered some heady words concerning the limited relevance of accounting measures:

Bringing to bear more useful information in social and economic processes . . . involves a new conception of what constitutes human welfare . . . . Under current accounting traditions . . . . our concept of profits allows incentives for types of economic growth exemplified by . . . rapid environmental deterioration . . . . accounting concepts in any balance sheet do not weigh the costs to a business of social deterioration or decay in its environs . . . . corporate management . . . is going to be involved in "piercing the fiscal veil" that accounting concepts cast as a shroud over the reality of social processes . . . .[3]

While these words may have some general applicability, they are likely to be most relevant for transnational corporations operating in countries with a high level of environmental consciousness and an orientation toward direct and immediate impacts upon human welfare. Perhaps the accounting profession should consider the need to "pierce the fiscal veil" visualized by Madden.

It has been suggested that a useful personal benchmark to distinguish between ethical and unethical behavior is to consider if public disclosure would be discomforting or embarrassing to those reported on. Increased disclosure of organizational performance based on objective criteria could make a noteworthy contribution to international business ethics.

The question of the amount of organizational performance information to be put into the public sphere is a matter for public action and decision. We may well question whether the SEC is justified in adopting a posture on the sensitive payments issue which is contemplated to alter business conduct rather than to inform investors. Yet accountants may justifiably be expected to reflect some favorable bias toward increased disclosure since information and communication is their forte. The current tendency toward disclosing more organizational information is, I think, a favorable sign for international business. With the usual restraints of the cost of information and the threshold for public information overload, let us hope the tendency will continue.

Now to the accountant's audit or attest function. Recognizing fully the responsibility to be accepted and thus the risks involved, I suggest that the accountant should undertake a broader role in the attest function as it relates to ethical matters and international business. To do so can make a real difference.

There is no easy way. It will simply require a commitment first to the law of the land, second to the accounting profession, and third to human conscience. These commitments must, of course, transcend concerns for short-run monetary compensation, whether in the form of improper payments, salary, bonus, or client billings. This is admittedly expecting much, but the accountant may be assured that it is in his own best interest. The society or public which is pressing for this kind of behavior will produce the rewards, at least in the long run. As Lee Seidler has pointed out for those in public practice:

A licensed profession might be characterized as a state-sanctioned monopoly, under which the practitioners are given the exclusive right to certain activities and titles. However, the privileges are not given free; there is an implicit bargain with the state. The beneficiaries of the monopoly status agree in turn to maintain high standards of professional competence, performance and reliability. Essentially the theory is that the general welfare will benefit more from the improved performance and safeguards enforced by the profession than it will lose from the added costs which result from a monoply supply of services . . . . the state and society are attempting to revise the terms of the bargain with the accounting profession. Whatever the implicit terms of the bargain were in years past, society is now clearly saying that it wants more. Since there is little doubt that the state and society possess the greater power, if the accountants are to continue to receive the benefits of professional monopoly status—and the present prosperity of the profession is tangible evidence of the value of such benefits—change may be required in the "public" part of certified public accountants.[4]

Now becoming more specific, accountants as auditors should clearly accept responsibility to see that many matters of law are being adhered to by the client corporation. This is a big order and there needs to be some bounds to it. Matters included in such responsibility must be made unmistakably clear, but they should include the more obvious financial matters as well as some of the manageable social matters such as employment practices, the environment, and product attributes. This does mean that experts outside of the current field of accounting must be utilized. It also means that the accountant must become aware of the many differing laws of the different countries in which the client operates, and it may call for the utilization of legal council. These are areas, I think, in which the accountant must serve.

Second, accountants should not only take responsibility for certain matters of law—they should also accept responsibility in all areas in which the credibility of the profession may be at stake. This means that they should adopt a frame of mind that emphasizes "what others will think." They are members of an information-providing profession. If they have any reason to wonder about the integrity or adequacy of their clients' public reports they must not yield—and the plea that to satisfy such wonder would involve a prohibitive cost or that good internal control systems are more effective anyway should not be allowed to beg the question. This is a posture that will sometimes be hard to take but one now critical and demanded of every member of the accounting profession.

Third, accountants, like all human beings must answer to their own consciences. This is an area that cannot be legislated by government or disciplined by a profession. It is a personal matter for each and every member of the profession. Yet we can hope that by heritage, by training, and by life's experiences, the accounting profession is now and will in the future be habitated by men and women with conscience and conviction. This is the only *real* possibility that the profession will fulfill its highest calling.

Earlier, I commented on the current work of the International Accounting Standards Committee and the possibility of the formation of an International Federation of Accountants. Organizations such as these provide obvious vehicles for the accounting profession to use in improving the impact of accounting on international business ethics. At the present time the charge of the International Accounting Standards Committee is too narrow to offer much hope—although the charge and the whole construct could change and become useful. The prospective International Federation of Accountants could be most effective in this area. I see no compelling deterrents to such a Federation's leadership in enacting a code of ethics for accountants the world over and developing an understanding of the dimensions of accountants' responsibility in the field of international business ethics. These programs could of course be given more strength if coupled with a world-wide licensing of accountants—a possibility that has been discussed for some time. Let us hope that such matters will be given high priority on the early agenda of the Federation.

Now I realize that my comments may seem a bit idealistic and at least as much moralistic exortation as hard substance proposals. Yet I am convinced that the future of the profession depends far more on its success in keeping the confidence of the public and its success in fulfilling the legitimate and deeply felt needs of society in the next decades than it does on the resolution of all of the controversial technical issues that it considers day after day or on the success of its major firms in winning their day in court in connection with pending litigation. I am also convinced that the profession must resist understandable tendencies to find comfort in safe, continually more limited areas of decreased overall relevance. The influence and stature of our profession can be markedly improved if we step up to the job and serve well our publics by improving international business ethics.

Paul Hazard, a distinguished humanist and member of the French Academy, wrote of the elements of resistance in time of war and invasion just after the liberation of France in 1944, and the same elements seem to apply equally well in our time and in our international economic and social setting:

What has to be preserved . . . are certain ideas . . . the idea that there must be in life, at the same time, clarity, beauty, and gentleness, the idea that the truth is not in what is vague and obscure; the sentiment of individual liberty; the sentiment of justice; the sentiment of law, which tries to introduce an element of stability into the eternal flow of things . . . . for each one of us to have in his heart an impregnable fortress—that is the way to our salvation.[5]

NOTES

1. W. M. Blumenthal, "Ethics, Morality, and the Modern Corporate Executive." An article in *Dividend* (Spring 1976) adapted from a speech. (Ann Arbor, Mich.: University of Michigan), pp. 6, 7.

2. American Institute of Certified Public Accountants, *Discussion Draft: Plan for Voluntary Quality Control Review Program for CPA firms with SEC Practices or with General Audit Practices* (New York: AICPA, July 23, 1976).

3. Carl H. Madden, *Clash of Culture: Management in an Age of Changing Values* (Washington, D.C.: National Planning Association, 1972), pp. 29, 36, 53.

4. Lee J. Seidler, "Accountant: Account for Thyself," *The Journal of Accountancy*, Vol. 135, no. 6 (June 1973), 40, 41.

5. Paul Hazard, "The Soul of France Shall Live," in *Resistance*, (September 1944). From *Books, Children, and Men*, Preface to the Fourth Edition by Bertha Miller Mahony (Boston: The Horn Book, 1960), p. xxiii.

The Role of the Accounting Profession

in International Business Ethics

Michael N. Chetkovich

AICPA Chairman-Elect
Managing Partner, Haskins & Sells

I share Professor Brummet's concern, as I believe we all do, over the ethical standards of some of our largest and, until now, more respected business institutions. There probably is cause for equal or even greater concern with respect to some of our social institutions, starting with government. I too believe that the accounting profession has an important role to play in the tumultuous and somewhat disoriented changes stemming from the heightened public concern over this issue. I tend to differ with Professor Brummet, not in goals—except perhaps in degree—but about who should be expected to do what and how much. Before we address specifics, some background remarks might be appropriate: I refer to the subject of sensitive payments.

BACKGROUND

In the past few years, as the title to a recent book goes, *Something Happened,* and most of us are not only attempting to determine what to do about it, but also to understand why it happened, and even exactly what it is that has taken place. We have witnessed a myriad of revelations which have seriously affected many of our traditional assumptions about the way in which businessmen and our political and other leaders transact with one another.

Watergate may have opened the doors, but other events also have coalesced to effect pronounced changes in our perceptions of our business and social institutions. Disclosures of illegal political contributions and surreptitious payments on an international scale continue to occupy our attention. A significant number of the largest U.S. companies have made public disclosures of illegal political contributions, bribes, kickbacks, and other improper or questionable payments at home and abroad extending over a period of years. There is hardly a company of any significant size today which is not devoting attention to the issue in one way or another. The net result of all of this has been a decrease in confidence in and respect for many of our institutions, our political system, our business establishment, and our assumed ethical standards. Yet it is very difficult to gauge the depth and real significance of this reaction. For example, it would seem to have much greater political-legislative impact than market-investor effect.

Historically, the issue arose as a by-product of the Watergate controversy, from which information concerning political slush funds and U.S. illegal campaign contributions was generated. Further investigations, such as those conducted by the SEC and other U.S. regulatory agencies, in addition to testimony before the U.S. Senate Committee on Multinational Corporations resulted in further and broader disclosures of questionable or improper activities. It was learned that disbursements from secret funds had found their way not only into U.S. political campaigns, but also into those of countries outside the U.S.—in some cases to gain concessions or other favorable treatment. In other instances, corporation records were falsified to disguise the purposes or payees of certain disbursements which were tantamount to bribes or kickbacks.

The issue took on rather tangible and direct international dimensions when, in early 1975, the chief executive officer of United Brands Company apparently committed suicide by leaping from his midtown Manhattan office in New York City. Subsequently, and partially as a result of an ensuing SEC investigation, United Brands publicly disclosed the payment of $1.25 million to a Honduran official to obtain favorable tax treatment. Since that time, over 200 U.S. companies have come forward to admit various types and amounts of improper or questionable payments, most of them having to do with overseas operations.

Definition and Purpose of Sensitive Payments

These disclosures pose a difficult and frustrating problem, particularly to the interested reader who *wants* to evaluate their significance: what wrong has been done, and by whom, and what does it mean? As in any problem area, it is difficult to understand and discuss the issues unless we are able to focus on just what it is that concerns us. However, efforts at arriving at a workable definition of the problem and a sharper focus have not been fruitful. Certainly, legal standards alone have not been a sufficient basis. Although various forms of new legislation are being considered, present American law does *not* necessarily make it illegal for U.S.-based companies to make political contributions or to pay bribes in foreign countries. Foreign legality standards are equally insufficient. Although it is illegal under the laws of most foreign countries to pay outright bribes and kickbacks to government officials, standards as to what constitutes a bribe and the level of enforcement effort vary considerably from country to country.

Moreover, in some foreign countries, actions which usually would be considered improper in the United States and elsewhere have been legitimized and even institutionalized. For example, the *despachante* system in Brazil is a means whereby an intermediary is paid a fee to expedite certain transactions (such as in obtaining visas for foreigners, customs permits, and even drivers' licenses). Without the *despachante's* assistance, applications such as these generally can die at the bottom of some official's desk drawer, or at the least, be delayed for many months. The *American Journal of Comparative Law*, in a 1971 article on the system, cited the yellow pages of the Rio telephone book as an example of just how entrenched the system is. These pages contained more than 300 entries for *despachantes*—and this was only a partial listing.

The purposes for which "questionable" payments are made vary. Some payments are made in the "normal" or, at least, every day course of business to avoid red tape and possible harassment. In other cases, payments may be made to obtain a competitive advantage or to influence government officials in providing special favors, such as in awarding or renewing contracts. For example, one corporation has said that $450,000 in payments made to a sales agent and allegedly passed to two generals of a foreign nation were demanded as a precondition for their approval of the purchase of the company's product.

Other payments are made to support or influence political processes or parties in a host country. The United Brands payment to influence tax legislation favorable to the company is an example of this type. In other cases, contributions have been made to political parties that generally supported policies or programs favorable to the contributing company. Corporate political contributions are legally permissible in a number of countries, for example, Canada and Italy; but in the United States they are generally illegal. It has been common for corporations to make regular contributions to Canadian political parties, without any indication of impropriety. In other countries, though, (and particularly in Italy) it has been alleged that political contributions of a number of companies were made in order to influence the recipients' decisions on various matters of particular and immediate interest to the contributors.

One must recognize that it is not always possible to determine clearly and objectively the reason the payments were made, or even the identity of the ultimate recipient. This problem frequently arises in connection with the payment of agents' fees. In the Middle East and certain other parts of the world, an agent generally is required for the successful completion of a commercial transaction. In fact, in some areas of the Middle East it is a legal requirement to have a local agent before a proposal is even considered.

The agent's fee usually is related to the size of the order, and can range anywhere from, say, 4 to 25% of the selling price. The agent, in return for his fee, uses his influence to close the deal. The difficulty arises in determining the extent and the nature of this influence. It can range from normal friendships or family ties between the purchasing official and the agent to the payment of substantial sums of money, commonly called *baksheesh,* to government officials. In most cases, it is extremely difficult to monitor the actions of the independent agent, even if one wished to do so.

If business is to be transacted in certain countries, however, the use of such agents is necessary. There is the classic example of a new vice-president of a U.S. firm who, after reviewing company agents' fees, decided that a certain Middle East agent's contract should be cancelled. Within forty-eight hours after cancelling that agent's contract, all local work permits of the company's employees were withdrawn.

ROLE OF THE ACCOUNTING PROFESSION

One can see from all this that we just simply are not facing a one-dimensional problem, but a multifaceted issue that defies simple resolution. Undoubtedly, the recent SEC *Report on Questionable and Illegal Corporate Payments and Practices* has clarified the SEC's position on which kinds of payments must be disclosed in filings with the Commission; the legislation which the commission has recommended indicates its views as to how these practices should be controlled. But there are still a number of unanswered questions and a need for careful judgment and legal consultation in gray areas. As a result, most multinational corporations are reexamining their existing policies and are establishing strict guidelines and controls.

Against this backdrop, the accounting profession in the United States has attempted to define more clearly the role of the auditor in this environment. Specific questions have been raised about the responsibility of auditors to uncover illegal acts and to require disclosure of such acts by their clients. Some even have suggested, as Professor Brummet does in his paper, that "auditors should clearly accept responsibility to see that many matters of law are being adhered to by the client corporation . . . . [and, further, that] accountants should not only take responsibility for certain matters of law—they should also accept responsibility in *all areas in which the credibility of the profession may be at stake.*" Such suggestions have undergone extensive consideration by the Auditing Standards Executive Committee of the AICPA. As a result of its deliberations, the committee recently issued an exposure draft of a Statement on Auditing Standards titled "Illegal Acts by Clients."

Comments were due by July 30 and issuance of the statement in a form substantially similar to that of the exposure draft is expected soon. The statement, when issued, would provide the following guidance to an auditor vis-à-vis *illegal acts:*

An examination made in accordance with generally accepted auditing standards cannot be expected to provide absolute assurance that illegal acts will be detected. The basic objective of such an examination is to form an opinion as to whether the financial statements are fairly presented in conformity with generally accepted accounting principles.

Although an auditor's training and experience should provide a reasonable basis for an awareness that some acts by a client coming to his attention in performing his examination might be illegal, the determination of the legality of such acts usually is beyond his professional competence.

Further, the draft recognizes that there are inherent limitations in the auditor's ability to uncover illegal acts, even if he had the prerequisite knowledge to make a legal determination:

The auditor's resources and authority for obtaining information are significantly less than those of a law enforcement or regulatory agency conducting an examination. He does not have subpoena power or the force of the courts behind him. Obtaining information and support depends to a considerable extent on the willing cooperation of management.

The further removed an illegal act is from those events and transactions specifically reflected in financial statements, the less likely it is that the auditor will recognize the illegality or even become aware of the act. Examples of this type include violations of . . . OSHA [Occupational Safety and Health Act], employment discrimination laws, and environmental regulations.

If these limitations are considered serious inadequacies of the present system and in need of change, then the auditing function as we know it today would have to be significantly altered. Not only would the audit necessitate the use of outside experts, but there would have to be a significant change in the nature of the audit function, making it more of a detailed total investigation of the client's conduct and affairs rather than an examination of his financial statements. This change would have to be accompanied by a modification in the method of obtaining information and probably would involve extending subpoena power (or something similar) to the auditor. The resulting increase in the cost of an audit and probable delay in issuing audited financial results would, in my opinion, not be offset by the utility of the information obtained and additional assurance gained. Further, such extensions of the auditor's role, toward making him more of a policeman, could significantly impair the effectiveness of the audit function as we know it.

The proposed statement does more than recognize the present limitations on the responsibility of auditors, though. It goes on to offer practical suggestions for the auditor who has uncovered a possible illegal act as a result of his financial statement examination. Of course, disclosure in the financial statements *is* necessary if there are potential material adverse financial effects. The statement, however, requires the auditor to consider not only the direct effects on the financial statements in evaluating materiality. He also is required to consider related contingent monetary effects (such as fines, penalties, and damages), the possible effects of expropriation threats, and the potential loss of a significant amount of business.

The implications of a possible illegal act also should be considered in respect to the reliability which the auditor assigns to internal control and management representations. Further, illegal acts that are uncovered should be reported to a proper level of authority in the client's organization, usually to the audit committee or board of directors. If the effects of the illegal act do not have a material effect on the financial statements, but the client does not give appropriate consideration to remedial action, the auditor then should consider withdrawing from the engagement and also consider, in consultation with legal counsel, whether to notify third parties.

I believe that the position taken by the profession in this document is a sound one, and one that will provide both guidance for the auditor and a definitive benchmark against which the auditor's performance in this sensitive area can be measured. Admittedly, though, it does not significantly expand the range of auditor responsibility, as advocated by Professor Brummet.

EXPANDED RESPONSIBILITY

Professor Brummet's call for auditor assumption of additional responsibility in the enforcement of international business ethics raises, I think, a separate issue. He has asked auditors to adopt a broader view and to take a greater responsibility for performance measurement, public disclosure, and audit assurances. Although he lauds the profession for certain favorable developments he has perceived over the last few years, he observes that our response to the developing needs of the profession and the public have been too slow, that we should have anticipated those needs by means of futures planning, and should have initiated responses on a more timely basis, rather than as a reaction to an already existing and festering problem.

We would all concede, I am sure, that in any human endeavor there always is *more* that could or should be done. And certainly any institution or organization needs some prodding to keep it moving in the right direction. But expectations should be kept within the bounds of reason and critics should temper their criticism with understanding.

The AICPA Planning and Finance Committee has a primary role in looking to and planning for the future. In addition to reviewing the Institute budget, the committee is expected periodically to appraise the current state of the profession and the developing trends which might affect it. Its objective is to recommend long-term strategies to enhance the profession's ability to respond effectively to changing conditions. The major areas of concern presently being considered by the committee are the following: (1) credibility and responsibilities of auditors, (2) legal liability alternatives, (3) structure and role of the profession, (4) education and recruitment, (5) statutory authority of the profession, (6) external and internal relations and communications, and (7) public service obligations. So, I believe that we at the Institute *are* giving consideration to the concept of futures planning, and the Planning and Finance Committee, in particular, is committed to this concept.

Concerning the acceptance of broader responsibility, I think we have to take a look at the institutional environment faced today by the accounting profession to understand some of the reluctance to move boldly in this area. Warren Bennis in a recent essay on the subject of leadership has, I believe, captured the essence of the problem in his discussion of the erosion of institutional autonomy. A major factor in this erosion is the litigious environment in which all institutions find themselves today. And this is especially true of the accounting profession. The growth of class action suits, in particular, has significantly increased the profession's liability exposure in the performance of the audit function. It is fair to say that these suits and their financial and related consequences are a serious concern to the profession.

In this kind of an environment it is a small wonder that we as professionals might tend to resist additional responsibility, particularly when that responsibility could well result in increased exposure to litigation and a geometrical risk progression. Indeed, Murphy's Law—the doctrine of anticipating the worst possible outcome because that is the one that frequently results—tends to be applied and as a result, there is a certain instinctive reluctance to accept an expanded range of responsibility.

But this reluctance, while it tends to be inhibiting, is far from being the most important factor restraining a significant expansion of the auditor's role into new areas—for example, examining and reporting on management performance and social responsibility and accountability.

To begin with, it should be recognized that even if the CPA profession concluded that it wanted to take on this responsibility, I doubt it could be done unilaterally. If there were to be public reporting, it seems to me that it would require some authority, conveyed by or stemming from some authoritative body or bodies outside the profession. We might work with clients, helping them in this area; but I don't see how we could just volunteer to take on a responsibility for public reporting, even if we were to be so inclined.

Further, as Brummet indicates, this area of service would require additional skills, a special competence, and certainly the profession would have to be confident that it possessed the competence in what still is a rather vaguely defined and uncharted area before it undertook to proceed.

The profession *should* devote research and study to these possible new areas of service, and as Brummet points out, we *are* doing that. Certainly, we should apply those particular skills we possess, such as in measurement and attestation, in helping to move the art forward. But, it is my belief that, as accountants, there is a distinct limit to how much we can do. If it is concluded that there should or must be reporting on compliance with social responsibilities, it will have to be developed and refined by a multidiscipline approach—including businessmen, accountants, lawyers, sociologists, the government, and so on. Certainly we should participate, particularly in shaping our own role. But I'm not for our taking on the whole burden, for I'm afraid we can't handle it.

There is still another important constraint that should be considered—that is, that the profession already has quite a lot on its plate in terms of effectively discharging its present responsibilities in the attest area: examining and reporting on financial position and results of operations. While we should *not* ignore extensions of the attest function where there is a need, or a public interest we can serve, we must guard against unnecessary diversions of our time or resources. I contend that, in our current environment, there is sufficient challenge in the field of financial reporting and enough unresolved problems to warrant pretty much all our time and interest. We don't need to look for challenges—some of which sometimes seem to be in the category of "insurmountable opportunities."

There is no simple answer to this dilemma of the auditor's role, but a proper recognition and understanding of the problem is important. There also is a need to examine another pressing matter—that of the unsatisfied needs of readers of financial statements. We must do our best to be responsive to this public need, but a better definition of what information is really needed and which "public" it is that we are trying to satisfy would be a great help to us. Hopefully, the work of the Commission on Auditors' Responsibilities and the SEC-appointed Disclosure Commission, headed by former Commissioner Sommer, as well as the FASB's conceptual framework project, will provide us with some of the information we need to answer these questions.

But we must realize that, regardless of how helpful these studies may be, we cannot be all things to all people. We need to zero in on our objectives—to define just what it is we are trying to accomplish and who it is we are trying to serve. To the extent that our sense of duty to the public and our own judgment as to what is appropriate lead us to assume added responsibilities, we necessarily must consider what can be done to minimize exposure to added legal liability.

To go back to the sensitive payments problem, and it has been and is a difficult one, I believe that the profession has been responsive to what reasonably could be expected of us and perhaps even more. We would not claim to have been heroes, but we *have* faced up to our responsibilities under some trying conditions.

It could well be that here in the USA we are on the threshold of an important new era, where there will be a greater emphasis on ethics and ethical behavior, from both an institutional and an individual point of view. I believe that the accounting profession can and will play an important role, one of which we can all be proud.

My closing is on a philosophical note. In appraising standards of behavior and passing judgment on the moral significance of such acts as are encompassed in sensitive payments, we must try to be fair and reasonable, and avoid hypocritical conclusions. We should be careful about making retroactive value judgments, that is, appraising actions of a different time and environment against more recent standards. We should not expect significantly higher standards of conduct of institutions and organizations than we are prepared to live up to as individuals.

At the same time, we should guard against a tendency to rationalize departures from proper standards of conduct on the basis that "everybody does it." While customs and standards of business conduct may vary somewhat—and even considerably—from country to country and area to area, I doubt that there is any place in the world where honesty is looked down upon. And in the eternal struggle to match conduct with ideals, it is much better that we try to raise conduct closer to ideals than to lower ideals to match conduct.

THREE

Multinational Enterprises and the SEC

An in-depth presentation on the elements necessary to ensure that financial statements provide a fair presentation to governmental agencies. Accounting firms' relationships to multinational enterprises and the SEC are discussed.

Ernest L. Ten Eyck

*Assistant Chief Accountant
Securities and Exchange Commission*

Mr. Ten Eyck holds a B.B.A. degree from George Washington University. He is responsible for research and development of changes to the Commission's rules and regulations governing financial statements, as well as providing assistance to other staff departments in the areas of compliance and enforcement. He is also in charge of matters related to SEC international policies.

James J. Quinn

*National Director of Accounting
Auditing and SEC Practice
Coopers & Lybrand*

Mr. Quinn holds a B.S. degree from Fordham University. He is a member of the firm's technical policy committee and chairman of the firm's SEC review board. He has authored numerous papers and articles on SEC matters.

Multinational Enterprises and the SEC

Ernest L. Ten Eyck

Assistant Chief Accountant
Securities and Exchange Commission

There has been a substantial expansion of interest by American investors in the securities of foreign issuers in recent years.* While the total magnitude of this interest is difficult to pinpoint,[1] one aspect is reflected by public offerings in the U.S. by foreign issuers. Such offerings, for cash, increased from about $34 million in 1973 to approximately $634 million in 1972.[2] The abandonments in 1974 of the interest equalization tax, the Fed's Voluntary Foreign Credit Restraint Guidelines, and the Commerce Department's rules controlling direct overseas investment have generally been regarded as the impetus for this growth.

While the growth curve of new foreign issues is impressive, the impact of these issues on the U.S. Securities markets is anything but monumental when compared to a new issue volume of over $80 billion for similar offerings by U.S. companies during 1975.[3] The practical, philosophical, and political problems which are associated with the issuance and trading of foreign securities, however, have insured a continuing interest in this area which is unrelated to mere financial statistics.

---

*The commission disclaims responsibility for any private publication by any of its employees. The views expressed are those of the author, and do not necessarily represent the views of the commission or its staff.

51

FOREIGN ISSUERS AND THE ROLE OF THE SEC

Although it is sometimes difficult to recognize a direct correlation, the activities of the SEC—like those of all federal regulatory bodies—are circumscribed by the intent of Congress as articulated in enabling legislation. Both the Securities Act of 1933 and the Securities Exchange Act of 1934 clearly were not drafted with any intent of erecting barriers to foreign entrance to U.S. securities markets. The barriers which do exist are primarily the result of diverse legal and economic environments, rather than of any isolationist tendencies on the part of federal legislators. On the commission's part, fairly broad discretionary powers granted by Congress are utilized to ease the impact of these natural barriers. Within the commission's mandate for the protection of U.S. investors, a highly pragmatic approach has historically been used in addressing the peculiar registration and reporting problems of foreign entities. This pragmatism is generally reflected in both the rules of the commission and in the solution to specific problems handled by the commission and its staff.

The Regulatory Framework

The Securities Act of 1933, while not erecting barriers for foreign issuers, made few concessions either. The only basic statutory distinction in the registration requirements of this Act relates to foreign governments and their political subdivisions, which are required to present somewhat less or different information than a corporate or other business entity. A corporate issuer, however, is technically required to make the same disclosures regardless of its national domicile. Neither the rules nor the registration forms promulgated under the Securities Act differentiate between domestic and foreign companies. As a matter of administrative discretion, however, broader disclosures are sometimes required, and narrower disclosures are sometimes permitted in certain circumstances. Discussions of the political environment in certain countries is often deemed appropriate, for instance. In addition, financial statements are generally required to be presented both in local currency and in a "convenience" U.S. dollar format. On the other hand, foreign registrants are frequently permitted to reveal simply the aggregate remuneration of management in lieu of specific amounts paid to individuals, since such disclosure is practically unheard of in many parts of the world. Similarly, certain quasi-political units (such as the European Coal and Steel Community) have been permitted to utilize a registration statement format similar to the Schedule B filings by foreign governments. Among other things, this avoids the necessity for audited GAAP basis financial statements for such entities.

With respect to corporate financial statements, administrative discretion is used quite liberally to permit registrants much the same flexibility provided more formally with respect to financial statements included in 1934 Act reports, discussed in some detail below.

The 1964 amendments to the Securities Exchange Act of 1934[4] recognize the potential problems of foreign issuers much more explicitly than any previous legislation. Section 12(g)3 gives the SEC broad discretion to ". . . exempt partially or completely [from the continuous reporting requirements] foreign securities . . . when such action is appropriate."[5] The commission's response to this carte blanche authority was the adoption of Rule 12(g)3-2, which—when roughly translated from legalese—grants substantial relief for foreign issuers from many of the continuous reporting requirements to which most U.S. companies are subject, such as Forms 10-K, 10-Q and 8-K. No exemption is available, however, for companies: (1) with securities listed on a national securities exchange such as the New York Stock Exchange or the American Stock Exchange, or (2) which issued securities registered under the 1933 Act. For convenience of discussion, these nonexempt issuers will be referred to as Class I companies. Other companies fall into one of two categories. If the company does not meet the general requirements for Exchange Act registration which applies to all issuers (assets of $1 million and 500 shareholders) or does not have 300 shareholders resident in the U.S., it is exempt from substantially all reporting requirements. If the issuer *does* meet the shareholder and asset tests, it may either:

1. register under the Exchange Act and thus become subject to the same reporting requirements as a Class I company, or
2. furnish the commission promptly with whatever information it otherwise makes public and thereby obtain exemption from the reporting requirements of Section 12(g). (These will be referred to as Class II companies.)

For most Class I companies, the periodic reporting forms are the 20-K and the 6-K. North American companies in this category, however, are subject to the same reporting requirements as U.S. firms, i.e., they must file 10-Ks, 10-Qs and 8-Ks.

For all practical purposes, *North American* means Canadian, the wording of the regulations having apparently been drafted with an eye towards avoiding the appearance of political discrimination. This distinction has a heritage dating back to the original adoption of the Exchange Act regulations in 1935, when the commission noted:

> The large and continued interflow of business between the United States and its neighboring countries makes uniformity of registration requirements desirable. There is sufficient similarity between the corporate and accounting practices of the United States and those of other North American countries to make uniform registration requirements practicable. Furthermore, corporations in these neighboring countries are close enough to the United States to make the filing of the required information feasible within the required time.[6]

Form 20-K is an annual report somewhat similar to the more familiar 10-K. Unlike the 10-K, Form 20-K does not require an annual recitation of required information. Rather, it is used to update information concerning the registrant's business, properties and so on, and only changes during the year are reported. The form does require, however, the same audited financial statements as are included in Form 10-K, but at the same time provides considerable leeway to both issuers and the Commission in meeting this requirement. The principal concession to foreign accounting problems is the "reconciliation" to U.S. GAAP permitted by the instructions to Form 20-K: "Any material variation in accounting principles or practices from the form and content of financial statements prescribed in Regulation S-X shall be disclosed and, to the extent practicable, the effect of each such variation given."[7]

This accommodation has been applied in practice to permit presentations ranging from a complete conversion of the financial statements to U.S. GAAP, to a simple disclosure that the company did not possess sufficient data to calculate what a particular result would be under GAAP.

The instructions to Form 20-K also permit the omission or substitution of particular financial statements from those otherwise required, at the discretion of the Commission. Such discretion has seldom been used since most of the world either uses the U.S. approach to basic financial statements or has available sufficient information to permit their preparation. A similar expedience is provided for auditing standards and procedures applied by independent accountants. This too has been infrequently applied. As a practical matter, most 20-K filers have engaged offices or affiliates of U.S.-based international accounting firms. This typically has resulted in the auditors having made an examination in accordance with auditing standards generally acceptable in the U.S. Where this is not the case, the staff has generally been reluctant to permit exceptions. Unlike differences in accounting principles where the results of a deviation can normally be identified as to amount, it is not generally possible to quantify the reduced assurance provided when there has been a deviation from GAAS.

Unlike registration statements filed under the 1933 Act, there is no requirement in connection with Form 20-K that registrants provide "convenience" U.S. dollar financial statements or similar information designated other than in the local currency. The filing must be in English, however.

Form 6-K is the only other commonly used form for Class I companies. It is really not a "form" so much as a cover document under which such issuers are generally required to file documents which they make public overseas. English translations of these documents are not required unless prepared in the normal course of business. Financial information in the form of interim reports for instance is generally designated only in local currency, as well as being prepared in accordance with local accounting principles.

Class II companies technically do not even have filing requirements, since the documents submitted to maintain their exemption are not *filed* but *furnished.* This permits them to avoid certain legal exposures under the Act. Like the documents filed under cover of Form 6-K, these need not be in English unless a translation is otherwise prepared by the issuer.

PROBLEMS IN DISCLOSURE DOCUMENTS
OF FOREIGN ISSUERS

Enforcement may well be the largest single difficulty facing the commission in attempting to impose the federal securities laws on foreign entities. This very real difficulty is one of the bases underlying the traditionally practical and flexible approach adopted in implementing the securities laws. The commission's expressed disclosure requirements applicable to foreign registrants have been formulated, for the most part, based on what was perceived to be the maximum information that foreign issuers generally could or would provide on a voluntary basis. In adopting the exemptive provisions of Rule 12(g)3-2, for instance, the commission stated that:

> . . . the continuing improvement in the quality of the information now being made public by foreign issuers, together with improvement which may reasonably be expected to result from recent changes and current proposals for change in relevant requirements, warrants the pro-

vision of an exemption from Section 12(g) for those foreign companies
which have not sought a public market for their securities in the United
States through public offering or stock exchange listing, and which furnish the Commission certain information which they publish abroad
pursuant to law or stock exchange requirements or which they send to
their security holders . . .[8]

The enforcement problem is not particularly troublesome in connection
with registered public offerings.[9] Although the SEC technically cannot stop a
registered offering from proceeding except by legal action, both registrants
and broker-dealers participating in the offering proceed at their peril if they
are put on notice that the commission staff has reservations about the prospectus. As a practical matter, few, if any, are willing to run such a risk.

In the context of the 1934 Act, the commission's ability to correct any perceived deficiencies in the periodic reporting process is somewhat more
limited. While the author is singularly unqualified to discuss matters of international law, it is apparent that the commission, for all practical purposes, is
limited in the use of many of its traditional enforcement tools against foreign
companies.[10] Institution of civil suits or administrative proceedings might, for
instance, simply result in the company's failure to respond.

The sanction which is always available is simply to suspend trading in the
company's securities. This probably is not perceived as a particularly useful
device, since the hardship would fall principally on U.S. security holders
rather than on the foreign issuers, most of whom are not significantly dependent on the U.S. securities market.

These enforcement problems, the relatively small number of foreign
issuers, and the absence historically of any major problems have combined to
produce a relatively lax atmosphere with respect to administration of the
periodic reporting requirements for foreign entities. As a result, reports are
frequently delinquent[11] and questionable compliance is relatively com-
monplace. On the other hand, the issuers apparently are doing at least a
passable job of putting information in the hands of shareholders, since complaints are extremely rare. Like the majority of issuer filings under the
securities laws, Forms 20-K and 6-K, as well as the materials submitted to
maintain exemption under Rule 12(g)3-2, are available at the SEC's public
reference room and copies are supplied on request. The attitude of the investing public towards the availability of the majority of this material might
be characterized as one of sublime indifference, as requests are few and far between.[12]

Those that *are* interested in the filings may still face a formidable obstacle, since many of the documents are not in English and few investors are so diligent in their search for information that they are willing to bear the expense of translation. Foreign language documents also have the potential for aggravating other problems, including the enforcement problem faced by the SEC itself. The carefully constructed disclosures of many public companies are difficult enough to understand when the original is in English.

Even the many companies which make extraordinary efforts to comply with the disclosure requirements of the U.S. securities laws may run afoul of the laws of their own country. The book-tax conformity requirements imposed by the tax authorities in many nations carry the potential for awesome fiscal penalties for transgressors. This may ultimately result in clumsy financial statement presentations designed to comply both with local tax law and the requirement for disclosures of deviations from GAAP. In addition, countries with their own securities laws sometimes impose "conformity" requirements with respect to disclosures made in other documents, including SEC reports. Legal structures overseas also may place limitations on the flexibility of companies in conducting their operations, through restrictions upon such things as discharge of employees and currency exchange. Each problem in these and other areas is dealt with as it arises, generally through meetings with the SEC staff. There are no "country desks" at the commission, and the burden is largely on the issuer to identify and raise potential difficulties, a process which appears to have worked well.

This functional philosophy encompasses the accounting area as well. Although there are those who would challenge any contention that the U.S. is a leader in the development of accounting principles, there is little disagreement with the proposition that we are at least *different*. The wide variety of accounting principles employed in various nations give rise to some of the more interesting challenges faced by both registrants and the commission in attempting to effectuate "full and fair disclosure". In dealing with U.S. registrants, there is a basic principle generally employed at the SEC that deviations from acceptable accounting *measurement* principles cannot be cured by disclosure. That philosophy does not work particularly well when it is applied to foreign registrants for two principal reasons. First, there are numerous situations where foreign companies simply have not kept their records in such a way that the details necessary to prepare GAAP basis information are readily available. This has been a particular problem recently, for instance, for companies attempting to apply the requirements of FASB Statement No. 8 regarding foreign currency translation. In these situations, the commission staff generally weighs the benefits of strict compliance against the cost and other burdens placed on the registrant in order to arrive at a reasonable solution. As a result, the solution to the same problem may vary from company to company. Second, a few U.S. accounting principles are based on an economic or business environment which is markedly different from that overseas.

The leading example of this situation is the Japanese "free share distribution." Unlike its U.S. cousin, the "stock dividend," it is not designed as a placebo for shareholders, but usually as a device for maintaining the relative interests of new and old shareholders or preserving what is, in Japan, an almost sacrosanct relationship between cash dividends and par values. Although the necessary data for "capitalizing" these transactions at market value is available, doing so would usually produce large negative retained earnings and an equity picture wholly out of kilter with economic reality. The Japanese measurement principle is therefore permitted—accounted for at par value—with note disclosure of the deviation from U.S. GAAP.

Disclosure problems related to foreign financial statements are generally minimal outside those related to differences in accounting practices. As with other disclosures, problems peculiar to the company's operating environment are expected to be raised by the company and dealt with in an appropriate manner. Disclosures which necessitate the gathering of voluminous data at large expense are frequently waived, occasionally on the somewhat cynical grounds that nobody understands the information anyway. Pension cost disclosures are a typical example.

Foreign auditors may present several unique problems in attempting to fit particular situations to the U.S. regulatory framework. As mentioned previously, the commission staff is particularly reluctant to permit exceptions in this respect. The ultimate goal is always to obtain a U.S. style auditor's report from competent accountants which represents that an examination was performed in accordance with *generally accepted auditing standards* as that term is used in this country. Where that goal cannot be met, the problem is usually related to one or more of the following.

1. *Independence.* The concept of independence as U.S. practitioners understand it is virtually unknown outside North America. While a few exceptions have been permitted, the staff has generally insisted that overseas auditors take steps to conform to the independence requirements of Regulation S-X. Concessions which are made often consist of permitting corrective measures to be taken *ex post facto.* No independence issue has been raised, for instance, when an audit partner divests himself of

securities of the client prior to the most recent audit date, even though such securities may have been held during an earlier audit period included in the filing. Other independence problems may be virtually incurable, as when the auditing firm is owned by a bank with a substantial financial interest in the client, not an unusual occurrence in certain countries. In such instances the registrant may be forced either to engage new auditors or to find independent auditors who are willing to assume joint responsibility with the firm currently engaged.

2. *Familiarity with U.S. practices.* Even when a foreign firm has no independence problems, there may be inadequate expertise available to tackle the substantial problems associated with conforming financial statements to U.S. GAAP and with conducting an examination in accordance with U.S. GAAS. If a proposed filing reaches the commission before these problems are solved, there is little that can be done except to refuse the filing. This is an almost unknown occurrence, at least in '33 Act filings, thanks to the functions of underwriters in foreign offerings. As one major underwriter has noted: "Smith, Barney & Co. has found it beneficial when filing 1933 Act registrations on behalf of corporate clients based in countries with substantially different accounting principles, to suggest U.S. accountants as advisors to the issuer at an early stage of the proceedings to assist the issuer's own accountants to comply with SEC requirements pertaining to the financial statements."[13] As with domestic issues, underwriters are a virtual necessity for a successful offering. Since nearly all major underwriters follow similar policies, foreign issuers have a substantial incentive to engage a U.S. accounting firm.

3. *Local professional standards.* American public accounting practitioners generally tend to think of themselves as the best in the world, a view which is probably accurate, if somewhat less than modest. The SEC for its part has consistently reaffirmed its belief that the assurances provided by the association of auditors with financial information is a significant factor in the maintenance of a viable securities marketplace in the United States. As noted earlier, it is difficult for the SEC or anyone else to weigh the effects of a deviation from generally accepted standards or procedures on the degree of assurance which is provided by an independent accountant's report.

In numerous countries, this may be more than just a problem of compliance with technical standards. The local audit environment in many cases is one with its concepts and philosophies rooted in statutory compliance considerations, or in notions of "accounting" which are more akin to our definition of bookkeeping. Such abstractions as "form versus substance", "fairness" and "skepticism" are truly "foreign" and even the closest working relationship with U.S. professionals is not likely to overcome such a basic handicap easily. As a practical matter, this delicate dilemma has rarely been faced, since a solution to the more obvious difficulty of familarity with SEC reporting requirements has resolved the difficulties, usually via the engagement of a U.S. accounting firm.

The Outlook for the Future

There are several projects presently underway at the SEC which may eventually have an impact on the participation by foreign companies in the U.S. securities markets. Two of these projects may see the light of day in the relatively near future.

Guide 24[14] for 1933 Act filings concerns the use of "convenience" financial statements by foreign registrants. As presently written, its guidance is minimal, merely noting that ". . . where necessary to a clear understanding, the U.S. dollar equivalent should be shown in parallel columns or otherwise, as appropriate." In practice, the financial statements for each period presented have generally been converted to U.S. dollars at the exchange rate as of the most recent balance sheet date. Since the advent of "floating" exchange rates, there have been some variations, usually conversion at the prevailing rate at each year-end presented. More recently, rampant inflation and other factors have caused exchange rates for several currencies to move erratically, giving rise to serious questions about the appropriateness of any particular exchange rate. These and other considerations—including a continuing concern with the potential for misinterpretation of convenience financial statements— are causing the commission staff to reexamine Guide 24. This could result in a proposal either to eliminate the use of convenience financial statements or to provide much more specific guidelines for their preparation.

Forms 20 and 20-K were last amended in 1967, and even with those changes, they still require considerably less information than the much revised Forms 10 and 10-K required to be submitted by most U.S. companies. There is also a general perception that the bulk of foreign issuers are now both willing and capable of providing considerably more data than nine years ago. A significant effort is presently underway in this respect, and may result in proposed revisions in these forms. It is not likely, however, that the proposals will go quite so far as requiring information as extensive as that required for 10-K filers.

Perhaps more significant than these and other particular projects is the general rise in the attention being devoted to international matters. One indication of this enhanced awareness is the recent creation of a Directorate of International Policy at the commission, augmenting the existing Office of International Corporate Finance and various other functions throughout the SEC concerned with international capital markets and similar matters.

A somewhat less academic interest in multinational phenomena is reflected in the ongoing succession of revelations concerning U.S. corporate involvement in "transnational influence payments," triggered by the SEC's version of an amnesty program. Reverberations from these disclosures have produced many threatening noises in the halls of Congress, but as yet not a great deal in the way of direct action. When the preoccupation with elections is over, our legislators may yet be heard from.

The increase in foreign involvement in our securities markets is likely to continue in any case. As it does, largely *ad hoc* practices currently employed will become more difficult to apply to the attendant problems, and an increasing formality is likely to emerge, with rules and regulations gradually replacing staff discretion.

In another aspect of the SEC's work, an ambitious project is underway by the commission's Advisory Committee on Corporate Disclosure. Among other things, this group is reexamining what many perceive as a highly questionable concept that "more is better". It is not inconceivable that the results of that committee's work could eventually lead to a substantially reduced disclosure framework for registered U.S. companies, perhaps moving closer to what is currently required of foreign issuers.

Things are by no means static in other parts of the world. Several international and transnational political organizations, including the United Nations, the European Economic Community and the Organization of American States, are beginning to exert considerable influence. Much of this activity is directed towards establishing uniform or minimum standards for reporting by public companies. In addition, several countries are in the process of establishing or expanding regulatory organizations similar to the SEC; some have sought and found guidance from the commission in this effort.

In the accounting arena, the International Accounting Standards Committee has raised hopes among its member nations that the establishment of at least minimal principles of accounting and disclosure can be agreed upon and enforced. In addition, organizations such as the International Accountants Study Group have added considerably to an understanding of the accounting framework as it functions in the major industrialized nations.

All of these factors taken together make it temptingly easy to project a continuing trend towards uniformity and increased access to foreign securities markets by all concerned. The kicker to this scenario may well be accounting itself, which traditionally has presented a major obstacle to the efficient conduct of multinational business. Despite the encouraging results of international efforts, there are some indications that the future could hold even more difficult problems than the past.

Until fairly recently, the historical tendency overseas was for accounting principles to develop somewhat more slowly than those in the U.S., but generally in the same direction. One of the more meaningful breaks in that trend came with the adoption of Statement No. 8 of the Financial Accounting Standards Board: "Accounting for the Translation of Foreign Currency Transactions and Foreign Currency Financial Statements." Aside from the chorus of anguished groans produced among this country's financial executives, that Olympian pronouncement has at least two significant implications for students of international accounting. Whatever the tendencies in other areas towards uniformity, it is fairly obvious that one of the last differences to disappear will be local units of exchange. The principles used in accounting for those differences are therefore critical in the effort to promote the usefulness of the world's basic disclosure vehicle—financial statements. FASB No. 8, while achieving the admirable goal of eliminating alternatives at home, simultaneously put us out of step with the rest of the world. While a considerable array of alternatives is available in most countries, the particular scheme of FASB No. 8 is rarely chosen from that array. The chances appear very slim that any major authoritative body overseas will follow the U.S. lead in this area.

In addition, FASB No. 8 is considered by many to be the clearest of several indicia of where the board may be headed with the "Conceptual Framework" project. If that is indeed the case, the signs point toward a framework whose foundation is the historical cost model. While it is by no means certain that this is necessarily a bad idea, it is a sharp contrast to the direction our fellow professionals are taking in several countries. Most significant of these is probably the United Kingdom, where rapid progress is being made toward implementation of the "Sandilands Report" recommendations. If that project continues as scheduled, our British counterparts will have virtually abandoned the historical cost model by 1979. The Dutch, who embraced something close to the Sandilands current cost accounting concept years ago, but in a more limited way, may well follow suit.

The crystal ball is, thus, not all that clear. Given these conflicting tendencies around the world, only change itself seems reasonably certain.

NOTES

1. The total volume of American purchases of foreign securities is probably unknown since most such purchases take place outside the jurisdiction of the U.S., principally on foreign stock exchanges.
2. SEC Bulletin 142 (March 1976).
3. *Ibid.*
4. Specifically, Section 12(g)3 of the Act.
5. House Committee Report No. 1418, 88th Congress, 2d Session, 1964, p. 11.
6. Securities Exchange Act Release No. 34-158.
7. "Instructions As to Financial Statements," Form 20-K.
8. Securities Exchange Act Release No. 34-8066.
9. Unregistered public offerings (absent an exemption) are dealt with by the maintenance of the "Foreign Restricted List" which is periodically updated. This serves to keep brokers and dealers on notice concerning foreign securities being offered and sold illegally in the U.S.
10. North American-based issuers are in somewhat of a different posture due to the traditionally close cooperation of U.S. law enforcement agencies with those of our immediate neighbors.
11. Certain foreign political units with debt securities in the hands of U.S. residents have not filed appropriate reports since prior to World War II.
12. A few reports are relatively popular, but these are generally from registrants which consistently return to the market with new issues and therefore have both a broad U.S. shareholder base and a continuing incentive to comply.
13. Smith, Barney & Co., Inc. *The U.S. Securities Market: Reemerging Source of International Capital;* undated booklet published in 1974.
14. Guides are neither rules nor regulations of the commission but rather represent policies and practices followed by the commission's Division of Corporation Finance in the administration of the securities laws.

Multinational Enterprises and the SEC

James J. Quinn

National Director of Accounting, Auditing, and SEC Practice
Coopers & Lybrand

The growth of multinational business entities has been accompanied by significant increases in international investing and financing. It is no longer unusual for corporations to raise significant amounts of equity capital or debt in foreign capital markets. In addition, a growing number of corporations have found it advantageous to list their securities on exchanges outside the country in which they are domiciled.

Among the matters a company must evaluate in deciding whether to offer or list securities in foreign countries are the registration or listing requirements in those countries. A significant portion of those requirements deal with financial statements which have the potential of creating certain difficulties because of the lack of uniformity in accounting principles and auditing standards throughout the world

The following discussion, which is presented in outline form, analyzes these differences in accounting and auditing and the present movement to greater international conformity.* It then presents the problems in this area which may be faced by a non-U.S. company registering its securities in the United States and it cites the solutions to these problems which have been effected in practice. It also deals with the problems a U.S. company may face in the financial statement area in offering or listing securities in four of the major international capital markets: Canada, the United Kingdom, Germany,

---

*The author gratefully acknowledges the helpful comments of Professor Dhia D. AlHashim, California State University at Northridge, with regard to an earlier draft.

and Japan. The discussion concludes with a summary of the current movement within the European Economic Community for greater harmonization
of financial statement requirements and company law.

OVERVIEW

What I would like to do here is to take a trip around the world and from a
regulatory concept look at the problems that companies face in various areas
of the world, particularly as they relate to the question of security issuances
for listing applications on exchanges and to that of how accounting and auditing are involved.

I would like to start first with an overview of the situation. I think it goes
without saying that we all know there is a lack of uniformity throughout the
world in accounting in terms of financial statement presentation and disclosure, and certainly with respect to auditing standards and procedures, including independence. That's a given. Now, in looking at the problem from
the perspective of the non-U.S. company entering our own marketplace, a
subject that Mr. Ten Eyck has dealt with in great detail, it is first necessary to
understand the Securities Act of 1933 and the Securities Exchange Act of
1934. In essence, the 1933 Act relates to the issuance of new securities,
whereas the 1934 Act governs the trading of securities in the U.S. Neither of
those acts, as Ten Eyck has indicated, distinguishes between the U.S. company and the non-U.S. company; both are subject to the same requirements.
There is a problem here, then, if we both—the U.S. and non-U.S. companies—are subject to these requirements and have these fundamental
differences of accounting and auditing in financial statement presentation.
What do we do? Do we or does the regulatory authority—basically, the
SEC—impose our requirements on the overseas company, and thereby
perhaps deny access to U.S. capital markets to many foreign issuers limiting
the opportunity for U.S. residents to invest in such securities? On the other
hand, should the SEC accept financial statements and audit reports based on
the standards existing in the issuer's country, thereby establishing a dual
standard for registering securities in the U.S.? Well, what they've done, and I
think it is a reasonable compromise, is to follow a middle-of-the-road course
whereby certain deviations from U.S. requirements have been accepted on a
case by case basis, when such deviations are not inconsistent with the protection of the U.S. investor. I will talk later on about how that is done, at least in
the financial statement area.

The other main concerns to which I wish to address myself are the problems for a U.S. company going overseas in either listing their securities as many have done in the last few years, such as in Tokyo, or in raising money through debt offerings, such as in Germany. In terms of the Canadian marketplace, the problems for the U.S. company are not that severe, not that insurmountable. I will discuss later what those problems are briefly, and essentially how they are to be overcome. So, the message is, at least for the moment, that the U.S. company meeting the SEC requirements in terms of financial statements, auditing requirements, and disclosure requirements has a reasonably easy time in getting itself listed overseas or in issuing securities overseas.

The European Economic Community (EEC) has embarked on a long-term program aimed at harmonizing company law, which will eventually result in the standardization of accounting and reporting procedures of companies within the EEC. While this may ultimately simplify multinational offerings, it is still unclear whether it will affect the continued acceptability of U.S. financial statements and auditors' reports.

DIFFERENCES IN ACCOUNTING PRINCIPLES AND PRACTICES, FINANCIAL STATEMENT PRESENTATION, AND DISCLOSURE

While accounting may be the language of business, an international language has not yet been developed either for communication or for accounting. Differences in accounting principles and practices, as well as the form and content of financial statements, exist throughout the world. Two of the more frequently encountered reasons for these differences are the following:

a. Economists and economic thought having had an influence (notably in Europe) in the shaping of accounting practices, e.g., the theory of depreciation based on replacement value;

b. Provisions of tax laws and other statutes, such as revaluation of fixed assets for book and tax purposes on the basis of "coefficients" established by other governments, creation of mandatory and tax deductible reserves not found in the U.S., and the flow-through method of accounting for investment credit in the U.S.

It is important to understand that although there are differences among nations, this does not necessarily mean that the principles used in the United States are superior—or inferior—to those in other countries; they are simply different. For example, while replacement-value accounting is not yet accepted in the U.S., those who support it in other countries could argue that we have adopted it to some extent by the use of LIFO inventory methods.

While the possibility of attaining complete uniformity throughout the world is questionable, progress toward more uniformity among nations is being made. The following examples help to illustrate this point:

1. The formation of the Accountants International Study Group by the professional institutes of Great Britain, Ireland, Canada, and the United States in order to publish comparative studies (fifteen to date) of accounting and auditing practices in the participating countries;
2. The formation of the International Accounting Standards Committee in 1973 with the representation of selected professional accounting bodies from various countries in order to formulate and publish in the public interest basic standards to be observed in the presentation of audited accounts and financial statements and to promote their worldwide acceptance and observance; and
3. The development of a program by the EEC aimed at harmonizing company law and standardizing accounting and reporting procedures among member nations.

Some of the differences between principles and practices followed by foreign companies and those generally accepted in the United States include the following:

1. *Consolidated Financial Statements*
   Such statements have not been presented in many countries; however, the recent IASC Statement No. 3, "Consolidation of Financial Statements and Equity Accounting," is expected to result in significant changes in this regard.
2. *Cash*
   Restricted cash (particularly compensating balances) may not be segregated or disclosed in accordance with present SEC requirements.
3. *Inventories*
   a. The LIFO method, although accepted in the U.S., is not accepted in some other nations;
   b. Arbitrary write-downs accepted in some countries are not accepted in the U.S.;
   c. Replacement value is reflected in the basic financial statements of some companies in other countries. In the U.S., such values are not

reflected in the basic financial statements. However, the SEC does require footnote disclosure of replacement cost data by certain, but not all, registrants. The required disclosures include the current replacement cost of inventories at each fiscal year end for which a balance sheet is required, and, for the two most recent fiscal years, the approximate amount which cost of sales would have been had it been calculated by estimating the current replacement cost of goods and services sold at the times when the sales were made. (See ASR No. 190, SAB Nos. 7, 9, 10, and 11 and related SEC releases subsequently issued.) In some countries the basis for inventory valuation may not be disclosed.

4. *Investments*
   a. Investments accounted for under the "equity method" in the U.S. may be accounted for on the cost basis in other countries. However, the recent IASC Statement No. 3, "Consolidation of Financial Statements and Equity Accounting," is expected to result in significant changes in this regard.
   b. Omitted disclosures may include investor's interest in underlying equity of an affiliate and aggregate market value of marketable securities.

5. *Fixed Assets and Depreciation*
   a. Depreciation may continue to be provided on fully depreciated assets which are still in use.
   b. The basic financial statements of some companies in other countries reflect the write-up of fixed assets to reflect replacement values, with or without the benefit of government-computed "coefficients," and with depreciation based on such values. The SEC has accepted such depreciation in some form in the case of foreign issuers where the practice is sanctioned and controlled by the foreign governments and results in a new depreciation base for tax purposes.
   c. Replacement values are not reflected in basic financial statements in the United States. However, the SEC does require disclosure of certain replacement cost data by some, but not all, registrants. Such disclosures include the estimated cost of replacing (new) the productive capacity together with the current depreciated replacement cost of the productive capacity on hand at the end of each fiscal year for which a balance sheet is required, and the approximate annual depreciation, depletion, and amortization for the two most recent fiscal years estimated on the basis of average current replacement cost of productive capacity. (See ASR No. 190, SAB Nos. 7, 9, 10, and 11 and any related SEC releases subsequently issued).

6. *Reserves*
   a. In some countries, hidden or "secret" reserves are created by understatements of inventories, excessive depreciation, excessive provisions for expenses, et cetera.
   b. Disclosed reserves in some countries are sometimes created for general as opposed to specific purposes—e.g., broad contingency reserves or reserves for future losses on inventories not on hand or contracted for. When such reserves are provided out of income (as opposed to surplus which does not usually present a problem), the investor often cannot judge whether they are provided for specific known losses or as a mechanism to effect income stabilization.
   c. Reserves are sometimes provided merely because they are deductible for tax purposes only when they are recorded on the books.
   d. Creation of reserves such as the foregoing by charges to income, the use of such reserves to absorb charges or losses, and the return of such reserves to income are not accepted practices in the U.S.
   e. FASB Statement of Financial Accounting Standards No. 5, "Accounting for Contingencies," which is effective for fiscal years beginning on or after July 1, 1975, contains requirements applicable to accounting for reserves for loss contingencies which are more restrictive than those formerly in effect in the United States.
   f. Accounting for reserves may create significant problems for foreign companies attempting to register securities in the U.S. as the adjustment of their operating results to reflect accounting on a U.S. basis may be a difficult, if not impossible, task.

7. *Stock Dividends*
   a. The accounting for stock dividends generally accepted in the U.S. (capitalization at fair value) is not followed in many countries, where capitalization is generally at par value.
   b. Practice to date indicates that, in general, the SEC will not require a foreign registrant to account for recurring stock dividends retroactively on a U.S. basis, but will expect the company to account for future dividends on such basis.
   c. However, a possible exception to this requirement is included in SEC Staff Accounting Bulletin No. 8 issued June 4, 1976. The applicable interpretation therein indicates that the SEC staff will not object to the Japanese practice of accounting for "free distributions" of common stock at par value if the Japanese registrant and their independent accountants believe that the institutional and economic environment in Japan with respect to the registrant is sufficiently different that U.S. accounting principles for stock divi-

dends should not apply. However, financial statements in such cases should include footnote disclosure of the method used, the accounting required in the U.S. for such stock dividends, the fair value of any such shares issued during the year and the cumulative amount of the fair value of shares issued. The cumulative amount may be shown in the aggregate or may consist of a listing of amounts by years.

8. *Treasury Stock*
   a. Treasury stock is classified as an asset in some countries, while generally deducted from the capital section of balance sheet in U.S.
   b. Profit and loss arising from transactions in treasury stock are accorded varying treatment in different nations; they are treated as a capital transaction in the U.S. with no income statement impact.

9. *Bonuses*

   Amounts accrued or paid to management and employees are charged to income in some countries, including the U.S., and to surplus in others.

10. *Interperiod Allocation of Income Taxes*

    This method of accounting—deferred taxes—is not followed in some countries. In other countries the method used is at variance with that used in the U.S.

11. *Business Combinations*
    a. U.S. accounting for these transactions is either not accepted or not followed in many other countries.
    b. In some cases a modified form of "pooling-of-interests" accounting is followed. The accounts of the merging companies are combined on an historic-cost basis except that income statements are only combined on a prospective basis; there is no retroactive combination as in the U.S.
    c. Goodwill may be amortized over substantially shorter periods or may not be amortized at all in other countries. In some countries it may be written off immediately. Amortization and immediate write-offs of goodwill are made to profit and loss accounts in some countries and to surplus accounts in others.

12. *Other Items*

    Differences in accounting principles, financial statement presentation, or disclosure may also exist with respect to the following: earnings per share, changes in accounting, pension costs, deferred research and development costs, exchange gains and losses, reserves for bad debts, periods in which dividends are recorded, commitments, subsequent events, contingencies, translation of foreign currencies, and marketable securities.

A Move Toward More Uniformity

The International Accounting Standards Committee, representing organizations of professional accountants in various countries, was formed in 1973 for the purpose of formulating and publishing, in the public interest, basic standards to be observed in the presentation of audited accounts and financial statements and to promote their worldwide acceptance and observance.

The Preface to International Accounting Standards, issued January 1973, provides:

> . . . the Founder and Associate Members have agreed to support these objectives by undertaking the following obligations:
> a. to support the standards promulgated by the Committee:
>> i. to ensure that published accounts comply with these standards or that there is disclosure of the extent to which they do not and to persuade governments, the authorities controlling securities markets and the industrial and business community that published accounts should comply with these standards;
>> ii. to ensure that the auditors satisfy themselves that the accounts comply with these standards. If the accounts do not comply with these standards the audit report should either refer to the disclosure of noncompliance in the accounts, or should state the extent to which they do not comply;
>> iii. to ensure that, as soon as practicable appropriate action is taken in respect of auditors whose audit reports do not meet the requirements of (ii) above. . . .

Although the International Accounting Standards do not override local regulations, the Preface to the Statement of International Accounting Standards states in part, "The obligations undertaken by Members of IAS . . . are designed to ensure that when the International Accounting Standards differ from, or are in conflict with, the local regulations, the financial statements and the auditor's report will indicate . . . in what respects the International Accounting Standards have not been observed."

The Council of the American Institute of Certified Public Accountants has not designated the IASC as a body whose pronouncements on generally accepted accounting principles would be enforceable under Rule 203 of the

AICPA Code of Professional Ethics. When IASC Standards contain significant differences from U.S. GAAP, the AICPA will urge the FASB to give early consideration to such differences with a view to achieving harmonization.

DIFFERENCES IN AUDITING STANDARDS AND REPORTS

Auditing Standards

As in the case of accounting principles and financial statement presentation and disclosures, there are important differences in the nature and scope of the examinations of financial statements made by independent public accountants all over the world.

Two of the major differences commonly encountered involve confirmation of receivables and observation of physical inventories. Although generally accepted in the U.S., these procedures are not followed in most countries (notable exceptions are Canada, England, and Wales).

There are also other procedures, taken for granted in the U.S., which are not normally employed by foreign auditors unless special arrangements are made.

These differences in procedures should not be construed as reflecting on all examinations by foreign auditors; while the scope of their examinations and procedures employed are different from those in the U.S., their examinations in many cases are more than adequate.

The SEC generally insists that the auditing standards followed by foreign auditors be the same as those required of U.S. auditors. Accordingly, foreign companies should promptly inform their auditors of any plans to register securities for sale in the United States. This may enable the foreign auditors to conform their examination to U.S. standards. Often, all that is necessary is the confirmation of receivables and the observation of physical inventories.

In some cases where such advance planning has not been possible, the SEC has demonstrated a willingness to adapt its requirements where consistent with the protection of investors. In such cases, the reports of the foreign auditors must disclose the deviations from U.S. practice.

However, there is no assurance—and there should be no presumption— that the SEC will continue to permit deviation from U.S. auditing standards. Any deviations from U.S. standards should be discussed with the SEC in advance of filing to ascertain whether such deviations will render the foreign auditor's report unacceptable.

Auditors' Reports

There are also significant variations in auditors' reports all over the world. Even where the objectives of the audit are similar, the reports in one country may bear no similarity to those in another country. The differences have their roots in professional and statutory requirements as well as in custom and tradition. Generally, the differences in the *form* of auditors' reports do not present problems which cannot be resolved in some manner.

Independence

The concept of independence is quite different in foreign countries from what it is in the United States. In some countries, for example, auditors are not only permitted to invest in securities of their clients, but they are also expected to be shareholders. Therefore, it is not uncommon for a foreign auditor to find, much to his surprise, that he is not independent according to SEC standards.

The rules and regulations of the SEC make no distinction between the independence of domestic and foreign auditors. However, Accounting Series Release No. 112 permits a slightly less restrictive interpretation of the independence of accountants examining a nonmaterial segment of an international business.

Recognizing that U.S. standards of independence generally do not exist abroad, the SEC has been *slightly* more lenient in interpreting its rules where foreign auditors are concerned. This does not mean that all of the commissions's rulings have been favorable to the foreign accountants. Accounting Series Release No. 81, for example, reported a case where foreign accountants were deemed not independent because of the ownership of a stock interest in the proposed registrant.

As in the case of domestic accountants, questions relating to the independence of foreign accountants should be discussed with the SEC, prior to filing, to determine whether or not the facts in the case will render the foreign auditor's opinion unacceptable.

FOREIGN COMPANIES REGISTERING IN THE UNITED STATES

The 1933 and 1934 Acts do not differentiate between foreign and domestic private issuers. However, the SEC has accepted certain practical deviations from U.S. requirements or practices in the case of some foreign issuers when such deviations are not inconsistent with the protection of the investor. The following classical cases illustrate the development of related SEC practice.

KLM Prospectus—Effective May 1957

The company presented its financial statements and summary of earnings in Netherlands guilders and U.S. dollars. The important matter was the manner in which the company reconciled its customary reporting practices as a Dutch company with accounting principles generally accepted in the U.S. The principle difference related to depreciation accounting. Aircraft and engines were being depreciated over a five-year period on a straight line basis to a residual value of 10%. During each of the three years following such a five-year period, the company charged income with an additional amount of 7.5% of the cost of aircraft and engines, and credited such extra depreciation to a surplus reserve entitled "extra depreciation reserve." In addition, gains on the sale of aircraft to be replaced were included in income and were offset by charges for "extra depreciation" and applicable tax. The total provision for "extra depreciation" was made because of the company's calculations that the replacement cost of aircraft would require increased amounts to maintain the same productive capacity in terms of available ton miles.

In the summary of earnings in U.S. dollars, depreciation was first shown on the basis of original cost under "operating expenses." Near the bottom of the statement, just before the provision for income taxes, was a special deduction for "extra depreciation on aircraft and engines." At the bottom of the statement, following "net earnings" and the per share amount of earnings and dividends, a special section was appended with the title "Additional Statement for United States Prospectus." This section disclosed net earnings and net earnings per share of common stock adjusted to reflect depreciation of aircraft and engines on the basis of historical cost in accordance with generally accepted accounting principles in the United States. Footnotes to the summary and the financial statements explained the procedures which had been followed.

The balance sheet presented was not "adjusted" to a U.S. basis. The company also stated that adjustment to reflect depreciation on a U.S. GAAP basis was not included in the company's published annual reports. The auditor's report, after indicating that the financial statements had been prepared "in conformity with generally accepted accounting principles in The Netherlands applied on a consistent basis," included an additional explanation paragraph. This paragraph indicated that, while there were differences between the accounting principles followed by the company and those generally accepted in the United States, the only difference with a material effect was that relating to the "extra depreciation." The paragraph went on to state, in effect, that conformity to a U.S. basis for this item would have required the adjustment shown under the "Additional Statement for United States Prospectus."

In 1969, KLM filed another registration statement in which only one difference in accounting principles required reporting because of materiality. This dealt with the distribution of certain profits to directors, members of management, and employees as provided in the company's Articles of Association. A note to the summary of earnings indicated that such amounts were deducted in calculating the net earnings for 1968 and 1969 shown in the summary and that the company did not deduct such distributions in determining net income in its annual report to shareholders.

In light of this adjustment, the additional explanatory paragraph of the auditor's opinion indicated that the differences in accounting principles followed by the company and those generally accepted in the U.S. would not materially affect net earnings.

The Philips N.V. Prospectus—effective May 1962

The earnings summary was presented in Netherland guilders and in U.S. dollars.

The headnote to the summary stated that it had been prepared on the basis of accounting principles customarily followed by the company and generally accepted in The Netherlands. It also indicated that these principles differed from those generally accepted in the U.S. in a number of respects. Material differences were described in Note 1 following the summary:

1. Depreciation was based on replacement values of fixed assets;
2. Fully depreciated fixed assets still in use were depreciated at 50% of normal depreciation based on replacement values;
3. Inventories were stated at replacement value, and such amounts were used to determine cost of goods sold;
4. Gain on resale of shares of the parent company was included in income; and
5. Profit sharing bonuses for management and employees were shown as a deduction *after* net income.

The earnings summary arrived at net income on the basis of the accounting principles customarily employed by the Philips companies. From this amount was deducted profit sharing bonuses and preferred stock dividends leaving a "balance of net income," to which was added an amount *estimated* stating the latter amount on the basis of U.S. accounting principles.

The adjusted balance sheet approximated the amount of net income available for common stock on the basis of U.S. principles and these amounts (not the Dutch amounts) were also given on a per share basis. A footnote to the summary explained how the company had attempted to estimate the adjustment as required in order to arrive at income on a U.S. basis. The note also indicated that there were other items to which differing accounting principles were applicable, but that the effect of using U.S. principles for such items would not have a material effect on net income. The balance sheet was not adjusted; it was presented in both currencies on the basis of the company's customary practice.

The Copenhagen Telephone Company Prospectus—1962

The company was a public utility operating under a concession from the Danish government. The government owned and voted 50.65% of the outstanding capital stock of the company and had the right to purchase at least one-half of any capital stock issued. The majority of the members of the board of directors of the company were appointed by, and the nomination by the board of the senior managing director was subject to the approval of, the government, which also supervised important activities of the company, including the determination of rates for telephone service and alteration of the accounting regulations prescribed for the company. The company's summary of earnings was presented in Danish kroner and U.S. dollars.

The headnote to the summary called attention to a note (captioned "General") in the financial statements regarding differences between the accounting principles employed by the company and those generally accepted in the United States. The footnote listed briefly the major areas of differences which were described in more detail in other notes to the financial statements.

1. Under Danish tax laws the company had discretion to decide the rate (with certain limitations) at which undepreciated assets were written off. The company was, therefore, deducting depreciation in such amounts as to eliminate all taxable income. At the same time, the company was not providing for deferred taxes. The company stated that due to its construction program there was no likelihood that it would be necessary to pay income taxes in the foreseeable future. Furthermore, in view of the company's relations with the Danish

government (particularly in regard to rate making) the company believed that "flow through" accounting was appropriate in the circumstances.

2. Deferred taxes were not provided for other timing differences.
3. Subscribers' contributions to construction were credited, in part, to property accounts and, in part, to the liability to the pension fund.
4. Depreciation was provided on property before it was placed in service.
5. A reserve fund had been set up out of earnings in prior years to meet part of the capital expenditures requirement. Transfers from the fund were made in round amounts to write down the telephone plant account.
6. Debt discount was included in property accounts and written off over 25 years.
7. Debt expense was written off to income as incurred.
8. Aggregate profits from the sales of property were included in the equity section of the balance sheet.
9. The company capitalized interest during construction of buildings but not of other property.

The financial statements and summary of earnings were based upon the previously published financial statements of the company with certain revisions in form; *there was no adjustment of the figures to reflect the application of U.S. accounting principles.* The company stated:

. . . . It is impossible, without unreasonable effort and expense, to state what the Company's net income would have been if the Company had followed principles of accounting generally accepted in the United States in lieu of those actually employed. . . . Moreover, the company's rates for service have always been set at a level which enabled the Company to cover its costs and, in addition, to pay a fixed dividend which can exceed . . . only with the approval of the government. The government has authorized the Company to pay a dividend of . . . for 1961, 1962 and 1963. In setting rates, the Company and . . . have been governed by the financial statements customarily prepared by the Company in accordance with the regulations prescribed. . . . The rates are appropriate to the costs and expenses shown by the prescribed accounting. Accordingly, the Company believes there is a proper matching of costs and revenues.

It is clear that what was appropriate in the KLM and Philips cases was not appropriate in this case. To have put this company's financial statements on a U.S. GAAP basis would have resulted in a meaningless conglomeration of figures having no relationship to reality.

In 1967, the company filed a registration statement on Form 20 under the 1934 Act. The financial statement treatment reflected in that filing was, for all practical purposes, identical to that included in the 1962 registration statement.

The Tokio Marine Prospectus—1971

The accounting and financial reporting practices of the company are regulated by Japanese law and the reporting requirements of the Japanese Ministry of Finance. Such practices varied in a number of respects from those of American insurance companies.

The basic financial data—including the summary of earnings—and financial statements of the company were presented to reflect the financial position and operating results on a basis comparable to American insurance companies in conformity with the Convention Annual Statement Form of the National Association of Insurance Commissioners (commonly referred to as the "statutory basis") and the then applicable requirements of Regulation S-X. It should be noted that this presentation was not just a bottom line adjustment to the financial statements prepared on the basis of the company's customary practice; on the contrary, it involved a complete conversion of the company's financial statements to a U.S. "statutory basis".

A note to the financial statements described the basis of presentation for the basic financial statements and indicated the differences between that basis and the accounting and financial reporting practices of Japanese insurance companies. The primary differences related to the computation and treatment of the following: unearned premiums, loss reserves, severance and retirement reserves, admitted assets, and special reserves.

The company also presented, in a note to the financial statements, a reconciliation of net income and earned surplus after appropriations as reported by the company in reports to its shareholders, with net income and realized gains on investments and earned surplus as reported in the prospectus. For each of the five years presented in the reconciliation, net income previously reported to shareholders was substantially increased to arrive at net income and realized gains on investments as reported in the prospectus.

As a further complication, the prospectus also included supplementary statements of adjusted earnings and capital stock equity. The purpose of these supplementary statements was to reconcile the net earnings and capital stock equity data prepared in conformity with the U.S. "statutory basis" of accounting with similar data presented in conformity with generally accepted accounting principles (GAAP) in the U.S.

The AICPA audit guide relating to fire and casualty insurance companies was issued and in effect at the time of the Tokio Marine filing. That guide dealt with the conversion of "statutory" accounting to GAAP accounting, which raises the question of why the basic financial data and statements, were not presented on a GAAP basis instead of on a "statutory" basis converted to GAAP in the supplementary statement. One reason for the presentation used may have been the fact that the form of financial statements then set forth in Regulation S-X for insurance companies were "statutory" in nature. That portion of the regulation was revised in ASR No. 183 (November 14, 1975) and the revised article calls for the presentation of insurance company financial statements on a GAAP basis. Accordingly, the presentation used in the Tokio Marine filing may no longer be indicative of current SEC practice.

The auditor's opinion contained a standard scope paragraph, a middle paragraph disclosing the variances between "statutory" accounting principles and generally accepted accounting principles, and an opinion paragraph dealing with the fair presentation of the financial statements in accordance with "statutory" accounting principles, as well as with fairness of presentation in accordance with generally accepted accounting principles of the financial data set forth in the supplementary statements.

The Plessey Prospectus—1971

The summary of earnings and financial statements of The Plessey Company Limited included in the prospectus were presented in pounds sterling and United States dollars. The reporting chartered accountants used a standard American short form report and stated that the financial statements were "in conformity with generally accepted accounting principles applied on a consistent basis."

A note to the financial statements indicated that property and equipment located in the United Kingdom and the company's related reserves for depreciation had been revalued as of June 30, 1964. The revaluation resulted in a net increase of property and equipment carrying values which were credited, in accordance with accounting principles in the United Kingdom, to intangible assets arising from acquisitions.

Another note to the financial statements described the composition of a balance sheet account entitled "Intangible Assets Arising from Acquisitions" as:

. . . the excess of the cost of the company's investment in subsidiaries over their net assets reduced, in accordance with accounting practice in the United Kingdom, by the following credits, which would require different treatment (indicated parenthetically) to conform with generally accepted accounting principles in the United States . . .

The note went on to list four items, rather significant in amount, which under generally accepted accounting principles in the United States would have been credited to surplus arising from revaluation (1 item), extraordinary credits (2 items), and paid-in surplus (1 item).

This presentation and the report of the chartered accountant are an interesting contrast to what was reflected in the 1969 KLM prospectus. Plessey was apparently permitted to use its customary reporting practices and simply disclose in the notes to the financial statements the differences between the accounting principles it followed and those generally accepted in the United States.

The Plessey Company Prospectus—1975

The consolidated financial statements included in the prospectus were presented in pounds sterling and in U.S. dollars. The report of the chartered accountants differs from that which appeared in the 1971 prospectus in that their 1975 report indicates that the financial statements were "in conformity with United Kingdom generally accepted accounting principles, which differ in certain respects from those followed in the United States (See note 6 to financial statements) applied consistently." As indicated above, the 1971 prospectus contained a standard American short-form report, which stated that the financial statements were "in conformity with generally accepted accounting principles applied on a consistent basis."

Note 6 describes various differences in accounting and quantifies some of them, but no reconciliation of net income between the two bases is provided. However, Note H to Statement of Consolidated Income of the Company indicates that the differences disclosed in Note 6 did not, in the aggregate, materially affect net income of the company, except for the recognition, as an extraordinary item, of 1,894,000 ($3,869,000) of the unrealized portion of the net gain after tax on the revaluation and sale of shares in an associated company. Recognition of this item as income would not be permitted under U.S. GAAP. The effect of this item on net income, in total and per share, was also disclosed.

The case examples discussed heretofore may be categorized as classic cases, despite their age, because they served as models for many registrants. These cases demonstrated to foreign registrants:

1. The need to describe the material differences between the accounting principles prevailing in their home countries and those generally accepted in the United States;
2. The need to quantify such differences when they are material and where such disclosure would be meaningful and significant to the investor; and
3. That there is some flexibility, depending on particular circumstances, in how quantified disclosures may be presented ranging between:
   a. presenting the basic financial statements on a U.S. GAAP basis;
   b. including a one-line adjustment to the statements of income and shareholders' equity to reflect the effect of the differences between U.S. GAAP and the accounting principles reflected in the financial statements; or
   c. disclosure in a footnote of major differences without reconciling net income and shareholders' equity.

A review of recent filings of foreign registrants with the Securities and Exchange Commission will confirm that the foregoing basic principles are still applicable, as illustrated by the following cases:

BP North American Finance Corporation Prospectus—August 1975

The financial statements of British Petroleum Company Limited (owner of 100% of BP North American Finance) were presented in pounds sterling and U.S. dollars in conformity with accounting principles generally accepted in the United Kingdom consistently applied.

The auditor's report states:

While such United Kingdom principles vary in certain respects from the accounting principles generally accepted in the United States, during the period under review the application of the latter would not have materially affected the determinations of net income, except for the treatment of back service pension charges in 1973 and 1974 referred to in Note M and Iranian receipts in 1973 and 1974 referred to in Note O. Under United States generally accepted accounting principles the profit on sale of production interests in 1974 referred to in Note D would have been reflected in income before extraordinary items.

Note M indicates charges had been made to income in 1973 and 1974 for back service pension obligations which arose from specified causes and which, if they had been amortized over twenty years in accordance with U.S. GAAP, would have increased net income by $56 million and $74.1 million, respectively, and earnings per unit of ordinary stock before extraordinary items by 14 cents and 45 cents, respectively.

Note O indicates that certain receipts from the Iranian government and participating oil companies, as a consequence of the nationalization of certain assets in Iran in 1951, had been credited in 1970 and 1971 to earned surplus whereas under U.S. GAAP then in effect, the amounts would have been included in income as extraordinary items.

No reconcilation of net income to a U.S. GAAP basis is presented.

BP North American Finance Corporation Prospectus—February 1976

The financial statements were again presented on the basis of accounting principles generally accepted in the United Kingdom. In addition to the two items previously identified as U.S. GAAP differences (back service pension costs and Iranian receipts), the auditor's opinion also indicated that the basis of conversion of overseas currencies reflected in the U.K. financial statements differed from the basis required under U.S. GAAP.

This latter item was discussed in Note O to the financial statements which indicates that under U.K. GAAP, nonsterling assets and liabilities are converted into sterling at the applicable period-end rates. The note also indicates that had the method established by the FASB in their Statement No. 8, issued in October 1975, been followed it is estimated that the net income for the periods under review would have been affected approximately as indicated in the tabular presentation included in the note.

A reconciliation of net income from a U.K. to a U.S. GAAP basis was provided in Note (a) to the Consolidated Statement of Income with this introduction: "The following are the material adjustments to net income which would be required if generally accepted accounting principles in the United States had been applied instead of those generally accepted in the United Kingdom."

Imperial Chemical Industries Limited Prospectus — June 1975

The consolidated financial statements are presented in pounds sterling and U.S. dollars in conformity with accounting principles generally accepted in the United Kingdom.

The independent accountants' report:

1. States in a third paragraph, ". . . as explained in Note 1 to the consolidated statements of income certain restatements have been made, for the purpose of this prospectus, to the United Kingdom accounts previously presented to shareholders;"
2. Indicates in a fourth paragraph that the financial statements being reported upon and expressed in pounds sterling were in conformity with accounting principles generally accepted in the United Kingdom consistently applied after giving effect to the restatements; and
3. Indicates in the fifth and concluding paragraph that U.K. and U.S. GAAP vary in certain respects and that the application of U.S. GAAP would not have a material effect on consolidated income for the five years ending December 31, 1974, and would have affected the consolidated financial position at that date to the extent summarized in Note M.

Note M presents the principal effects of differences between U.K. and U.S. accounting principles on consolidated capital and reserves to December 31, 1974, for the following items:

1. Deferred taxes — to give effect to full deferred tax accounting;
2. Revaluation of fixed assets — to eliminate the effect of revaluations of fixed assets;
3. Translation of fixed assets and noncurrent investments — to apply historical exchange rates to such assets (ICI applies year end rates and reflects net differences in reserves); and
4. Translation of long-term debt — to apply historic exchange rates to such items (ICI applies year end rates and all differences are charged directly to reserves).

It should be noted that the foregoing disclosures as to differences related to the accounting for translation were based on U.S. GAAP then in effect; FASB Statement No. 8 has subsequently revised U.S. GAAP in this area.

An additional variation from U.S. GAAP is identified in footnote A(10) to the financial statements, which indicates that, in general, finished goods are stated at the lower of average cost or net realizable value, raw materials and other inventories at the lower of cost or replacement price, but that in determining cost for valuation purposes, depreciation is excluded.

Kyoto Ceramic Co., Ltd. Prospectus — January 1976

The accounts of the company in Japan are maintained in conformity with Japanese accounting practices, which in many respects do not conform with U.S. GAAP. The company's periodic reports to stockholders are prepared in accordance with provisions of the Japanese Commercial Code and do not reflect the consolidation of subsidiary companies.

The financial statements included in the prospectus, however, were presented on a consolidated basis reflecting the financial position and results of operations on a U.S. GAAP basis. It should be noted that this presentation was not just a bottom line adjustment to the financial statements prepared on the basis of the company's customary practice; on the contrary it involved a complete conversion of the company's financial statements to a U.S. GAAP basis.

In a separate section of the prospectus entitled *Japanese Financial Reporting Practices*, disclosure was made of net sales and net income (on an unconsolidated basis) previously reported to stockholders on the basis of the provisions of the Japanese Commercial Code. The net income (loss) of the company's only significant subsidiary is also disclosed in this section of the prospectus.

The consolidated financial statements are presented in Japanese yen and U.S. dollars and the independent accountant's report is a standard U.S. short-form report.

Between January 30, 1971, and March 31, 1975, the company made six free distributions of its common stock to its stockholders. In Japan, such free distributions of common stock (to be distingished from stock dividends paid out of profit) are accounted for as stock splits. Accordingly, these distributions were accounted for by transfers of the applicable par value from paid-in capital to the common stock account, in accordance with the provisions of the Japanese Commercial Code.

Note H to the Consolidated Financial Statements indicates that publicly traded companies in the U.S., in accordance with SEC Accounting Series Release (ASR) No. 124, generally account for free distributions of less than 25% by a transfer from retained earnings to other capital accounts of an amount equal to fair value of the shares distributed. If the company had accounted for the free distributions in this manner, annual transfers would have been made as follows:

	Japanese Yen	U.S. Dollars
1972	1,848,000,000	6,119,000
1973	2,604,000,000	8,623,000
1974	16,495,000,000	54,619,000
1975	8,104,000,000	26,834,000

Consolidated retained earnings at September 30, 1975, were=15,887,000,000 Yen ($52,606,000).

This presentation was apparently made in response to the provisions of SEC Staff Accounting Bulletin No. 8, dealing with stock dividends of Japanese Companies. (See earlier discussion under Differences in Accounting Principles and Practices, Financial Statements Presentation and Disclosure.)

Carter Hawley Hale Stores Inc., Prospectus—December 1975

The registrant, a U.S. company, owns a 20.5% interest in House of Fraser Limited, a U.K company, for which separate financial statements expressed in pounds sterling and U.S. dollars are presented.

The independent auditors' report indicates that the separate financial statements of the U.K. company were prepared on a U.S. GAAP basis and that they include certain adjustments to the U.K. accounts to convert them to a U.S. GAAP basis. The nature of various adjustments made, and related reconciliations of sales, earnings, and shareholders' equity is presented in Note A to the consolidated financial statements of House of Fraser Limited and Subsidiaries.

With respect to FASB Statement No. 8, which is effective for fiscal years beginning on or after January 1, 1976, Note Q to the financial statements notes in part that, "since the effects, if any, of applying Statement No. 8 on the company's financial statements have not yet been determined, the financial statements herein do not reflect such Statement."

It is interesting to note that shareholders' equity as originally reported by the U.K. company was reduced from $320,368,000 to $174,934,000 at January 25, 1975, as a result of the various adjustments made to the U.K. statements to conform them to U.S. GAAP. Net earnings as originally reported to shareholders was increased—or decreased—during the five years. then ended, as shown in Table 3.1.

Table 3.1
EFFECT OF ADJUSTING U.K. STATEMENTS
TO CONFORM WITH U.S. GAAP

Years ended January	Net Earnings Originally Reported	Net Earnings Based on U.S. GAAP	Net Increase (or Decrease)
	(thousands of dollars)		
1971	$10,329	$11,475	$ 1,046
1972	14,918	17,127	2,209
1973	25,216	22,121	(3,095)
1974	24,039	28,858	4,819
1975	23,140	19,856	(3,284)

Électricité de France Prospectus—January 1976

EDF, one of the largest enterprises in France and one of the largest electric utilities in the world, was created by the Nationalization Law of April 28, 1946, for the acquisition by the French government of certain privately owned public utilities. It is a national public establishment owned and controlled by the French government.

The prospectus was issued in connection with an offering of $100,000 Guaranteed External Notes due September 15, 1976, the payment of which is unconditionally guaranteed by the Republic of France. Accordingly, the filing evidently qualified under Schedule B of the 1933 Act (applicable to registration of securities issued by a foreign government or political subdivision thereof).

Although Schedule B does not contain a requirement for financial statements, EDF's financial statements, expressed solely in French francs, are included in the filing and consist of a balance sheet as of December 31, 1974; statements of capital and surplus and statements of income for the five years ended December 31, 1974; and statements of sources of funds used for construction for the five years ended December 31, 1974.

No auditor's report is included in the prospectus. The accounts of EDF are subject to examination by a minimum of two French statutory auditors *(commissaires aux comptes)* and in a note preceding the index to the financial statements, it is stated that " . . . such examination and review (by the Commission for Verification of Financial Statements of Public Enterprises) are not comparable with an 'audit' as such term is generally understood in the United States."

EDF's financial statements are prepared in accordance with accounting principles prescribed by the National Accounting Council, created by government decree to standarize accounting principles in France.

In general, the government policy has been to balance EDF's revenue and expenses. Accordingly, as indicated in a footnote, an attempt to change the timing of recognition of costs and expenses in accordance with U.S. GAAP would not result in a proper matching of revenue and expense. While the official published financial statements of EDF are presented for purposes of the prospectus in a form more customary in the U.S., no reconciliation of net income to a U.S. GAAP basis is presented. However, differences between the accounting policies followed by the company and U.S. GAAP are described in the financial statement footnotes.

The differences between the accounting policies followed by the company and U.S. GAAP include, among other things, the following:

1. Pension costs are accounted for on a "pay-as-you-go" basis instead of on the accrual basis;
2. Income taxes are accounted for under the "flow through" method, which generally would not be acceptable under U.S. GAAP (unless exempted under Addendum 2 of APB Opinion No. 2);
3. Plant is valued at and depreciated on the basis of 1959 appraisal values;
4. Borrowing costs are expensed and are not deferred and amortized over the life of the related debt; and
5. Mandatory debt redemption premiums are deferred and amortized over the life of the related debentures on a straight-line basis instead of being included in income as part of the gain or loss on redemptions.

Registration and Listing of Foreign Issuers

Financial statement requirements of Form 20 (1934 Act) are given as follows:

1. Financial statements, schedules, and accountant's reports must be given as would be required if the registration statement were filed on Form 10 (similar to Form S-1);
2. Any material variation in accounting principles or practices from the form and content of financial statements prescribed by Regulation S-X must be disclosed and, to the extent practicable, the effect of each variation must be given;
3. Upon request of the registrant and where consistent with investor protection, the SEC may permit:

    a. Omission of one or more of the required financial statements or the substitution therefor of statements of comparable character, and

    b. Omission of one or more generally accepted auditing standards or procedures or the substitution of other appropriate auditing standards or procedures.

4. SEC may also require the filing of other financial statements in addition to, or in substitution for, the required statements in any case where such statements are necessary or appropriate for adequate presentation of the financial condition of any person whose financial statements are required or whose statements are otherwise necessary for the protection of investors.

5. Under Rule 12b-12(d) of the 1934 Act Form 20 must be prepared in the English language, and any exhibit, other paper or document which is filed with the form and which is in a foreign language must be accompanied by a translation into the English language.

Form 20-K requirements are the same as those for Form 10-K with respect to financial statements, schedules, and accountant's report. Any material variation in accounting principles or practices from the form and content of financial statements prescribed in Regulation S-X must be disclosed, and to the extent practicable, the effect of each variation must be given. Upon request of the foreign issuer and where consistent with protection of investors, SEC may permit omission of one or more of the financial statements required to be filed or the substitution therefor of appropriate statements of comparable character, or omission of one or more generally accepted auditing standards or procedures or the substitution therefor of other appropriate auditing standards or procedures.

SEC may require the filing of other financial statements in addition to, or in substitution for, the required statements in any case where such statements are necessary or appropriate for adequate presentation of the financial condition of any person whose financial statements are required or whose statements are otherwise necessary for the protection of investors.

Under Rule 12b-12(d) of the 1934 Act Form 20-K must be prepared in the English language, and any exhibit, other paper, or document which is filed with the 20-K and which is in a foreign language must be accompanied by a translation into the English language.

Current Reports and Quarterly Reports—Form 6-K

Issuers required to file the form must furnish whatever information such issuers: (1) are required to make public in the country of their domicile or in which they are incorporated or organized pursuant to the law of that country; (2) have filed with a foreign stock exchange on which their securities are traded and which was made public by such exchange; or (3) have distributed to their security holders.

The required information that must be furnished is that which is significant with respect to the issuer and its subsidiaries concerning financial condition or results of operations, changes in business, acquisitions or dispositions of assets, changes in management or control, granting of options or payment of other renumeration to directors or officers, transactions with officers and directors or principal stockholders, and, finally, any other information which may be of material interest to investors. Form 6-K is to be filed promptly after this information is made public.

Material in other than the English language need not be accompanied by a translation into English. However, existing English language translations should be furnished, but they need not be accompanied by the original foreign language version.

Information and documents included in Form 6-K are not deemed to be "filed" for purpose of Section 18 of the 1934 Act or otherwise subject to the liability provisions of that section. Finally, under Rule 13a-13 of the 1934 Act, Form 10-Q does not have to be filed by foreign private issuers who file reports on Form 6-K.

U.S. COMPANIES REGISTERING OR LISTING THEIR SECURITIES IN FOREIGN COUNTRIES

Canada

The registration, distribution, and trading of securities in Canada is governed by provincial rather than federal law. While not identical, the securities laws of most provinces are very similar. The following example is based on the laws and practices of the Province of Ontario.

Financial Statements—Prospectus. As a general principle, financial statements included in a prospectus must conform to accounting principles generally accepted in Canada. This has rarely been a problem for U.S. companies registering in Canada, as financial statements prepared on a U.S. GAAP basis have almost invariably been in accordance with Canadian GAAP. The relationship between GAAP in the two countries has permitted that virtually anything that was generally accepted in the U.S. was generally accepted in Canada; on the other hand, some alternatives which were generally accepted in Canada were not accepted in the U.S.

However, this situation has changed because of alterations in accounting principles in the two countries. These changes include the following.

1. *Business combinations:* The Canadian position on pooling-of-interests transactions is far more restrictive than the U.S. position.
2. *Marketable equity securities:* FASB Statement No. 12 requires entities subject to its requirements to carry marketable equity securities at the lower of aggregate cost or market value. In Canada, the cost basis of accounting generally has been retained unless the market value of temporary investments has declined below the carrying value by a significant amount or the decline in value is other than temporary.
3. *Translation of foreign currencies:* FASB Statement No. 8 is applicable to *Accounting for the Translation of Foreign Currency Transactions and Foreign Currency Financial Statements.* The requirements of this Statement differ in certain respects from practices followed in Canada.
4. *Deferred taxes and the petroleum industry:* FASB Statement No. 9, "Accounting for Incomes Taxes—Oil and Gas Producing Companies," contains the requirements for U.S. entities. There are certain differences in the related accounting requirements and tax laws of the two countries.
5. *Other Differences:* There are also, presently, differences between the two countries in the earnings per share and pension accounting areas; the effect of the differences is usually not material.

With respect to deferred tax accounting in the petroleum industry, the Ontario Securities Commission will accept deferred tax accounting (which differs slightly from the Canadian practice) provided that the differences arise from differing tax laws and not from differing accounting.

The effect of other accounting differences on the registration and trading of U.S. companies' shares in Canada, cannot be precisely predicted at this time, but the commission has begun consideration of a policy to be applicable when such accounting differences exist. Hopefully, these differences will require only footnote disclosures; however, that is not totally clear at this time.

The format of the financial statements presents no problem as it is the same for both countries. However, certain "compliance" disclosures must be made, usually in the form of footnotes, to meet Canadian statutory requirements. These present no great problem and, in most cases, are less detailed than disclosures required in Form S-1. One important requirement is that all "significant" figures in the financial statements must be converted to Canadian funds as supplementary information if the financial statements themselves are not already converted to Canadian funds. The question of which figures are "significant" is usually resolved by discussion with the Securities Commission.

Financial Statements—Annual and Interim Reports.   There are no Canadian equivalents to U.S. annual or interim reporting forms (10-K, 10-Q, et cetera). However, a U.S. corporation registered in Canada would be required to send semiannual and annual financial statements to its shareholders with copies being filed with the relevant Canadian Security Commissions. The financial statement requirements of annual reports to shareholders for both countries are quite similar; the essential differences are a number of minor statutory disclosures which are required in Canada and which would otherwise not be made.

A U.S. corporation registered with the SEC and in good standing can usually obtain a ruling to meet this requirement by sending copies of the financial statements and annual report distributed to its shareholders in the United States to its shareholders in Canada as well. If this exemption is not available or granted, a corporation may comply with these requirements by filing with relevant Canadian Securities Commissions copies of such financial statements as it does send to shareholders together with any additional information necessary to bring the disclosure in the financial statements up to Canadian statutory standards. Any such additional information relating to audited financial statements must be covered by the auditor's report.

Auditing Standards and Reports.   There are no differences in auditing standards between Canada and the United States. The form of auditors' report used in the U.S. is acceptable for annual report purposes in Canada. It may also be acceptable in a prospectus but the more usual practice is to use the similar wording of a standard Canadian auditors' report. This presents no significant problems.

Qualifications of auditors' reports are acceptable in a prospectus if they relate to inconsistencies in the application of accounting principles, to uncertainties (e.g. unresolved litigation), or to unavoidable limitations in the scope of examination (not usually acceptable for SEC purposes). The latter two types of qualifications are not looked on with favor by underwriters. A qualification in an auditors' report is not acceptable in a prospectus if the qualification is capable of being removed through a change in the underlying financial statements, which is also true for SEC purposes.

Germany

The listing of securities on an exchange in West Germany is governed by the Stock Exchange Law as amended and supplemented. The issuance of Deutsche-mark bonds by a foreign issuer must also be passed on by the Subcommittee of the Central Capital Market Committee. The Subcommittee consists of the five banks most active as managers of "foreign" DM-bonds issues. The main objective of the Subcommittee is to reconcile the volume of "foreign" DM issues with the capacity of the market. There is presently no requirement for "federal" approval or review of the issuance and listing of securities.

Decisions on listing are made by the Listing Committee of each stock exchange. In principle, it is *not* the task of the Listing Committee to check the financial soundness of securities submitted for listing. Rather, it is their concern to ensure that the listing prospectus contains all the data required from the legal and practical viewpoint for the formation of an opinion on the securities and the issues.

Applications for listing must be made in writing to the Listing Committee of the stock exchange on which the securities are to be traded. The application must be submitted through a credit institution (bank) which is itself a member of the stock exchange involved. It is customary for several banks to form a consortium for the introduction of one or more issues of securities with one of the banks undertaking to act on behalf of the consortium. Each application for listing must be accompanied by a prospectus signed by the company and the sponsoring banks in addition to a number of supporting documents.

More than fifteen principal items of information are required in a prospectus for an industrial registrant. The requirements vary for banks, insurance companies, and certain other types of registrants. The audited financial statements of the issuer or, where applicable, consolidated financial statements are required for the latest fiscal year, the closing date of which must not be more than thirteen months earlier. If the closing date is more than nine months earlier, more recent interim financial statements will also be required. The supporting documents to be supplied must include among others the annual shareholders' reports, including financial statements for the last three years.

The listing application must also be accompanied by several undertakings. One of these requires the publication of the company's annual financial statements in the *Federal Gazette* and in one other periodical designated by the stock exchange.

Financial Statements and Data. United States companies should not be faced with any major problems in this area. The financial statements included in the listing application closely resemble those presented in a U.S. annual shareholder report. Companies have sometimes preferred to present the financial statements in the form which would be required by the SEC; there is no requirement to change or modify the U.S. presentation or to explain the effect of differences in generally accepted accounting principles between the two countries.

In addition to the financial statements mentioned above, the following additional financial information is required to be included in the prospectus:

1. Conditions of long-term liabilities and commitments;
2. Description of any contingent liabilities not reflected in the balance sheet including detailed explanations of any exposures facing the company as a result of pending or expected claims, and
3. Detailed information on sales for the last three years including, if possible, *units* of sales and production.

These requirements should not present major problems to a U.S. company. In fact, if the first two items are material to the understanding of the financial statements they will already be disclosed, to some extent, in the financial statements or the notes thereto. The third item is somewhat related to the line of business disclosure requirements in the United States.

One item of disclosure required by the prospectus is the outlook of the business for the current year. Companies frequently include unaudited financial data in their response to this requirement similar or identical to the "capsule" data included in the paragraph following the summary of earnings in an SEC filing.

Auditors' Reports. The standard U.S. auditors' report is acceptable in Germany including, generally, such qualifications as would be acceptable to the SEC in a U.S. filing. The final decision as to the acceptability of any qualification rests with the stock exchange. In some cases the stock exchange may require expanded disclosures about the issues giving rise to the qualification.

Translation Into the German Language.   The prospectus as well as the full financial statements and auditors' report must be presented in the German language.

Japan

In December 1973, the Tokyo Stock Exchange decided to permit the listing and trading of certain "foreign" securities. The related requirements are outlined below. The first companies listed were Dow Chemical Company, First National City Corporation, General Telephone and Electronics Corporation, IU International Corporation, First Chicago Corporation, and Banque de Paris et des Pays-Bas. Subsequently, additional companies became listed including IBM, IT & T, General Motors, AMAX, Sperry Rand, Borden, Atlantic Richfield and Chase Manhattan Corporation.

Listing on the Tokyo Stock Exchange.   Presently, securities eligible for listing are restricted to those foreign company shares which are listed on specified stock exchanges in their home countries. The exchanges are the New York, American, Toronto, London, Paris, Luxembourg, Brussels, Amsterdam, Frankfurt, Zurich, Milan, and Sydney exchanges.

Listing applications are sponsored by a member firm of the Exchange. A listing applicant must meet certain financial tests before his application will be considered, but meeting the tests does not guarantee listing. The tests to be met include, among other things, net assets of 20 billion yen (approximately $69,500,000) and net income before tax applicable to common stock in excess of 3 billion yen (approximately $10,400,000) for each of the last three fiscal years. Other criteria include a sliding scale ratio of pretax net income applicable to common stock, net assets, dividend history, and share distribution.

An applicant must also place sufficient shares of stock through a managing securities company, which is a full member of the Exchange, by the date of the actual listing to ensure a smooth distribution of shares and the formation of fair stock prices. The rules of the Exchange with respect to this matter are very specific and complex, and deal both with the number of shares and number of shareholders. The requirements to be met rest to a significant degree on the price of the company's shares on its domestic stock exchange.

Upon acceptance of the listing application, the exchange will review the eligibility of the company for listing. Upon completion of this review, the application is passed to the Ministry of Finance, which makes a further study of the company. The listing is officially approved when the Ministry of Finance gives its approval pursuant to the Securities and Exchange Law.

Upon listing, the company would be subject to certain requirements under the Japanese Securities and Exchange Law. This would include, among other things, the filing of annual Securities Reports (which include audited financial statements for two years) with the Ministry of Finance within *three months* after the close of each fiscal year. The company would also be required to file a semiannual report which includes comparative unaudited financial statements for the first six months of each year and the corresponding six-month period of the preceding year; this report is due within three months after the close of the six-month period.

Financial Statements to be Submitted to the Tokyo Stock Exchange for the Listing of Shares. A company applying for the listing of shares must file a Securities Report for Listing Application in almost the same form as the Registration Statement to be filed with the Minister of Finance for the public offering of securities. The report must contain the applicant's financial statements for the latest five consecutive fiscal years. The statements for the latest three years must be audited by public accountants licensed or registered in Japan.

Interim financial statements, including a balance sheet dated at least six months after the end of the latest fiscal year, are required if the application is made more than six months after the end of the latest fiscal year. These statements need not be audited.

Financial statements of major subsidiaries for the latest three years, translated into Japanese, are also required. However, consolidated financial statements for the latest five years may be substituted for this requirement. These statements need not be audited. The Tokyo Stock Exchange policy on financial statements of foreign companies will follow the Decision of the Corporate Accounting Deliberation Council described subsequently.

Financial Statements—Ministry of Finance. Registration statements filed with the Minister of Finance must contain financial statements for the preceeding five consecutive fiscal years. The statements for the latest two years must be audited. The registration must also contain interim financial statements with a balance sheet date six or more months after the end of the latest fiscal year, if it is filed later than eight months after the close of that fiscal year. Such statements need not be audited. If the registration is filed on an unconsolidated basis, unaudited consolidated financial statements on a home country basis must be attached. The annual report must contain audited financial statements for the two most recent fiscal years. If the annual report is filed on an unconsolidated basis, consolidated financial statements on a home country basis must be attached; they need not be audited. The semiannual report must contain comparative unaudited condensed financial statements for the first six months of the current and preceding year. If filed on an unconsolidated basis, the report must have attached thereto consolidated financial statements.

On September 4, 1973, the Corporate Accounting Deliberation Council (an advisory organ to the Minister of Finance) reached a decision to amend two regulations pertaining to the requirements for financial statements of foreign companies, as follows.

1. New provisions of regulations concerning terminology, form, and method for preparation of financial statements: Effective March 23, 1974, financial statements of foreign companies prepared in accordance with laws and customs of their home countries became acceptable for use in Japan in connection with public offerings of securities or listing securities on any exchange in Japan. The revised regulations provide that:
   a. Generally, any foreign company may prepare its financial statements on a home country basis, unless the Minister of Finance deems this to be inappropriate for the public interest and protection of investors;
   b. A foreign company may prepare its financial statements on the basis of the requirements of a different country where the company periodically reports on such a basis, if the Minister of Finance deems the home country basis to be inappropriate and the other country basis appropriate for the public interest and protection of investors;
   c. A foreign company shall prepare its financial statements on the basis of the requirements in any country which the Minister of Finance designates as appropriate for the public interest and protection of investors, if the requirements in the home country or in the other countries are not deemed to be appropriate by the Minister of Finance;
   d. When the accounting principles, procedures, or method of application reflected in the financial statements of a foreign country differ from those in Japan, the nature of the differences shall be disclosed in footnotes to the statements, and, where possible, the monetary effects of such differences should also be disclosed; and
   e. Financial statements must be presented in the Japanese language and money amounts therein must be presented both in the company's home country currency and in Japanese yen.

2. New provisions of Ministry of Finance ordinance concerning the registration of public offering or secondary distribution of securities: The changes made to this ordinance clarify the question of whether or not consolidated financial statements would be acceptable in filings with the Ministry of Finance. The ordinance now provides that registration

statements, annual securities reports, or semiannual reports required to be filed with the Ministry of Finance are to include:

a. Consolidated financial statements if the company reports on that basis in its home country;

b. Separate company financial statements if the company regularly reports on that basis; and

c. For companies that regularly report on both basis, both types of financial statements must be included.

Some Recent Developments Pertaining to Requirements in Japan for Consolidated Financial Statements. The Financial Accounting Standard on Consolidated Financial Statements was promulgated in June 1975 by the Business Accounting Deliberation Council, Ministry of Finance. This Standard takes into consideration the requirements of International Accounting Standard No. 3, *"Consolidated Financial Statements."*

On July 13, 1976, the Ministry of France issued an outline indicating the effective dates on which companies will be required to report on a consolidated financial statements basis for fiscal years beginning on or after April 1, 1977, for reporting under the Japanese Securities Exchange Act. The Ministry of Finance plans to issue regulations applicable to consolidation, principally covering its scope, form of statements, and disclosure requirements. The Japanese Institute of Certified Public Accountants has prepared and disseminated a manual to help interested persons understand the records and procedures necessary for the preparation of consolidated financial statements.

The extent to which the foregoing developments may affect foreign companies wishing to list their shares on an exchange in Japan is not presently known.

Auditors' Reports. Under Article 193-2 of the Securities and Exchange Law, an accountant authorized to issue audit certifications must be licensed under the Certified Public Accountant Law of Japan. A foreign accountant licensed under foreign law is authorized to issue audit certification in Japan if he has been approved to do so by the Minister of Finance and is registered as a member of the Association of Japanese Certified Public Accountants in accordance with the requirements of the Certified Public Accountant Law.

On December 5, 1972, the Corporate Accounting Deliberation Council reached a number of decisions on the audit of financial statements of foreign companies by public accountants licensed or registered in Japan. They included this significant item: In conducting the audit of financial statements of foreign companies, such accountants may rely on the evidence used for audit obtained by home country accountants from the company. In relying upon such evidence, such accountants must take primary responsibility for the capability and experience of the home country accountant.

These regulations would seem to present at least three basic alternatives for the Japanese authorities:

1. Acceptance of the report of the "home country" accountant (if he is licensed in Japan, approved by the Minister of Finance, and registered as a member of the Association of Japanese CPAs);
2. Acceptance of the report of a Japanese accountant which is based on his review of the underlying working papers of the home country accountant and any other procedures he deems necessary; and
3. Acceptance of the report of a Japanese accountant based on a complete independent examination.

Under present requirements of the Ministry of Finance, the second alternative is the prevalent practice. In cases where international accounting firms are the "home country" auditors and have partners who are licensed Japanese CPAs, the Ministry of Finance requires that the Japanese CPAs must either have had substantial participation in the audit done by the "home country" auditors or else must perform a postaudit review of the working papers and also obtain a firsthand knowledge of the business by visiting plants and interviewing corporate management.

United Kingdom

Since in almost all cases the issuance of a prospectus in connection with an offer to sell new securities is accompanied by an application for the listing of such securities for trading on The Stock Exchange, the requirements for both are considered jointly.

The principal regulations for the issue of securities in the United Kingdom are, in practice, those contained in *Admission of Securities to Listing* issued by The Stock Exchange and known as the "Yellow Book." It is also necessary to observe the following pertinent legislation:

1. The Companies Act of 1948 which contains, among other things, a section dealing with the contents of prospectuses;
2. The Prevention of Fraud (Investments) Act of 1958 which, in general, prohibits the issuance of circulars relating to the securities except by

licensed dealers in securities or by institutions such as merchant banks
or stockbrokers which are exempt from such requirements;

3. The Exchange Control Act of 1947, which does not affect a U.S. issuer
   directly but does affect the U.K. purchaser of its securities.

The "Yellow Book" deals with, among other things, the contents of the
prospectus (the requirements of which are more comprehensive than those
contained in the Companies Act of 1948), the form and content of financial
statements, the auditors' report, and the periods to be covered by both. Chapter 8 of the "Yellow Book" deals specifically with the requirements for foreign
companies. A review of the detail requirements set forth in that chapter leads
to the conclusion that they present no significant problems to most U.S. companies.

The financial statements which are required and which must be covered by
an auditors' report are briefly summarized below.

1. Prospectus
   a. Consolidated income statement for five years.
   b. Balance sheets of company, and company and consolidated subsidi-
      aries as at the end of the latest fiscal year.
   c. Consolidated balance sheet at the end of each previous fiscal year
      covered by the income statement and at the beginning of the five-
      year period. (This may be given in summarized form, if desired).
   d. If, after the date of the most recent audited balance sheet included in
      the prospectus, the company, or any of its subsidiaries, has acquired
      or agreed to acquire or is proposing to acquire a business or shares in
      a company which will, by reason of such acquisition, become a sub-
      sidiary, and no part of the securities of that company is already listed,
      financial statements as in (a) and (b) above will be required for such
      company.
2. Annual Accounts
   As a condition of listing, a company must undertake to prepare and cir-
   culate to its shareholders in the U.K. or the Republic of Ireland a copy
   of its annual accounts within six months after the close of its fiscal year
   comprising the following:
   a. Consolidated income statement for the year;
   b. Balance sheets of the company, and of the company and its consoli-
      dated subsidiaries as at the close of the year.

Paragraph 2 of Chapter 8 contains *a very significant exemption for U.S. companies:* "In the case of companies incorporated in the United States of America which are listed either on the New York Stock Exchange or on the Ameri-

can Stock Exchange the Council's requirements as to accounting ma.ters will be satisfied provided that such companies observe the requirements of such Exchange combined with those of the Securities and Exchange Commission." Effectively, this means that such a company seeking listing on the London Stock Exchange would not have to issue a prospectus, although financial information from past annual reports would be summarized in statistical cards published by the Extel Statistical Services, Limited.

Paragraphs 8 and 12 contain very significant statements with respect to auditors' reports: (1) Prospectus (paragraph *8*): "A report containing a significant qualification would not normally be regarded by the Department as acceptable;" and (2) Annual Accounts (paragraph *12*): "An audit report which conforms to U.S. auditing practice would be acceptable."

The European Economic Community

The EEC has embarked on a program aimed at harmonizing company law which will, it is hoped, eventually result in the standardization of accounting and reporting procedures of the companies within the EEC. So far, there have been published seven directives (six proposed and one effective) and a proposed statute for the European company.

1. The first directive, which has been adopted, deals with matters of basic company law.
2. The second proposed directive (issued March 1970, and amended October 1973) deals with matters relating to a company's capital stock.
3. The third proposed directive (issued June 1970, and amended January 1973) deals with mergers between companies which are subject to the laws of the same member state.
4. The fourth proposed directive (issued November 1971, and amended February 1974) deals with the form and content of financial statements and a management operations report. It contains standard forms for the balance sheet and profit and loss statements of a company, and provides for mandatory headings. A company would be permitted to use one of the limited number of standard forms included in the directive. The directive also specifies the principles to be applied in valuing the various items in the annual financial statements and requires that the forms be accompanied by notes in which the items in the balance sheet and profit and loss statement are explained. Under the proposal, a report on operations containing a detailed business analysis and status report would also have to be prepared by the company. There is also a pro-

posed requirement to publish the annual financial statements, auditors' report, and the report on operations.

5. The fifth proposed directive (October 1972) deals with the structure of the company. It proposes a two-tier board system and employee participation in the supervisory board. It also outlines the requirements for an annual audit and the independence of auditors. The proposals would require the auditors' report to include, among other things, any observations concerning any:

   a. Infringements of law or of the statutes which have been found in the company's accounts, in its annual accounts, or in the management report, and

   b. Facts noted which constitute a serious danger to the financial situation of the company.

6. The sixth proposed directive (issued October 1972, and amended December 1975) deals with the content, checking, and distribution of the prospectus to be published when securities issued by companies subject to Article 58(2) of the Treaty are admitted to official stock exchange quotation.

   Chapter 5 of Schedule A (admission of shares) and Chapter 5 of Schedule B (admission of debentures) set forth the information required with respect to the net worth, financial situation and results of the company. Briefly summarized, the financial statement requirements, as presently proposed, are as follows:

   a. Comparative table summarizing the annual accounts for the past five years;

   b. The annual accounts relating to the last two fiscal years (only one year called for by Schedule B) as approved by the general meeting of shareholders—presumably covered by an auditor's report;

   c. Unaudited interim financial statements depending on the time of filing; and

   d. Substantial supplementary detail information.

7. The purpose of the seventh proposed directive (issued April 1976) is to institute a system of Community legislation on consolidated accounts as a necessary extension to the Fourth Draft Directive on annual accounts and with the same objectives.

   The proposed directive, which is lengthy and complex, should be studied carefully by entities which may be subject to its requirements. An idea of the scope of the draft and its accompanying explanatory memorandum is indicated by its table of contents which is as follows.

Section	Articles	Subjects
1	1-5	Definitions
2	6-8	Scope
3	9-21	Drawing up of group accounts
4	22	Group annual report
5	23	Audit
6	24	Publication
7	25-27	Final provisions

The draft directive deals with, among other things, the following subjects:

a. Requirements and methods for preparing overall consolidated financial statements and subgroup consolidated financial statements;
b. Requirements as to accounting principles to be followed;
c. Required disclosures to be made, including:
  i. Various information with respect to the entities included in the required consolidated financial statements; and
  ii. Operations information, including sales by category of product, activity and by geographical market, the respective contributions to group income of each category and market, and information with respect to employees and personnel costs included in profit and loss.
d. A requirement that the required financial statements be audited; and
e. A requirement that the required consolidated financial statements, the group annual report, and the report submitted by the person responsible for auditing the accounts shall be published.

The proposed statute for the European company (issued June 1970, and amended May 1975) is a draft company law for a "Societas Europa," which would be a company wholly subject to a specific legal system that is directly applicable in all the member states. The proposed statute, as amended, provides for a supervisory board consisting of one-third representatives of the shareholders, one-third representatives of the employees, and one-third representatives of general interests which are independent of the shareholders and the employees. (Note that these provisions differ from those contained in the proposed Fifth Council Directive.) The proposed statute contains a section dealing with the preparation of the annual accounts and the audit thereof which is similar to the proposals made in the fourth and fifth proposed directives.

It is clearly premature to evaluate the impact of these proposals on U.S. issuers wishing to raise capital within the EEC. Registration and listing could be more complicated than heretofore in terms of the individual member nations; on the other hand, multinational offerings could be less complicated.

In sum, a U.S. company encounters considerably greater difficulties in raising money within the U.S. than does a U.S. company going overseas. In the major capital markets of the world, any well-run U.S. company meeting the stringent SEC requirements should have no problem in the regulatory area when raising capital, providing, of course, that market conditions are right.

FOUR

Accounting for Foreign Currency Translation

Adjusting, translating, and consolidating accounting reports—prepared on the basis of different national accounting standards and kept in various currencies—to provide a common base of understanding is explored.

Lee J. Seidler

Professor of Accounting
New York University

Joseph E. Conner, Jr.

Managing Partner-Western U.S.
Price Waterhouse & Co.

Dr. Seidler, who formerly worked at Price Waterhouse & Co., holds an A.B., an M.S., and a Ph.D. degree all from Columbia University. He has authored many books, articles, and papers on different aspects of accounting. Dr. Seidler has taught accounting courses at universities throughout the world. He has been actively involved in numerous professional organizations, including the AICPA.

Mr. Connor holds an A.B. degree from the University of Pittsburgh and an M.S. degree from Columbia University. He has written numerous papers and articles on various aspects of national and international accounting. Mr. Connor has been very active in different professional organizations, including the AICPA.

Accounting for Foreign Currency Translation

Lee J. Seidler

Professor of Accounting

New York University

There is a real problem in discussing or criticizing FASB Statement No. 8, "Accounting for the Translation of Foreign Currency Transactions and Foreign Currency Financial Statement."[1]

In an article in *Institutional Investor,* John Thackray examined the twelve standards that the Financial Accounting Standards Board had then issued, for which the FASB spent $16 million[2]. If you divide $16 million by twelve pronouncements, you get $1.3 million per pronouncement. However, if you are an accountant you would examine the underlying data and note that FASB Statement No. 8 reverses Statement No. 1 and that FASB Statement No. 10 corrects Statement No. 5. Therefore, the FASB produced a net of ten pronouncements, which results in a cost of $1.6 million per pronouncement. I have little doubt that the faculty members here, working under research grants, would be willing to produce pronouncements at a substantially lower unit price.

Nevertheless, even at $1.6 million per, the general quality of these pronouncements has been disappointing. Some of them, such as FASB No. 2, suffer from an antiintellectual bias. This pronouncement says, in effect, that research and development costs are money "down the drain" and, therefore, should be expended immediately. Other pronouncements, such as Numbers 6 and 12 (on obligations to be refinanced and classification of marketable securities) deal with comparatively inconsequential problems, as compared to the enormous unresolved issues facing accountants. Others, such as No. 5 on contingencies, appear to introduce as much new confusion as existed before issuance.

The problem in discussing FASB No. 8 is that it is *not* in the same class as these other pronouncements. It is probably, in terms of quality if not end result, the best piece of work issued by the board.

It is the only pronouncement that reflects a thorough research-oriented approach. The task force, of which I was a part, was quite effective. The board took more care to explain itself than in any other pronouncement. It is reasonably strongly grounded, yet I think it has the wrong answer and is thus subject to criticism. Nevertheless, I hope that future pronouncements look more, rather than less, like FASB Statement No. 8.

I do not know how many have seen the recent exposure draft on "Accounting for Leases."[3] which bears an unfortunate resemblance to the worst of the pronouncements issued by the Accounting Principles Board in its last days. It is another cookbook: a hundred and eleven pages of "do this and don't do that," which clearly reflects that the FASB was split in two and sometimes three factions. It is another political patchwork which seems to suggest that they locked up the theory books while writing it.

First of all, a little history on Statement No. 8 and reflection on the board operations are in order. The board establishes a task force when it starts to study a subject. They appointed a task force on accounting for foreign currency translation and, in due modesty for the part I played on it, it was an excellent task force. It was "excellent" because it included most of the supposed "experts," on the subject, such as Professor Gerhard G. Mueller, Len Lorensen, and Don Parkinson from Canada. The board was able to isolate the talent on the subject. They cannot always do that; clearly, it is difficult to find a group of experts on "materiality."

As part of our work on the task force, we discussed various elements of translation, which led to the FASB discussion memorandum. Here is where I have my first differences with the FASB. They issued a discussion memorandum which broadly reflected the different theoretical approaches that had been taking shape in the area of translation; a reasonable amount of coverage was accorded to the so-called "temporal method," which is the approach they ultimately adopted. The discussion memorandum was, as all are, unweighted. It ignored the fact that during the operations of the task force, the predominant view within the Task Force was to pay no attention to the temporal method.

This unbiased presentation has a certain apparent look of impartiality, but it results in a dilution of the efforts of the concerned members of the task force. The board then committed, as usual, the greater error of disbanding the task force. The board has finally reversed itself on this manner of operating. In "Accounting for Leases," for example, they have kept the task force together to review comments and reactions to the pronouncement. But in the case of FASB Statement No. 8, the board had a task force with a number of differing views which the board largely ignored and then, following the disbanding of this group, went ahead with a method in which the task force showed no real interest.

Now, let's talk about the method they adopted. Intending to bring some order out the chaotic variety of methods used to translate the results of foreign operations, the Financial Accounting Standard Board's Standard No. 8 has instead substituted a new chaos of its own. The former profusion of methods so useful to managements, but so confusing to analysts, has given way to a single method which now infuriates many managements, but which has managed to keep analysts about as confused as ever.

The new pronouncement mandates the use of the so-called temporal method for translation. Actually, the stipulation of the particular method is of less significance than another requirement: that gains and losses from translation be reflected immediately in income—which effectively means a quarterly basis for publicly held companies. As will be noted below, it is the combination of an illogical method, together with the rigid immediate recognition requirement, that has caused so many difficulties with this pronouncement.

On the other hand, the fear of many analysts that the immediate recognition of gains and losses will cause undue fluctuations in reported earnings appears to be considerably exaggerated.

THE TEMPORAL METHOD: A WEAK THEORY

It is difficult to provide a clear explanation of the temporal method or its rationale, since neither is really very clear.

Essentially, the underlying basis for the temporal method is an ideal that translation of foreign financial statements should not alter the basis of accounting used in the statements. That is, if an item is carried in the foreign balance sheet on the historical cost basis, the translation method should not change that basis. If an item is carried at other than historical cost, such as at market, the translation method should preserve that basis.

Assets and liabilities that are stated in terms of foreign money, such as cash, accounts receivable and payable, and most debts, are carried in the balance sheet, by definition, at current value as expressed in local (foreign) currency terms. Therefore, according to the temporal theory, these items should be translated at the exchange rate that reflects the current value of foreign money, the current rate.

Assets and liabilities that are carried at historical values in the balance sheet, such as fixed assets and, generally, inventory, are in the foreign balance sheet at values that existed when they were acquired. Therefore, they should be translated at the exchange rate in effect at that earlier date, the historical rate.

If an asset's carrying basis changes so should the translation rate. Thus, inventory is usually carried at cost and translated at the historical rate. However, if inventory is written down to market (in local currency) then it should be translated at the current rate. Similarly, marketable securities carried at cost should be translated at the historical rate; marketable securities carried at market are translated at the current rate.

It all sounds innocuous and somewhat consistent. Unfortunately, in application, and coupled with the requirement that all translation gains and losses be taken directly to income, the results are sometimes bizarre.

Why Does the FASB Cling to the Temporal Method?

The fascination of the FASB with the temporal method is not easily explained. The method has never had wide support in accounting literature and has been advocated principally by only one writer. The board's own discussion memorandum did not accord great attention to the method: many negative comments were received during the exposure draft period. A number of corporations, such as Schlumberger, are in virtually open rebellion. Yet a few days ago, the board announced that it had looked into the complaints, had heard them before, and would not change its mind.

One can only assume that at this point the issue has become one of pride and authority, rather than financial reporting. As such, it will probably be decided on the basis of relative power, an arena where the FASB does not fare too well. As a practical matter, the real power lies in Washington at the offices of the SEC. If the commission or its chief accountant wishes to interfere, they have abundant authority to do so. In fact, they are the only ones who do. At the moment, there is no indication that they will move, but the SEC has not been noted, at least recently, for advance announcements of many of its actions.

ANALYSTS PREFER THE MONETARY-NONMONETARY METHOD

Most analysts are reasonably familiar with the monetary-nonmonetary method of translation which had achieved fairly wide usage prior to FASB No. 8. In application, the temporal method is almost identical to the monetary-nonmonetary method. The only significant difference, as noted above, is that when the local currency carrying value of a nonmonetary asset is changed from original cost to current value (or market), the translation rate changes from the historical rate to the current rate.

This switch is of limited significance in most cases. Insurance companies may feel its greatest impact: the accounting for their portfolios of marketable securities is generally controlled by local (foreign) law and varies from country to country. Thus, a bond carried at cost in one country will be translated at the historical rate, while a similar bond carried at market in another country must be translated at the current rate. The dollar value of the bond carried at cost remains constant; the dollar value of the bond carried at market will reflect changes in the exchange rate, as well as changes in market values.

In the past, however, companies that used the monetary-nonmonetary rate often deferred gains and losses so as to avoid the strange fluctuations due to foreign currency debts that are discussed below. That option is no longer available.

Thus, as with the monetary-nonmonetary method, under the temporal method assets and liabilities which are fixed in terms of local (foreign) currency are translated at the current rate of exchange—the rate prevailing at the balance sheet date. Such monetary items are best typified by a local currency banknote. That is, a 100 franc bill carried in the balance sheet as cash will always be worth 100 francs, regardless of the exchange rate, inflation, or other changes. The 100 francs may change in purchasing power, but they will still be worth 100 francs. Receivables and payables in local currency, without regard to length of maturity, have the same characteristics and are also translated at the current rate.

On the other hand, inventory and fixed assets will vary in local currency value. They may originally have been purchased at one price in local currency say 100 francs, but changes in inflation, exchange rates, et cetera, can alter their value in local currency. These nonmonetary items, usually assets, are translated at the historical rate; that is, the rate of exchange in effect when they entered the balance sheet. There are a few nonmonetary liabilities, such as service warranties, that are satisifed by the delivery of services rather than money.

When an item is translated at the historical rate, it is translated at the same rate as long as it is in the balance sheet; thus, it simply holds a fixed dollar value; it will not give rise to exchange gains or losses. Since fixed assets hold a constant dollar value, some companies keep their foreign fixed asset records in the U.S. and merely compute depreciation in dollar terms without bothering about translation.

Note that a loan payable in a currency other than that of the foreign subsidiary is a nonmonetary liability since it can change its value in terms of local currency. If the debt of the foreign currency is in dollars, it will simply hold a constant dollar value.

A Simple Balance Sheet Illustration

Tables 4.1, 4.2, and 4.3 illustrate FASB No. 8 in the balance sheet.

Table 4.1 shows the balance sheet of a French subsidiary at the moment of its incorporation. The company has been established with cash, accounts receivable, inventory and fixed assets, each in the amount of Fr. 100. On the liability side, there are accounts payable of Fr. 100 and capital of Fr. 300. The exchange rate at the time of incorporation is Fr. 4 = U.S. $1.

If the balance sheet were translated at the moment of incorporation, clearly there would be no difference between the current and the historical rate. Therefore, all items are translated at the prevailing 4:1 rate. There is no gain or loss on translation.

Table 4.2 illustrates the translation of the balance sheet at some later date (but assuming no business operations) after the exchange rate for the franc has fallen to Fr. 5 = $1, or Fr. 1 = $0.20. The cash, receivables and payables, are translated at the new *current rate*, which is 5:1. The inventory, fixed assets, and capital are translated at the historical rate, the rate that was in effect when they entered the balance sheet, or 4:1. Note that these latter items simply keep their original dollar value, even though the franc-dollar exchange rate has changed.

Now, add both dollar sides of the balance sheet. The left or asset side adds to $90; the right or liability side to $95. In order to make the translated dollar balance sheet add, a negative $5 must be put in the retained earnings, called in this case, *exchange loss*. Thus, the translated retained earnings figure simply balances the balance sheet.

The exchange loss can also be derived by direct calculation. The company's position in assets and liabilities translated at the current rate (the only ones that matter) consists of Fr. 200 of assets (cash + receivables) and Fr. 100

TABLE 4.1
BALANCE SHEET TRANSLATION: TEMPORAL METHOD

Starting Exchange Rate: Fr. 4 = U.S. $1

Cash	Fr.	100 ÷ 4 =	$ 25	Accounts Payable	Fr.	100 ÷ 4 =	$ 25
Receivable		100 ÷ 4 =	25				
Inventory		100 ÷ 4 =	25	Capital		300 ÷ 4 =	75
Fixed Assets		100 ÷ 4 =	25				
	Fr.	400	$100		Fr.	400	$100

TABLE 4.2

Dollar Gains, Franc Weakens: Fr. 5 = U.S. $1

Cash	Fr.	100 ÷ 5 =	$ 20	Accounts Payable	Fr.	100 ÷ 5 =	$ 20
Receivable		100 ÷ 5 =	20				
Inventory		100 ÷ 4 =	25	Capital		300 ÷ 4 =	75
Fixed Assets		100 ÷ 4 =	25	Exchange Loss			(5)*
	Fr.	400	$ 90		Fr.	400	$ 90

TABLE 4.3

Alternatively, Dollar Weakens, Franc Gains: Fr. 3 = U.S. $1

Cash	Fr.	100 ÷ 3 =	$ 33	Accounts Payable	Fr.	100 ÷ 3 =	$ 33
Receivable		100 ÷ 3 =	33				
Inventory		100 ÷ 4 =	25	Capital		300 ÷ 4 =	75
Fixed Assets		100 ÷ 4 =	25	Exchange Gain			8*
	Fr.	400	$116		Fr.	400	$116

*Charged or credited directly to profit or loss of period.

of liabilities (accounts payable) for a net asset position of Fr. 100. Under the pre-devaluation rate of 4:1, that net asset position was worth $25; however, after devaluation and with the new rate of 5:1, the Fr. 100 net asset position is worth only $20. There has been a loss of $5, the amount that was necessary to balance the balance sheet.

In the past, the company could have disposed of the $5 in virtually any way it desired: deferral, direct charge to income, offset against fixed assets, et cetera. Under FASB No. 8, as we have noted, the amount of $5 must be passed through the income statement of the period; it then goes to retained earnings.

The same exercise is duplicated in Table 4.3, but with the assumption that at the later date the franc strengthened to Fr. 3 = $1, rather than weakened. The translation process is identical. However, with the strengthened franc, the figure necessary to balance the statement is a gain of $8, an amount which is also taken directly to the income statement.

The $8 can also be directly calculated from the unchanged net position in assets translated at the current rate of Fr. 100. In the alternative case, the translated dollar value of that position went from Fr. 100 = $25, to Fr. 100 = $33 at the new 3:1 rate; the difference is $8. Note, that if we had considered that the Table 4.3 balance sheet was at a date *after* that of Table 4.2, and not suggested it as an alternative, possible condition at the same date, then the translation gain would have been $13, the difference between the debit balance of $5 in retained earnings in the Table 4.2 balance sheet and the credit balance of $8 in the Table 4/3 balance sheet.

Relax, The Past Is Not the Future

Many analysts have allowed the restatements of prior years' earnings which some companies have provided under FASB No. 8 to run their blood pressure to new highs. In the past, companies were able, with relative ease, to program the recognition of translation gains and losses. But, the past *restated* for immediate recognition of gains and losses, provides some scary results. These restatements demonstrate how future earnings will fluctuate, reason some analysts. Don't be one of them.

In this instance, restatements of the past are only limited guides to the future. Far more likely is that most companies—except those with large amounts of long-term foreign currency debt—will show only minimal translation losses or gains if FASB No. 8 remains in force. In substance, we expect most companies to try to "opt out" of the game.

The reasoning underlying this prediction is fairly simple: During the

1950s, 1960s and into the early 1970s, exchange rates were fixed. That is, fluctuations (usually against the dollar) were held in narrow bands by central banks that stood ready to buy or sell unlimited amounts of currencies. When a currency's apparent value grew too far out of line with the fixed exchange rate, it would be devalued (or in very rare cases, upvalued). Eventual devaluations were reasonably easy to predict, since they were almost always preceded by a period in which a "weak" currency stayed at the lower limit of its exchange rate against the dollar. As increased central bank sales of dollars became necessary, devaluations became inevitable.

It required only minimal intelligence on the part of the treasurer or controller of a multinational corporation to assure translation gains. Liabilities would be moved into obviously "weak" currencies, so that with the inevitable devaluation, they would be worth less dollars, resulting in a translation gain. Assets would be moved into apparently strong currencies for safety and possible translation gain with an upward revaluation.

The ease with which such asset and liability arrangements could assure translation profits, and loss avoidance, undoubtedly had the effect of luring international controllers and treasurers into substantially more foreign exchange transactions than were warranted by normal operations. Indeed, the possibility of transforming the accounting department—normally a *cost* center—into a *profit* center was particularly tempting.

The end of fixed exchange rates in the early 1970s also ended the easy aspects of the game. Foreign exchange markets under floating rates are surely "efficient markets"; it is not easier to pick an undervalued currency than an undervalued stock. However, the lack of rules on gain and loss recognition meant that controllers could still play the exchange markets, if not with assured profits, at least with losses that could be spread, amortized, or otherwise immediately avoided.

However, FASB No. 8, with its requirement for immediate recognition of gains and losses, removes that last bit of protection to the controller. To the corporate financial executive, foreign exchange markets are now even-money bets, with immediate counting of gains and losses. This is approximately equivalent to playing the "Don't Pass" line on a Las Vegas craps table and sending the results immediately to the shareholders.

Most corporate executives prefer better odds, and they are usually available. Thus, our conclusion: The translation game is now too uncertain and most corporate executives will try to avoid it.

The idea that corporate financial executives will avoid the possibility of foreign exchange losses (and therefore gains) does not mean that they will end foreign operations—although there must be some marginal effect on the pro-clivity to invest abroad. Rather, expect companies to minimize exposure to exchange fluctuations by various "hedging" operations, most simply by keep-ing assets translated at the current exchange rate about equal to liabilities translated at the current exchange rate, on a country-by-country basis. That is, net assets (assets minus liabilities) translated at the current rate should be about zero.

Returning to Tables 4.1, 4.2 and 4.3, note the possibilities for hedging. If the foreign subsidiary portrayed here existed in a high tax country (e.g., Western Europe, Canada, or Japan), a simple expedient would be to convert the Fr. 100 to dollars and remit it to the United States. Assuming an adequate foreign tax credit, this could be accomplished at little cost and would result in a balance sheet with a net position of zero in assets and liabilities translated at the current rate.

Alternatively, the company could purchase inventory or fixed assets with the Fr. 100 of cash. This too would reduce the net exposed position to zero. Of course, a little better initial planning might have suggested financing the sub-sidiary with only Fr. 200 of capital and using Fr. 200, rather than only Fr. 100 of debt, again a hedged position. Another possibility would be to cover the ex-posed position by taking a forward position in the appropriate currency. However, as noted below, such transactions involve considerable complexity and are eschewed by many companies.

MERCK SHOWS THE WAY

The changes in the foreign net asset position of one major international drug company are a good demonstration of the actions that will be taken by many companies to "opt out" of the foreign exchange loss and gain game.

Merck adopted FASB No. 8 in its 1975 financial statements and, therefore, began to recognize all exchange gains and losses in income immediately. Before the change, Merck followed the AICPA's suggested method of recog-nizing realized gains and losses immediately, but of deferring unrealized gains. As many enthusiastic controllers understood, the unrealized gains could be realized, when necessary, to offset translation losses.

Merck provides an unusual but useful analysis of its foreign net assets, dividing them not only in the conventional geographical manner, but also as between "Net Assets Subject to Exchange Fluctuation" and "Net Assets Not Subject to Exchange Fluctuation." The net assets *not subject* to exchange fluctuation consist of items, such as fixed assets, which are translated at the historical rate, and whose dollar values will therefore be unaffected by variations in exchange rates.

The net assets *subject* to exchange fluctuations represent net positions in assets or liabilities that must be translated at the current rate of exchange and which, therefore, can generate gains or losses. Our illustrative company in Table 4.1, for example, has a net asset position, subject to fluctuations of Fr. 100 (Fr. 200 of cash and receivables less Fr. 100 of accounts payable). A negative figure would indicate a net exposed liability position.

In its 1974 annual report, Merck showed $72 million of net assets subject to exchange fluctuations of a total of $356 million total net (foreign) assets. In the 1975 annual report, although net foreign assets have increased 28% of $455 million, the exposed position (net assets subject to exchange fluctuations) was reduced to an insignificant $9 million net liability position.

Of course, since both the $72 million in 1974 and the minus $9 million in 1975 are total net positions, Merck may still have substantial exposed balances in individual countries which may cancel out in the total. Indeed, a glance at the five-area geographical breakdown of the net asset position indicates a net exposed asset position of $13 million in Latin America and an offsetting net exposed liability position in Continental Europe of $9 million. However, the average picture confirms the idea of a reduced exposed position. In the 1974 statement, the average exposed position for the five areas was over $14 million and all were asset balances. At the end of 1975, the average exposed area balance was less than $7 million with both net asset and liability balances on the chart.

Thus, despite a sharp increase in foreign net asset balances, Merck has also sharply reduced its worldwide exposure to foreign exchange fluctuations in its balance sheet. We expect this mode of operations to become the predominant pattern for those companies who can assume hedged positions without great difficulty. In general, companies that are "cash rich" overseas should be able to even up their balance sheets with little difficulty by merely remitting more earnings to the U.S.

Restatements Are Not Valid

FASB No. 8 requires the company to restate prior years' results—five years in the 10-K—as if the company had been using the current required accounting. If the hypothesis in the preceding section is correct, namely that corporate financial executives will act differently under FASB No. 8 than they have in the past, then the results of the restatements are not valid as predictors of the future. Controllers took certain risks in foreign exchange when the accounting treatment was favorable. It is doubtful that they will take the same risks when different accounting is required. The past, restated for different accounting rules that were actually not in effect, tells nothing unless the company will operate in the same manner in the future. In this context, consider Dow and Burroughs, discussed below.

It Will Be More Difficult for Dow Chemical

Some companies will find it more difficult, and possibly quite uneconomic, to put their balance sheets into the hedged position necessary to minimize exposure to translation gains and losses. Dow Chemical, for example, showed $219 million of long-term debt payable in foreign currencies in its 1975 balance sheet (Note G, pg. 33). Of that amount, $115 million is bonds, payable in Swiss francs; the remaining maturities are unidentified, but are often assumed to consist of Deutsche-mark loans.

Dow shows $1.1 billion of plant in Europe and Africa. Despite that nicely obfuscated aggregation, most of the plant is probably in Europe, much in Germany. In recent years, the Swiss franc and the Deutsche-mark have tended to fluctuate in tandem. Assuming that such will be the case in the future, from an economic point of view, Dow's foreign currency loans appear to carry no exchange risk.

Essentially, the company has plants in Germany which will earn Deutsche-mark cash flow. That cash flow will go to repay the Deutsche-mark loans. The dollar-Deutsche-mark exchange rate is of little consequence for the lending transaction; only the dollar value of the *net* cash flow after debt repayment would be affected by a change in the exchange rate.

Through 1975, Dow reflected the essential economics of that situation by deferring gains and losses from translating the foreign currency loans over the life of the debts. In 1976 when it must adopt FASB Opinion No. 8, Dow will be required to translate the German loan values at the current rate, which will produce gains or losses while carrying the German plant at a constant dollar value (historical rate translation). The translation gains or losses can no longer be deferred; they must pass through income. Since the debt amounts are large, the translation gains and losses will also probably be significant — but they are not real. We have already noted that Dow does not bear any exchange risk on these loans. The accounting gains and losses which will be reported in the future will be false.

Dow could avoid the problem of translation gains and losses by changing its balance sheet structure. If, for example, the Deutsche-mark and Swiss franc loans were converted into Eurodollar loans, the accounting problem would disappear. The plant would still be converted at fixed rates and the loans, being in dollars, would require no translation. No translation gains or losses would arise.

There would, however, be one significant drawback to that debt restructuring: Dow would own an earning asset producing Deutsche-mark cash flow in order to repay dollar loans. Clearly, this is not a hedged position. Dow would be at risk if the dollar-Deutsche-mark exchange rate changed and it would have real economic gains or losses.

What about the accounting? As we just noted, the translation method indicates a hedged position; on an accounting basis there would be no gains or losses.

Dow, then, has a basic problem with FASB No. 8. While companies with positive cash flows overseas can avoid the problems of FASB No. 8 merely by greater remittances, purchasing inventory, or other easy expedients, the debt-heavy company has a basic tradeoff between economic reality and accounting gains and losses.

It is not clear what path will be taken by Dow and other companies in similar positions. It is interesting to note that while Dow's total long-term debt increased from $1.30 billion at December 31, 1974 to $1.56 billion at the end of 1975, foreign long-term debt decreased during the same period from $258 million to $219 million. This decrease took place even though Dow indicates unused foreign credit lines of $430 million ($320 million in Deutsche-marks), somewhat greater than its unused dollar credit lines.

Estimating the Impact of Foreign Debt: Burroughs as An Example

The Dow Chemical and Merck discussions suggest a reasonable route for analysts: look for large amounts of foreign currency debt. It is relatively easy for companies without heavy foreign debt to avoid the pitfalls of FASB No. 8, and they probably will. Those with foreign debt will have problems and should be considered more carefully.

While long-term foreign debt is the item of most obvious concern, where a company borrows heavily short term to finance inventory or a rental base, as does Burroughs, the entire foreign debt must be considered. The maturity date of a liability bears no relation to the translation gain or loss.

Burroughs' foreign debt appears to consist of the following:

	$ Millions
Short-term debt of foreign subsidiaries (per Note 4 of Annual Report)	$184.4
Long-term debt: (Note 5 of Annual Report)	
British (convertible)	14.8
Swiss	70.3
Japanese	19.5
French	22.1
	$311.1

The long-term debt is most likely against equipment held for lease, as is much of the short-term debt, the currencies of which are not given in the annual report. To the extent that the short-term debt is used to finance accounts receivable, it is hedged and will not generate gains and losses. However, it appears that the uncovered position, in total, is large.

In the past, Burroughs translated long-term debt at historical rates, thus avoiding the creation of gains or losses. At December 31, 1974, the company had $29 million ($0.74 per share) of such unrecognized losses. Exchange gains and losses on short-term debt were debited or credited to the reserve for international operations and also were excluded from the income statement.

For the analyst, it now becomes a question of keeping an eye on the exchange rates for the currencies in which the debt is payable and attempting to estimate the impact of such changes. They can be large. For example, if the Swiss franc strengthens by 10%, the $70.3 million of Swiss franc debt would produce a $0.19 per share loss for Burroughs.

HEDGING AGAINST TRANSLATION GAINS AND LOSSES

As noted in the previous discussion, direct rearrangement of the assets and liabilities in the balance sheets of foreign subsidiaries is probably the easiest and most economical way of avoiding translation gains or losses. Many businessmen and accountants refer to all such efforts as *hedging*. However, in a more restrictive sense, *hedging* is used to denote actual forward purchases or sales of currencies made to fix values, prevent losses, lock in gains, et cetera.

For example, the balance sheet in Table 4.1 could have been hedged against a translation loss by a forward sale of 100 francs (or forward purchase of $25) at Fr. 4 = $1.[5]

When the franc dropped versus the dollar to Fr. 5 = $1 (as in Table 4.3), the fixed-price contract would gain in value by $5. Thus, the increase in value of the forward contract would offset the loss on the balance sheet position. On the other hand, had the franc strengthened to Fr. 3 = $1, as in Table 4.3, having committed its extra cash to the forward contract, the company misses the profit it would have had on its asset position—which provides about the same result that would have occurred if the company had evened up its current rate asset position in another way.

Of course, if the franc does not fluctuate versus the dollar, then the company has lost whatever costs—such as commissions—that were associated with the forward contract. Many companies have taken the position that since currency values seem to fluctuate on a random basis (there's that Efficient Market Hypothesis again), the net result of active hedging through forward purchases and sales will simply be the expenditure of commissions. If it does not hedge, the company would save the commissions.

Some companies have told analysts that they are following a policy of "not hedging." We suspect that these companies are using the term *hedging* in the more restrictive sense of actual purchases and sales of currencies. It is doubtful that any company will eschew the possibility of *hedging* by rearranging its balance sheet at virtually no cost.

Note that hedging with forward market transactions involves a number of complications. For example, for U.S. tax purposes profits from forward market transactions are generally taxable. As noted below, translation gains and losses are generally not taxable. Thus, in the example immediately above, the $5 profit from the forward contract might actually be only about $2.50 on an after-tax basis. If the profit on the forward contract is taxable, it would take a double hedge, a Fr. 200 contract to actually hedge the balance sheet.

The taxability of forward contract profits varies from country to country. As an added complication, the U.S. Treasury has suggested that capital gains rates may be applicable, so that the loss (deduction) side of a forward contract may be less attractive. Considering the problems, uncertainties, and possible (long-term) futility of hedging, it is easy to understand why some companies do not intend to utilize forward market contracts extensively.

TRANSLATING THE INCOME STATEMENT

The previous discussion has been concerned totally with translation of the balance sheet, except, as it was pointed out, that balance sheet gains and losses must be passed through the income statement. The income statement itself must also be translated.

Table 4.4 illustrates income statement translation. The first example, the Black Forest Elf Clock Repair Company, is a pure service operation. All repair work is done by the elves who are salaried, and who provide their own tools and wooden sticks for repairs.

TABLE 4.4
INCOME STATEMENT TRANSLATION: TEMPORAL METHOD
Starting Exchange Rate: DM 4 = $1

Example I: *Black Forest Elf Clock Repair Company*

	at 4:1		at 5:1		at 3:1	
	DM	$	DM	$	DM	$
Sales	$100 \div 4$	$= 25$	$100 \div 5$	$= 20$	$100 \div 3$	$= 33.33$
Cost of Sales	$80 \div 4$	$= 20$	$80 \div 5$	$= 16$	$80 \div 3$	$= 26.67$
Gross Profit	20	$= 5$	20	$= 4$	20	$= 6.66$
Gross Profit (%)	20	20	20	20	20	20

Example II: *Superautomationfabriekenwerk*

	at 4:1		at 5:1		at 3:1	
	DM	$	DM	$	DM	$
Sales	$100 \div 4$	$= 25$	$100 \div 5$	$= 20$	$100 \div 3$	$= 33.33$
Cost of Sales	$80 \div 4$	$= 20$	$80 \div 4$	$= 20$	$80 \div 4$	$= 20.00$
Gross Profit	20	$= 5$	20	$= 0$	20	$= 13.33$
Gross Profit (%)	20	20	20	0	20	40

In the first period, the exchange rate is DM 4 = $1 during the entire period. The general rule for income statement translation is that amounts are translated at the rate in effect when they pass through the income statement. Thus, theoretically, it would be correct to translate each sale at the rate in effect on the date of the sale. Practicality suggests some modification of that rule in the interest of economy, and most companies translate income statement items at the average exchange rate during the period. Monthly sales weighting is probably the most common method.

Since all of Black Forest Elf Clock Repair Company's revenues and costs are of a current nature, sales and cost of sales are both translated at the rate during the period, 4:1. This results in translated dollar sales of $25 and cost of sales of $20, giving a gross profit of $5.

Note, that while in this example direct translation of the DM 20 gross profit would have yielded the $5 amount, the foreign current profit figure is never directly translated. The translated dollar profit figure is computed only after the individual items are translated. This is necessary, since not all the items in the income statement are translated at the same rate, as will be illustrated below.

Note, in the Black Forest example, if the rate in another period is 5:1, that is, a weaker Deutsche-mark, the translated gross profit drops to $4 in direct proportion to the change in the exchange rate. Similarly, if the DM were to strengthen to DM 3 = $1 in another period, the translated gross profit would rise, again in proportion to the change in value of the local currency.

This gives rise to a basic, although often abused rule: all other things equal, the translated dollar value of foreign earnings will vary in direct proportion to the change in the exchange rate, *if all the company's sales and expenses are current rate items.*

A variation on the general case is suggested in the second example, that of Super-automationfabriekenwerk (Super). This highly-automated operation has only machines, no labor; thus, cost of sales consists entirely of depreciation. The general rule that all income statement items are translated at rates prevailing during the period is modified for those items, such as depreciation, that represent the transfer to the income statement of an asset which was translated in the balance sheet at historical cost. Fixed assets are translated at historical cost; so is depreciation. Similar considerations apply when inventory, translated in the balance sheet at historical cost, is passed to the income statement as cost of goods sold.

The Super example follows the same changes in exchange rates as did the earlier one on the clock company. As long as the exchange rate is stable at 4:1, all the items translate at the same rate. However, when the exchange rate changes to 5:1 for a subsequent period, an odd effect occurs. The sales figure is translated at the average rate in effect during the period, that is, DM 100 = $20. However, the depreciation figure must be translated at the historical rate of DM 4 = $1, which means that DM 80 of cost of sales translates to $20. Sales of $20, less costs of $20, produce a gross profit of zero.

In the next example, when the DM strengthens and the exchange rate goes to 3:1 for the period, the reverse effect occurs. The DM 100 of sales translates at the new rate of 3:1 to $33. The depreciation (cost of sales) remains at the constant dollar figure of $20, producing a jump in gross profit to $13.

Thus, the basic rule relating to translated income figures to changes in the exchange rate must be modified when costs include items that were originally translated at historical cost in the balance sheet. If such costs are included, then the translated dollar profit figure will change at a greater rate than the exchange rate.

INVENTORIES PRODUCE JUMPS IN QUARTERLY PROFITS

Table 4.5 illustrates how the effect described immediately above will tend to cause wide fluctuations in translated quarterly profit margins when exchange rates vary.

TABLE 4.5

QUARTERLY INCOME STATEMENT TRANSLATION: TEMPORAL METHOD

Illustration of Trailing Effect on Gross Profit Margins When Exchange Rates Change

Assumptions: Initial exchange rate—Fr. 4 = $1
              Inventory balance = Fr. 80 at all times
              Inventory turnover = 4 times per year
              Inventory method = FIFO

Normal Conditions: *First Quarter of Year.* *Rate is Fr. 4 = $1*

	Fr.	$	Comment
Sales	100 ÷ 4	= 25	
Cost of Sales	80 ÷ 4	= 20	
Gross Profit	20	= 5	

Second Quarter of Year: *Exchange Rate Changes to Fr. 5 = $1 on March 31*

Sales	100 ÷ 5	= 20	translated at current rate
Cost of Sales	80 ÷ 4	= 20	inventory at first ¼ rate
Gross Profit	20	= 0	

Third Quarter of Year: *Exchange Rate Still at Fr. 5 = $1 Throughout Quarter*

Sales	100 ÷ 5	= 20	at current rate
Cost of Sales	80 ÷ 5	= 16	inventory at second ¼ rate
Gross Profit	20	= 4	

Fourth Quarter of Year: *Exchange Rate Goes to Fr. 4 = $1 on September 30*

Sales	100 ÷ 4	= 25	at current rate
Cost of Sales	80 ÷ 5	= 16	inventory at third ¼ rate
Gross Profit	20	= 9	

First Quarter of Next Year: *Exchange Rate Stays at Fr. 4 = $1*

Sales	100 ÷ 4	= 25	
Cost of Sales	80 ÷ 4	= 20	inventory at fourth ¼ rate
Gross Profit	20	= 5	

The assumed conditions of a constant balance sheet inventory amount of Fr. 80, the FIFO assumption (generally used in foreign countries), and the three-month inventory turnover period combine to provide a basis for the demonstration. With these assumptions, inventory costing Fr. 80 will be bought in each quarter and will be sold (passing through cost of sales) in the following quarter.

In the first quarter of the year, the "normal conditions," the exchange is and has been Fr. 4 = $1. With that rate, the foreign sales of Fr. 100 translate to $25, while the Fr. 80 cost of sales, representing inventory also acquired at the 4:1 rate, translates to $20, giving a gross profit of $5.

On the last day of the first quarter, assume that the franc weakens and the exchange rate goes to Fr. 5 = $1. All other conditions remain the same in the second quarter. The Fr. 100 of sales is now translated at the 5:1 rate of exchange in effect during the second quarter. Cost of sales, under the FIFO assumption, consists of the inventory that was acquired in the first quarter. When that inventory was acquired, the exchange rate was 4:1, and it must be charged to cost of sales at that rate. Therefore, the Fr. 80 of cost of sales translates to $20, giving a gross profit of zero.

Thus, as in the case of the earlier illustration with the depreciation charges of the super-automated German example (Table 4.4), the weakening of the local currency produces a disproportionate drop in translated dollar earnings.

During the third quarter, the exchange rate remains at 5:1. Sales of Fr. 100 are again translated at 5:1 to $20. Cost of sales, however, now consists of inventory that was purchased in the second quarter when the exchange rate was also 5:1. It therefore translates to $16, which produces a gross profit on a translated dollar basis of $4. Note that $4 is 20% less than the "normal" gross profit of $5 that was achieved when the exchange rate was 4:1. In short, the gross profit, after the dip caused by the translation method, is reduced by the same percentage (20%) as was the value of the local currency (from $0.25 to $0.20 per franc).

Table 4.5 then illustrates the effect in the opposite direction, when on the last day of the third quarter, the local currency rises in value to Fr. 4 = $1. The same distortion occurs in the following quarter, as translated gross profit jumps from $4 to $9 while the currency value rises by only 25%. Note that in the fifth quarter, when inventory and sales are translated at the same rate, gross profit stabilizes at $5, reflecting the 25% rise in the currency.

Note that in the general case, the unusual dip or jump is felt in the following inventory cycle, which for purposes of this example, was made equal to a quarter.

Watch for Second-Quarter 1976 Foreign Profit Dips

During the first quarter of 1976, several major European currencies, the French franc, the Italian lira, and the pound sterling all fell substantially. The effect described immediately above should have a large negative effect on the reported second-quarter profit margins of those companies that normally earn profits in these three countries. That is, second-quarter profits will show an abnormally large dip, while third-quarter profits will rise and reflect only the percentage dips in the currencies.

Note that if the affected companies have net debt positions in these same currencies, when the balance sheet translation gains from the debt will tend to offset the income statement effect just described. On the other hand, if the companies have net (current rate) asset positions in these weakened currencies, the translation losses on the asset positions will only accentuate the problem.

BALANCE SHEET VERSUS INCOME STATEMENT IMPACT

One of the greatest points of confusion in translation accounting is the difference in the presentation and results of translating the balance sheet and those of translating the income statement.

The amount that usually appears in the notes to the financial statements as a gain or loss from translation is the result of translating only the balance sheet. While there is an impact from translating the income statement, it does not show up as a separate and clearly identifiable gain or loss.

Translation of the balance sheet was demonstrated in Tables 4.1, 4.2 and 4.3. Under FASB No. 8, the resulting $5 loss shown in Table 4.2 and the $8 gain in Table 4.3 would both have been taken directly to income for the period ending at the balance sheet date. The $5 loss and $8 gain would also be the amounts that would have been given in the note to the financial statements as the gain or loss on translation.

Tables 4.4 and 4.5 demonstrate the translation of the income statement. When exchange rates changed there was an effect, but not one which is separately identified as a translation gain or loss in the financial statements. There can be no separate isolation of the income statement effects of translation because, in contrast to the balance sheet, each income statement is a new statement and is translated anew. That is, gains and losses in the balance sheet arise from first translating an asset, say cash, at one exchange rate and then later translating the *same* asset at a different rate. However, while assets (and liabilities) are carried forward from one balance sheet to the next, each item in the income statement, sales, expenses, et cetera, starts anew each period. There are no amounts to be translated at one rate on one date and at a different rate at a later date.

This is not to say that rate changes do not affect the income statement. As was noted in Table 4.4 with the Black Forest Elf Clock Repair Company, in the simplest case a constant stream of foreign currency profits will change in dollar value in proportion to the change in the exchange rate.

Thus, with a 4:1 rate, the Black Forest Elf Clock Company earned DM 20, or $5. In the subsequent period, with the exchange rate at 5:1, the same DM 20 earnings are worth only $4. The dollar value of the earning stream declined by 20%, the same percentage as the decline in the DM.

One might argue that the earnings of the second period were affected by $1, due to the devaluation of the DM. That contention might be correct, but only if one is willing to assume that, "all other things are equal." That is, the relative impact of the devaluation on the second quarter was $1, only if it is assumed that every other condition, such as sales volume, unit costs, et cetera, in the second period, was unchanged from the first period. Such unchanged conditions are not common, particularly when in most countries a significant change in the exchange rate *would* impact the sales volume.

As a practical matter, rarely would enough information on demand elasticity and other factors be available to permit an accurate calculation of the impact of a rate change on the income statement from period to period. Of course, many companies do disclose a figure for the "income statement impact," although generally in the text of the annual report, rather than in the financial statements or the notes. Since there is no unique number which will represent the income statement impact, companies obviously have a good deal of flexibility in how the figure is derived. Many companies appear to have calculated the figure in the past by merely translating the current income statement at the "old" exchange rate, and attributing the difference between that figure and the actual current result to the impact of the exchange rate change. This is obviously a simplistic view of the impact. Other companies appear at times to have snatched the figure from thin air. Unless an estimate of the income statement impact is accompanied by an explanation of the computational method and underlying assumptions, it should be treated with considerable scepticism.

This is one problem that the FASB appears to have understood. Paragraph

33 of FASB No. 8 requires that if a figure for the income statement impact is presented (as against a description of the impact) the methods and assumptions must be disclosed.

CONFUSION ON STARTING DATE FOR QUARTERLY REPORTS

FASB No. 8 is required for all periods that start *after* December 31, 1975. The FASB urged earlier compliance, and a number of companies did follow it for the year 1975. As a practical matter, the method described in FASB No. 8 was completely acceptable in the past (there were very few that weren't) and could have been applied at any time during the exposure draft period or even earlier.[6]

The starting date provides no complications for calendar-year companies. They must use it for the year 1976 and for all the quarters in that year. The situation is less simple for fiscal-year companies. Clearly, they must use it for the first *year* that starts after December 31, 1975. Therefore, Proctor and Gamble, with a June 30 year, will be required to use FASB No. 8 for the year ended June 30, 1977; Levi Strauss for the year ended November 30, 1977.

Unfortunately, FASB No. 8 is silent about the quarterly periods of fiscal-year companies which occur during 1976, but before the start of the year in which the company must adopt FASB No. 8. Thus, there is no clear answer as to what practice must be followed by P and G in the first and second (calendar) quarters of 1976.

Discussion with several accountants suggests that in those situations when a fiscal-year company does not voluntarily start using FASB No. 8 during the affected quarters, a pragmatic compromise will probably be reached. The company may actually report in the quarter under its pre-FASB No. 8 policy. However, if translation following FASB No. 8 would give a substantially different result, then a footnote would be required in the quarterly report, indicating the existence of FASB No. 8, its contemplated adoption date, and the results of the quarter *if* FASB No. 8 had been applied.

TAX EFFECTS ON TRANSLATION GAINS AND LOSSES

In the most common case, that of a foreign subsidiary's balance sheet being translated into dollars, the resulting gains or losses are not taxable (or tax effected). In the foreign country, the subsidiary files its financial statements in the local currency; there is no translation nor translation gain or loss in the foreign country. Since foreign subsidiaries are not consolidated for U.S. tax purposes, the translated balance sheet does not appear on the U.S. tax return either. U.S. taxability will arise only when the subsidiary remits earnings to the U.S.—if it does remit earnings at all. The provision of deferred taxes on unremitted foreign earnings is optional and is rarely done for translation gains and losses.

In some cases, however, translation gains and losses may have tax effects. While foreign subsidiaries (separate corporations) are only taxed for U.S. purposes when earnings are remitted, foreign branch results are immediately consolidated for U.S. tax purposes. Translation gains or losses are taxed under two different, somewhat complicated methods.

A translation gain of a foreign subsidiary, which owns another foreign subsidiary, may require deferred tax accounting, which will flow up to the U.S. parent company's consolidated financial statements. Other circumstances might also exist calling for tax effect accounting. However, the most common case remains as above: that of no tax effect from translation.

NOTES

1. Financial Accounting Standards Board, "Accounting for the Translation of Foreign Currency Transactions and Foreign Currency Financial Statements," Statement No. 8 (Stamford, Conn.: FASB, October 1975).
2. John Thackray, "Are the Days of the FASB Numbered?" *Institutional Investor*, vol. 10, no. 10 (October 1976), p. 67.
3. Financial Accounting Standards Board, *Exposure Draft (Revised): Accounting for Leases* (Stamford, Conn.: FASB, July 22, 1976).
4. Leonard Lorensen, *Reporting Foreign Operations of U.S. Companies in U.S. Dollars*, ARS no. 12 (New York: American Institute of Certified Public Accountants, 1972).
5. In practice, the rate for forward purchases would almost always be different from the current rate, reflecting a balance between forward expectations of currency values and short-term interest rates.
6. Note that when FASB *exposure drafts* are in conflict with existing accounting pronouncements, they cannot be followed until the exposure draft is formally adopted as a standard.

Accounting for Foreign Currency Translation

Joseph E. Connor, Jr.

Managing Partner-Western U.S.
Price Waterhouse & Co.

The subject is FASB No. 8, a statement widely criticized in the year since its birth. Before dealing with the subject of translating foreign currency, let me deal first with the proper bounds of criticism—reasonable criticism.

Criticism is the inescapable lot of any group that accepts an accounting standard which sets mission loftier than encouraging the equality of debits and credits. The Financial Accounting Standards Board is no exception, nor should it be. Honest, reasoned criticism is a main source of growth, and the board's demonstrated ability to hear and react gives promise to its continuing viability.

The FASB concept is sound. The board's dedication is unquestionable. The board needs and deserves active support, of which logical, constructive criticism is an inseparable part. It needs criticism, not static.

It has been just over a year since FASB No. 8 was adopted. The statement does basically two things: (1) it requires uniform translation procedures similar in practical effect to a translation method already followed in practice; and (2) it requires uniform inclusion of translation gains and losses in income, and outlaws preexisting practices which sanctioned some deferment of translation differences.

My own writings in this field differ from the FASB conclusions set forth in Statement No. 8. I continue to believe that there are circumstances in the complex world of international business where uniform, "do-it-this-way" translation standards simply don't provide the right answer.

Nevertheless, FASB has resolved a difficult and controversial question that has defied consensus for decades. This is precisely what FASB is supposed to do. And I should also note that this statement should undercut one of the criticisms to which the board has been subjected of late: an alleged failure to eliminate differences in practice.

It is of concern to me that Professor Seidler refers to the (a) limited support in accounting literature given the temporal method of translation, and (b) infers that the FASB's failure to reconcile its position might well end up in SEC activity. I think Professor Seidler is wrong on both counts.

First, it is true that the temporal method of translation has few supporters, at least when called by that name. In fact, however, the temporal method is substantially the same as the monetary-nonmonetary method which is widely used in practice. In fact, FASB No. 8 points out that the temporal method provides a conceptual basis for the procedures that are now used to apply the monetary-nonmonetary method. So, I believe it is unfair to identify the temporal method as some untried idea from academe. Its concepts had been applied for a number of years and its translation practices had been adopted by most of the major international companies, including a number whose financing base was drawn from a multitude of currencies.

In the second place, I know of no movement within the staff of the SEC to force reconsideration of FASB No. 8. Undoubtedly the staff has its own views of appropriate translation methods and these could well contrast with the FASB's view, but the latter has been accepted by the SEC staff. In fact, the uniform application of method—any method—undoubtedly eases the regulatory task and reduces criticism of the staff for permitting alternatives. Nor do I think that recourse to the SEC would result in action that would make the translation procedure more palatable to those companies which are critical of FASB No. 8. Specifically, (1) it is not likely that the SEC would opt for alternative translation methods, and (2) it is not likely that the SEC would opt for deferral and subsequent period amortization of gains or losses as an alternative to immediate income recognition.

Undoubtedly some companies truly believe that the FASB No. 8 translation rules are not appropriate in their situations or in all circumstances. I share that view. But, the SEC cure may be worse than the disease.

DISAGREEMENTS WITH FASB NO. 8

Turning now to Professor Seidler's views, it seems to me that he has identified a number of theoretical shortcomings in FASB No. 8, namely: (1) weaknesses in the temporal method itself, (2) absence of cash flow considerations in the translation of debt undertaken to finance fixed assets and inventory, (3) recognition of unreal gains and losses.

He has also identified the key practical objection which most companies have to FASB No. 8: namely, the distorting effect on recurring earnings which results from including exchange gains and losses in income. Let me deal with each in turn.

Translation Method

First as to the temporal method: I do not share Professor Seidler's evaluation of the temporal method of translation. While I have reservations as to the results produced by that method, I must in fairness acknowledge that there exists an acceptable conceptual basis for it. I have already stated that I believe that the temporal method is only a renamed version of the old monetary-nonmonetary method. But I must limit this analogy to present ground rules for asset measurement—historic cost. At present the translation procedures to apply the temporal method generally are the same as those following the monetary-nonmonetary method. This coincidence arises because under present generally accepted accounting principles, monetary assets and liabilities (like cash, receivables and payables) are usually measured at current exchange values and nonmonetary assets (like plant) at past values. Hence, the term *temporal*.

But what if we change the measurement base of fixed assets? What if we substitute current value accounting for historic cost of plant? Then a real difference arises in the translated value of plant following the temporal method as opposed to the monetary-nonmonetary method. The task of translating foreign fixed assets following the temporal method adopts itself to a situation where historic cost is abandoned. Plant values would be current, valued in foreign currency, and translated at current rates. Preservation of the intrinsic value of physical assets at historic dollar equivalent cost is no longer necessary under current value accounting and the nonmonetary translation technique loses its relevance.

So, if we are to follow one conceptual framework of translation, I think the

FASB has done well to identify a methodology which conforms to one accepted present practice and which can be expanded to cover the prospect that historical cost will be abandoned in the future.

My real concern with the present FASB No. 8 is that the temporal method fails to deal with economic reality. It prescribes a set of translation rules which consider each asset and liability as if they existed or came into being in a vacuum. It rejects the interrelationship of assets and the means undertaken to finance them. It does make a difference if a foreign plant is financed out of foreign currency debt as opposed to Eurodollar debt, but the FASB has ruled for a translation method that ignores the hedging protection of local currency debt and the exchange exposure of financing in currencies other than the one which will be earned in normal operations of the assets thus financed. In stating this criticism, I share Professor Seidler's concern that *cash flow considerations* have been forgotten in establishing translation rules and that as a result *unreal gains and losses* are being reported in some circumstances.

Since these theoretical translation points were not fully developed by Professor Seidler, let me do so now.

The key to understanding the history of foreign exchange translation practices is to realize that U.S. practice developed in relation to this country's experience in dealing with currencies which had a long-term history of devaluating relative to the dollar. Prior to World War II it was recognized that devaluation of foreign currencies did not in most cases mean a loss in intrinsic values of these assets. In many instances, it could be demonstrated that devaluation reflected severe inflationary conditions that existed in the country whose currency was devalued. Thus increased local selling prices were expected to compensate in large measure for the devaluation effect. Continuation of original dollar historic cost of fixed assets was justified since continued operation of the physical assets resulted, in many cases, in the maintenance of substantially the same translated United States dollar gross profit margin after a devaluation as before.

The reason for the use of historic rates for long-term foreign currency liabilities is a little more obscure, but it still ties to our experience with other currencies devaluating relative to the dollar. It is my opinion that historic rates were used as a conservative measure of cash profits. In the usual case, debt provided a considerable portion of the financing for plant, property, and equipment. There was a sound economic basis for this back-to-back financing package. Foreign currency debt would be extinguished from the cash flow resulting from operation of the plants thus financed. With the plant being translated at historic rates, translation of debt at current rates following a devaluation would have created an immediate profit in translated dollars but without either local currency surplus to which dividends could be charged or an increase in local currency cash to pay the dividend remittance. Accordingly, use of historic dollar translation rates for local currency long-term debt in effect deferred the potential foreign exchange gain until increased local currency cash flow from operating and depreciating the plant would permit not only recognizing the translation gain but also realizing on it through dividend remittance.

The more or less continuing history of foreign currency devaluations relative to the U.S. dollar following World War II progressively raised questions as to whether this translation method had been carried far enough. For example, it was seen that inventories—no less than property, plant, and equipment—had intrinsic value and were not affected usually by devaluation, unless price controlled. In the usual case, the demonstrated ability to sell such inventory at increased local selling prices following a devaluation led to the conclusion that inventory should also be translated to historic costs.

I have no quarrel with this extension of the historic dollar translation method to inventories as such. The problem arises because accountants in the post-World War II era forgot the rationale behind the translation rules affecting local currency financing of plant and inventory, both of which produced local currency cash throw off. In an era of constant foreign devaluations relative to the dollar, it became recognized that following a devaluation, foreign exchange gains on local currency debt were, in fact, permanent and real profits. It was also recognized that the devaluation gain merely compensated for high interest costs undertaken and charged to income in order to arrange the local currency financing. Such gains were, in the period up to 1970, increasingly taken into income despite the fact that the ability to remit such profits was, in many cases, absent until increased cash flow in local currency from depreciation of plant and equipment made possible realization of dollar dividends.

These rules are those incorporated in FASB No. 8, but they don't work when you are dealing with currencies which appreciate relative to the dollar and they may never work when foreign retail prices are not set in the marketplace.

What happens when an upward revaluation of a foreign currency occurs relative to the dollar? Of prime importance is the realization that the dollar has lost purchasing power relative to appreciating currencies. This acknowledged economic change is not one which dollar accounting must recognize—given today's convention, however unrealistic, of not recognizing losses in purchasing power generally. Foreign subsidiaries will continue to record local currency transactions without change. Manufacturing wages and overhead, sales revenue, cash collections, et cetera can reasonably be expected to remain stable and unchanged in local currency since the latter has not been subjected to the monetary pressures which have forced the revaluation of the dollar. Their translated dollar value will, however, be higher. Accordingly, the prospect is that dollar translated net income in the future will be higher. Plants will continue to be modernized, expanded, or replaced out of local currency cash flow.

FASB No. 8 can, however, produce a loss on revaluation, when none, in fact, has occurred, and it can over report dollar translated earnings in subsequent years. Assuming plant, property and equipment, and inventory exceeding or equal to long-term foreign currency liabilities, with other working capital financing provided by capital and retained earnings, upward revaluation of foreign currencies produces a foreign exchange translation debit which would be reported as a loss following FASB No. 8. This "loss" is not in accordance with the economic facts. Local currency cash flow from operating the plant will pay off the local currency debt. No loss really exists.

Future translated gross profit margins will increase over the level that would have been obtained prior to revaluation as the unrealistically low old historic dollar amounts for depreciation and inventory enter the income statement. Hence, recording a loss on date of revaluation following FASB No. 8 usually can be expected to be followed in succeeding years by increased translated dollar profits which is an undesirable pattern of reporting with a roller-coaster effect.

Let me illustrate this: Assume that a new corporation operating in a foreign country determines to finance its working capital through equity infusions and to finance its plant assets through long-term borrowings payable in foreign currency. The balance sheet at inception would be as follows:

Cash	Fr 100 ÷ 4 = $25	LTD	Fr 60 ÷ 4 = $15
Plant	60 ÷ 4 = 15	Capital	100 ÷ 4 = 25
	Fr 160 $40		Fr 160 $40

Now assume that an upward revaluation occurs to the extent the Fr 100 = US $2. The balance sheet would then look as follows:

Cash	Fr 100 ÷ 2 = $50	LTD	Fr 60 ÷ 2 = $30
Plant	60 ÷ 4 = 15	Capital	100 ÷ 4 = 25
		Earnings	10
	Fr 160 $65		Fr 160 $65

Retained earnings of $10 arises from the exchange gain of $25 on the upward revaluation of cash less the exchange loss of \$15 from translation of long-term debt at current rates.

Now let's assume that two things happen: the plant is sold at cost and the debt is paid off. The balance sheet would then look like this:

Cash	Fr 100 ÷ 2 = \$50		Capital	Fr 100 ÷ 4 = \$25
			Earnings	25
	Fr 100	\$50		Fr 100	\$50

Income for the period would show a net exchange gain of \$15, representing the gain on cash flow from the plant used to liquidate the long-term debt. This gain has nothing to do with the only external force which should trigger off an exchange adjustment: namely, a rate change.

Putting all transactions together we have the following schematic analysis of the next exchange gain:

	Exchange Effect
up valuation of cash at date of rate change	\$25 gain
up valuation of long-term debt at date of rate change	15 loss
up valuation of cash resulting from sale of plant	15 gain
	\$25 gain net

What has really happened is that the upward revaluation of long-term debt used to finance plant has not been matched at the revaluation date by an up valuation of the plant. It is only when the plant is sold and the resultant cash flow up valued that the increased cash translation equals the increased valuation given to long-term debt on the date of rate change.

The incongruity of this situation becomes particularly clear when the revaluation of long-term debt takes place at a considerable time interval from liquidating the plant. Then we have a situation where an exchange loss is reported in one period and an offsetting exchange gain in a later period. This is what I mean by the rollercoaster effect.

The problem seen here with FASB No. 8 is that the statement sets forth rules so that each asset and liability is translated in a vacuum without recognition that assets should be translated with reference to the particular liability which financed them. Professor Seidler talks in his paper about the need which corporate treasurers will feel to hedge their exchange position so that exchange gains and losses are avoided. But the biggest hedge of all is back-to-back financing of plant construction with foreign currency long-term debt— and FASB No. 8 fails to recognize this.

There are, of course, methods which would avoid the problem of unreal exchange losses when foreign fixed assets are financed in local currency which appreciates relative to the dollar.

The first corrective measure defers the exchange adjustment on long-term foreign currency debt for later amortization. The best justification for the deferral concept lies in the relationship of long-term obligations to the financing of assets—plants, property and equipment, and inventory. This approach would defer exchange differences relating to the translation of long-term liabilities used to finance those assets, which, following the translation practices prescribed by FASB No. 8, are to be carried at historic dollar translated amounts. In my opinion these assets are not properly being accounted for at cost under FASB No. 8 following an upward revaluation. In subsequent years these assets will be charged to operations at pre-revaluation dollar translated costs while revenues are stated at more favorable post-revaluation dollar translated amounts. The deferral at date of revaluation and subsequent amortization—over a period approximating the remaining life of plant—of the exchange debit arising from translation of long-term liabilities partially offsets this undervaluation of plant, property and equipment, and permits an improved future matching of income and expense.

This is the point made by the dissenting member of the FASB to Statement No. 8. Succinctly put, this method avoids the reporting of translation losses which are not economically justified relative to long-term assets—just as FASB No. 8 accomplishes the same end by use of historic rates for assets where foreign currencies depreciate relative to the dollar.

A second, more extreme correction to FASB No. 8 would be to allow plant and other fixed assets to be translated at current rates. The case for current rates is most easily seen when foreign currencies are revalued upward. As described earlier, local currency sales, costs, and earnings can reasonably be expected to remain stable, in the absence of other factors not related to the effect of devaluation. Dollar translated earnings should be more because the local currency is worth more. From a balance-sheet viewpoint, the current rate technique also produces realistic results. Foreign assets have, in fact, changed in relative cost values. Translation at current rates of exchange does not alter the basis of valuation—it is still cost, i.e., local currency cost. Remember that you buy foreign plant with foreign currency. Liabilities are fully valued at amounts which, in dollars, are the equivalent of local currency needed to settle them. The method acknowledges that a foreign subsidiary with net worth has a higher translation value following an upward revaluation than was the case prior. A revaluation gain is present and should be accounted for.

I admit this is a radical solution and it will aggravate the reporting of smooth earnings. This situation is best dealt with by explaining the effect of exchange fluctuation on earnings in earnings releases.

Effect on income

Since we are talking about smoothing earnings, a word must be said as to the practical problem of including in current period earnings exchange adjustments which can widely fluctuate.

I am sure that Professor Seidler is right that corporate treasurers will attempt to hedge this exchange exposure risk and avoid as much as possible the erratic effects on earnings. And I believe it is probably good financial management to do so. But in practice not all exchange risk can be avoided.

It is not popular to espouse erratic earnings. Nonetheless, foreign exchange rate changes are a visible fact of life. When rates change and a company has an exposed foreign currency position, it strikes me that the function of accounting is to report that event. There is an earnings impact.

This is the tack that the FASB has taken and I believe it is superior to the alternative of trying to smooth earnings by some artificial amortization of exchange gains and losses. The practical problem, of course, and properly of concern to corporate treasurers is that exchange fluctuations are just that— they fluctuate. One period's gain could reverse and be followed by a loss in succeeding periods.

In my opinion, however, the function of accounting is to report these changes and not cover them up. Exchange gains and losses follow upon rate changes which are real. It is not the function of accounting to smooth earnings.

Let me make one additional point while I am talking about the somewhat erratic effects which FASB No. 8 is having on corporate earnings. Professor Seidler illustrates the point well when he talks about the short-term inventory liquidation problem and its effect on quarterly earnings. I think his illustration lacks one important conceptual comment. FASB No. 8 translates inventory costs at rates reflecting those in effect during the period of inventory accumulation. These translated inventory costs are taken into income as cost of sales in the following quarterly period. If the normal inventory accumulation period is three months, it is fair to say that the exchange effects on the cost of this inventory are charged to income as cost of sales on a three-month lag basis. Professor Seidler illustrates this situation and is rightly critical of the mismatching of costs and revenue that it occasions. I am, too. The causative factor for this situation is that selling prices of goods following a revaluation, as shown in Professor Seidler's illustration, have not reacted to the revaluation change. In other words local inflation is not mirroring exchange changes. In this situation it is inappropriate to hold to historic translation rates. The cure

to the problem is to use current rates to translate inventory where local inflation and devaluation go in different directions. This again is a point raised by
the dissenting member of the FASB to Statement No. 8. But I must
acknowledge that similar mismatching or lag matching of inventory costs
with sales revenue is not alone a foreign exchange problem. FIFO costing in
domestic operations has the same effect during a period of rapid domestic
price changes.

So let me sum up my feelings about FASB No. 8. On the good side:

1. It adopts a long accepted translation method and doesn't invent a new
   and untried one;
2. It adopts a uniform rule for recognition of exchange gains and losses
   and removes the variety of practices which had heretofore existed relative to realized and unrealized exchange gains and losses and their
   deferment or inclusion in income; and
3. The immediate recognition in income of exchange gains and losses is
   consistent with other opinions of the FASB in that it is transaction-
   oriented and avoids income smoothing such as would result from an
   amortization method.

On the not-so-good side:

1. The translation method can produce unreal exchange gains and losses,
   since it fails to relate in the translation process those assets with the type
   of financing used to acquire them;
2. Poor financing decisions can result from attempts to hedge foreign exchange position, and poor financing decisions can result because translation rules relative to long-term debt removes the hedging, which I believe is inherent in such financing.

This analysis is said critically, but hopefully with constructive criticism. I
have outlined deferral mechanisms which should help fine tune FASB No. 8.
And I believe that it is fine tuning that will help eliminate the static the FASB
is hearing on its translation opinion.

FIVE

Financial Control and Reporting

in Multinational Enterprises

An exploration of the difficulty of providing worldwide consolidated financial reporting by multinational enterprises because of diverse financial reporting influences, requirements, and constraints.

George M. Scott

Associate Professor
The University of Texas
at Austin

J. Frank Drapalik

Partner
Ernst & Ernst

Dr. Scott holds both a B.B.A. and an M.B.A. degree from the University of Michigan and a Ph.D. degree from the University of Washington. He has earned numerous awards and has authored many papers, articles, and books on national and international accounting.

Mr. Drapalik holds a B.S. degree from Washburn University. He is a member of the firm's international operations committee and its banking committee. Mr. Drapalik has appeared as a speaker before a number of groups and recently was on the program at an Annual International Banking Seminar.

Financial Control and Reporting

in Multinational Enterprises

George M. Scott

Associate Professor
The University of Texas at Austin

Multinational enterprises are widely viewed as the most efficient organizational vehicles that have ever existed for mobilizing the world's scarce resources.

This paper examines significant differences between multinational enterprises and other international companies and how these differences provide opportunities for multinational enterprises to increase their efficiency further. Specifically, the quality control aspect of this efficiency is considered at the levels of subsidiary and headquarters managers. This translates roughly into what we accountants call "financial and accounting control."

THE IMPORTANCE OF INTERNATIONAL BUSINESS

The mushrooming growth of international business is sometimes regarded as a rival of the Industrial Revolution in importance. In 1957, 2800 U.S. parent companies controlled 10,000 foreign affiliates abroad—about 3.5 affiliates per parent company. In 1971, 3500 parent companies controlled 25,000 foreign affiliates, a growth from 3.5 to about 7 foreign affiliates per U.S. parent company. Thus the total number of foreign affiliates increased by a factor of two and one-half during this fourteen-year period, and the average number of foreign affiliates per company doubled. These trends have continued.

During the decade of the sixties, the total amount of direct foreign investment by U.S. companies doubled, while total sales abroad tripled and remitted profits increased from $3 to 8 billion. Again, the trend shown by these figures has generally continued.

Of the Fortune 500 companies, almost all have significant foreign operations. More than 20% of the total sales of about 200 of these companies represents foreign operations, and for some companies, e.g., IBM, *significant* means more than 50% of their sales. Further, the companies with extensive foreign operations appear to be more successful on average than are purely domestic U.S. companies; their long-term growth rate has been about double that of their domestic counterparts.[1]

Also noteworthy is the marked shift in the nature of U.S. foreign operations which has taken place during the last two decades. Purely import-export operations have declined in importance relative to the extension of active business operations abroad. Even some smaller U.S. companies are now involved in manufacturing, processing, components and raw materials sourcing, marketing, financing and even research and development in other countries on a permanent basis. Also, many companies that have traditionally manufactured only in the United States are now undertaking a full range of activities abroad with a vengeance.

An example of the latter is General Dynamics, which has sold its F16 fighter plane to European countries. Forty percent of the parts for planes to be purchased by other countries will be produced in Europe. Three assembly lines are being set up—one in Belgium, one in Fort Worth, and one in the Netherlands. The accounting and control problems that will face General Dynamics will be severe, and they will doubtless be exacerbated by the company's inexperience in these types of operations. To boot, this is but *one* product; IBM, ITT, Xerox, and hundreds of other companies have similar arrangements for dozens and even hundreds of products.

Not only U.S. companies have the international fever, however. Total foreign direct investment of non-U.S.-based companies is comparable in magnitude to that of U.S.-based companies—around $200 billion. In other words, U.S. firms provide only about half of the total foreign direct investments in the world. An increasing amount of this foreign investment is in the U.S. Standing at $25 billion now, this investment is increasing at a rate of about 20% per year.[2] For example, German companies are now said to have more capital invested in South Carolina alone, than in any other country outside of Germany.[3]

At present, approximately one-sixth of the world's GNP is generated by the foreign affiliates of international companies; if domestic operations are included, their share of GNP jumps to 50 or 60%.[4]

So the world is becoming multinationalized. So what, you say! How does this affect me as an accountant?

These questions will be addressed in detail in this article. Let me note at the outset, however, that we accountants are among the last in the business world to recognize the challenges and opportunities presented by the explosion of multinational ventures.

CHARACTERISTICS OF MULTINATIONAL ENTERPRISES

The multinational enterprise (ME) is different from other types of companies in international operations; it is a unique form of entity with respect to the way it conducts its business. The differences are subtle and difficult to pinpoint, but they are critical to an understanding of the ME.

The ME—as opposed to other international companies—is characterized by:

1. Significant operations abroad and operations in several countries— arbitrarily, at least 20% of total sales abroad and operations in six or more countries;
2. Foreign operations which encompass the full range of domestic activities, including foreign sourcing, production, and marketing;
3. Activities which are integrated across national borders at the operations and financial levels, as well as in terms of managerial control;
4. Coordination on a global basis—by means of a management system which forces the component parts of the total entity to cooperate rather than to go their separate ways.

The fourth characteristic above is probably the most important ingredient in the description of an ME. Coordination is essential to an entity's strategies and in the pursuance of its global goals. In the parlance of accountants, the component parts must "articulate." Clearly, the ME is not a decentralized company in the traditional sense of profit centers.

Having established these attributes of an ME, we must concede that the ME as defined is an abstraction which does not exist in pure form. However, many companies approach this definition—ITT, IBM, GE, Xerox, Unilever, Colgate, Philips Lamp, Shell, Mobil, Exxon, and Nestle, to name but a few.

No one of the above characteristics must necessarily be present in full measure; there are degrees of multinationalism. Also, a company may operate as a multinational with respect to only some of its functions. For example, a company can act like an ME in its management of cash but not in its logistics function and vice versa. The most important general distinction to be made is between the financial functions and the operations functions. Hundreds of companies integrate and coordinate global financial matters to a significant extent but have left sourcing, production, and marketing operations decentralized in the local country.

Literally thousands of companies are following in the footsteps of the leaders in multinationalism, by incorporating into their own organizational designs and long-range plans those ingredients of multinationalism which they perceive as relevant to their company. The general movement toward multinationalism has tremendous future implications for management in general and for accounting and accountants in particular.

ENVIRONMENTAL COMPLEXITY AND OPPORTUNITY

The movement toward multinationalism is largely in response to two factors: 1) The problems and complexities unique to, or exacerbated by, operations in the different environments of several countries, and 2) the unusual opportunities presented by the differences among these multiple environments. These multiple environments can be classified into four general types for each country.

The regulatory-legal-political environment. One important aspect of this environment is the regulation of accounting. Although all countries regulate financial reporting to some degree, the form of regulation differs significantly from one country to the next. In each country, control of financial reporting is comprised of a different mixture of inputs from statutes, government agencies, stock exchanges, professional associations, and so forth. The functions of the SEC, AICPA and FASB of the United States, for example, are replaced by legislation regulating many aspects of corporate behavior and reporting practices in other countries. Outside the American-British accounting orbit, concepts akin to "generally accepted accounting principles" are encountered far less frequently than are legal reporting requirements. A myriad of different disclosure requirements exist and serve to complicate the management of MEs. For example, affiliates may be required by law to provide local financial reports for stockholders, the public, tax authorities, regulatory agencies, stock exchanges, and lending institutions.

The array of financial reporting influences, requirements, and constraints confronted by MEs throughout the world, only a sample of which have been mentioned, makes worldwide consolidated financial reporting by MEs difficult. Most MEs find it necessary to maintain two or more sets of records in some affiliates, each set reflecting different needs.

The business and economic environment. This environment determines factor costs, product demands, competition, degree of economic stability and growth, and other elements.

The social-cultural environment. This environment influences product acceptance, labor patterns and costs, and consumer attitudes toward MEs.

The international monetary environment. This environment introduces a new set of problems to business dealings, namely those related to dealing with exchange rates. Fluctuations of exchange rates introduce financial risk and create the perceived need to reduce or protect an enterprise against this risk through managerial actions such as hedging.

THE PROBLEMS AND OPPORTUNITIES OF MULTIPLE ENVIRONMENTS

Since the environments of each country are different, the task of dealing with environment-related problems, complexities, and risks is several times more difficult than in a purely domestic company. As an example, it is more difficult in international operations even to remain aware of changes in the environments; the executives of domestic companies all live in one country and think in terms of "keeping up with current events," rather than "monitoring the local country environments." This problem of monitoring is best viewed as an information systems problem—the ME needs a kind of information system that is simply not needed by the domestic company.

The environments of the different countries are not only different, but they also change relative to each other, so that either the prime location for a certain activity or the most advantageous activity at a given location may change over time; for example, since it is no longer economical to export Volkswagens to the U.S., they must now be built here. Further, some environments are less stable than others and experience change at accelerated rates; environments may even change abruptly as with *coup d état*. These problems not only increase the complexity of operations for international companies, but also compound the uncertainty and risk of operations.

But multiple environments also provide more opportunities. The company that is wired into many environments and has learned to deal effectively with greater complexity and uncertainty has the potential to:

1. Provide its global operations with the lowest cost raw materials, labor, and other elements available within its region of operations;
2. Sell its products, no matter where produced, in the most lucrative markets of the world;
3. Borrow needed capital in the financial markets of the world at the lowest possible cost, and lend excess capital to achieve the highest returns;
4. Reduce total taxation costs by careful separation and judicious location of various activities; and
5. Utilize resources (including cash) more effectively by transferring idle or underutilized resources to other parts of the world.

What emerges is an optimization problem of great magnitude, with the objective functions being those of solving management problems economically and taking advantage of all available opportunities. Few of the constraints or variables involved are linear and many are not quantitative; but even if they were, no computer is capable of handling so large a problem. Further, the computer model needed would be rendered obsolete with every change in a significant environment factor—an almost daily occurrence.

How then can this optimization problem be solved? Precise solutions are not possible, but MEs are able to find approximate solutions. At first blush, it may appear that problems caused by greater complexity—including greater risk accompanied by greater complexity—are best dealt with by decentralization, allowing local managers to deal with local complexity. But appearances are deceiving. Complexity and risk caused by relative changes among the environments of different countries cannot be handled in a decentralized manner, because only managers who understand the implications of the interactions among the environments of different countries can effectively deal with these problems. Local managers cannot grasp opportunities presented by differences in the environments among countries effectively, because they cannot easily keep track of developments—such as production factor and money costs—outside of their own country.

Centralized management is another conceivable way to deal with complexities and risks. The interactions are too many and too complex, however, to be understood adequately by headquarters managers alone, since they are neither up on current events in local countries nor aware of all the attendant circumstances. Further, the information glut at headquarters in a large-scale centralized system introduces communications channel overload and over long delays in decision-making, which greatly reduces the company's flexibility of action in response time.

It is necessary that both headquarters and local managers play major roles in the management of MEs. The intimate knowledge of local managers about the local environments is critical in situations involving complex interactions, and headquarters managers cannot take advantage of available opportunities without the help of local managers. Headquarters must be kept aware of local needs and conditions, including changes affecting raw materials, working capital, production scheduling, et cetera, before decisions can be made that capitalize on the opportunities available. For example, as exchange rates vary, local managers must interpret local conditions, but only headquarters may be able to understand the implications of these changes for the global system well enough to formulate a management strategy. Where interactions among foreign subsidiaries are involved, complexity can be most effectively dealt with and risk most significantly reduced by a symbiotic relationship between local and headquarters managers.

The preceding suggests that neither decentralized nor centralized management is more effective in international operations. A new form of management seems appropriate—one that is based in a comprehensive way on the cooperation of local and headquarters managers in the conduct of a broad range of activities. The author has labelled this form of management *coordinative management*, since it is global coordination more than the other attributes which sets the ME apart from other international companies.

Coordinative management is already developing in international companies; some MEs have progressed far toward coordinative management without defining or naming it. However, coordination still remains essentially an alien approach that is quite different from the conventional management practices epitomized by decentralization and profit centers, which began to emerge as early as the 1920s. There is still a great deal of room for accountants to get in on the ground floor of coordinative management and to help erect this revolutionary management structure.

CONTROL AND COORDINATION SYSTEMS IN MEs

If a company is an ME, that is, globally coordinated, then its management processes are different. Because of the need for extensive collaboration of headquarters and local managers, a different management style called *interac-*

tive management emerges. Managers "interact" to make decisions by communicating extensively among themselves, ensuring that all of the major interactions among the environments are considered before a decision is made. The decision then becomes, in some sense, a "joint" decision no matter whose formal responsibility it is. While managers may interact in a number of ways to achieve this level of communication, the most effective means is face-to-face discussion based on careful advance preparation by all managers involved; thus, the formal management meeting has risen to new heights of sophistication in MEs.

Because of the global integration and coordination, and the interactive management style found in MEs, different types of managerial systems are required. These include different kinds of systems for financial control, performance evaluation, resource management, and information gathering. Additionally, MEs need a type of managerial system not required in companies during the past—a system of coordination tools and techniques.

Control Systems

The distinguishing features of control systems in a coordinated ME may be shown by drawing several contrasts between control systems in noncoordinated international companies (non-MEs) and those in MEs.

Control systems in non-MEs are intended primarily to serve local management. Reports to headquarters are infrequent and quite basic, providing only a few performance indicators supported by little detail. At an extreme, these reports may display only the variance of actual from budgeted profit. On the other hand, control systems in MEs serve both local management and headquarters. Standardized information in considerable detail flows constantly to headquarters, in order to help control and coordinate the global system.

Also, each entity in a non-ME is concerned only about itself. Headquarters in turn controls subsidiaries at the macro level. In an ME, interactions among subsidiaries are encouraged if the net result works to the advantage of the global system, and headquarters interacts with subsidiaries by participating in the local management processes. All of these interactions must be monitored and accounted for by the control system, imposing an additional burden on the system.

Local variances in a non-ME usually can be attributed to local causes, such as the local economy, or the performance of local managers. In an ME, variances are more difficult to pin down because the local manager is not in complete control of his own operations. Control systems in MEs must somehow compensate for the fact that managers from subsidiaries and from head-quarters contribute to and share responsibility for local results.

In a non-ME, local goals tend to remain fixed over a considerable period of time. Since local goals are subordinate to global goals in the ME, however, they tend to be considered a variable in the short pull, in order to help achieve global goals. This additional dynamism in operations requires an equally dynamic and responsible control system. For example, if a subsidiary procures its raw materials from subsidiaries in one or more other countries, its materials' costs fluctuate at least as frequently as exchange rates do. Either standard costs must vary to compensate for exchange rate shifts or the control system must be insulated from the effects of these exchange rates alterations.

The control system's sole purpose in a non-ME is to control. In an ME, the control system must also be designed to provide sufficient information to headquarters in order to aid the coordination process. Using the budget as an example, a variance in production quantity at one location can have an impact on a remote subsidiary, if that subsidiary is the intended recipient of the produced units. Also, the long-range plan in an ME is not merely a compilation of local plans; it places emphasis on the outlook for the entire global system and on the coordinative and other strategies necessary to maneuver the ME into its desired future position.

Accounting control systems of MEs must also be altered to facilitate accounting for inflation in managerial analyses. Although inflation provides a difficult control problem even in domestic companies, the problems for MEs are compounded by the fact that inflation rates are different in each country. Differential rates of inflation may confound the financial control system to the point where financial statements of related subsidiaries, prepared under different rates of inflation, completely lack comparability. For an ME, comparability of foreign subsidiaries is essential, because a rational basis is needed for the frequent resource allocations within the system.

Accounting systems of MEs can cope better with global inflation, if accounting is on a current-value basis. While current-value accounting is now receiving a great deal of attention with respect to external reporting, its importance for internal managerial purposes has been largely overlooked. Whereas historical-cost accounting provides comparability only in the absence of inflation, current-value accounting provides resource values and financial results on a basis which provides valid comparisons and allocations among organizational units, whether or not inflation is present. Using current-value accounting, resource values are stated in terms of their purchasing power in the local economy, where they will be used to generate earnings, and this information about local purchasing power is essential to the making of informed resource allocation decisions.

Performance Evaluation

Many of the problems of performance evaluation in MEs are implicit in the preceding discussion. As suggested, the integration and coordination of operations circumscribe the areas of operations controlled solely by the local managers. Evaluation of a local manager on the basis of his direct accountability is therefore difficult at best.

By virtue of his role in global coordination, the local manager participates in activities which impact on the operations of subsidiaries in other countries and on company-wide coordination. Although he should therefore be evaluated partly on the basis of these extra activities, systems do not exist which adequately appraise a manager's contribution to operations other than his own. While many possibilities exist, no single technique or set of techniques has been shown to yield effective evaluations.

Resource Management

The coordinative form of management in the ME suggests resource management approaches that differ from those of non-MEs. As one example, MEs attempt to "pool" the cash resources of their entire system to the extent permitted by local banking laws. While this provides greater efficiency in the use of cash, it also places heavy demands on cash management systems and managerial time and expertise.

In the related area of dealing with currency risk, MEs are adopting approaches which provide routine reports of exposed positions on transaction contracts, cash, and other resources for the entire global system. Based on these reports, specialized managers (some of whom are accountants) can take actions to hedge or reduce exposure for the entire system. Hedging may be accomplished for several foreign subsidiaries in a single hedging transaction to reduce transaction costs. On other occasions, exposed positions in various subsidiaries may be offsetting, so that no action is considered to be necessary; whereas, if each subsidiary were on its own, each might take separate action to hedge.

To cite another example, managers of MEs try to develop a balanced approach to tax coordination, thus giving attention to the interactions between tax considerations and nontax factors affecting well-being, such as remitability, inflation, exchange rate risk, and the goodwill of governments. To implement this approach, key tax personnel might be included on the global team of managers who interact in the coordinative process.

Complex and sophisticated global logistics and transportation networks are emerging as a result of the emphasis on coordination. One oil company, for example, is said to have a plotting board giving the up-to-the-hour location for each of its tankers so that they may be rerouted in response to changed oil prices, delays of other tankers, or fluctuations in demand at various locations.

Information Systems

Information systems of MEs are different from those of non-MEs in two major ways. First, the Management Information System must be integrated across national boundaries, particularly where the operations of subsidiaries are specialized by country. To quote Paul Hoffman, a manager at IBM:

> Now, in an integrated operation, each country has to get information from the other countries. Information has to cross borders, not only for finished product, but also for parts and raw material requirements. . . . with the advent of long-range requirements and added international operations and integration it became necessary to develop a new concept. The most important mechanisms used to achieve formal information integration in MEs are large scale computer communications systems, and computerized data basis.[5]

The second difference is that, in order for coordinative management to be effective, the information system of the ME must incorporate a scanning and intelligence system designed to provide all managers with the information they require about local environments. Since not all managers need all information, refined classification and filtering processes must be incorporated into the system.

Coordination Methods

The area of coordination tools and techniques is totally undeveloped and unstructured at the present time. To accountants, this is akin to the APB and FASB attempting to establish accounting principles in the absence of a general framework for the objectives of financial statements. There is ample opportunity, therefore, to develop or invent coordination tools, or even to develop a general theory or approach for coordination.

Coordination techniques employed to this time have been an amalgam of several kinds of approaches. A few of these follow:

1. *Meetings:* A body of academic literature about meetings is now emerging, and formal meetings are becoming an important means of coordination. It may be said, for example, that ITT's empire is run by meetings devoted to coordination, analysis, and planning, and that these meetings are supported by an elaborate information system tailored to provide each high level manager with the information needed to perform effectively during the meetings.

2. *Budgets and plans:* These have already been mentioned as coordination techniques.

3. *Project management techniques:* In coordinative management, tools such as PERT, which are normally associated with closed-end projects, can be adapted for use with routine operations of a continuous nature.

4. *Management science techniques:* A variety of management science techniques are suitable for coordination in MEs. Present experience, however, suggests that they are little or no more important in MEs than in non-MEs. Simulation and linear programming, for example, have similar shortcomings in both types of companies.

5. *Policy guidelines:* These are generally rule-of-thumb decisions promulgated by headquarters that provide a crude form of coordination. A simple example is the requirement that the excess of cash over current liabilities be placed in a regional cash pool to be drawn upon by subsidiaries in other countries as needed.

6. *Accounting-based policies:* These are similar to policy guidelines in that they represent a mechanical approach to directing certain activities within the system. For example, for certain subsidiaries, Philips Lamp permits an amount equal to 90% of depreciation on a replacement value basis to be reinvested in the same product line without headquarters approval, thus defining in a rational way the extent of reinvestment discretion permitted local managers.

7. *Corporate inculcation:* Inculcation is a by-product of an interactive system, whereby managers thoroughly absorb "the company way." High levels of interaction permit a manager to learn the collective thinking of the other managers so well that he is able to conduct his own activities in the way approved by the collective group of managers. This provides a form of direction to activities that, while not based directly on interaction, is nevertheless an indirect result of it.

ACCOUNTANTS AND MEs

The Management Revolution in MEs provides ample grist for accountants' mills. This includes accountants in international companies, as well as CPA firms, and especially those in CPA firms who provide advisory services. Auditors must also understand the nature of MEs, since auditors must have an appreciation of the economic substance of every company they audit.

As a digression, the following is an intriguing question for international CPA firms: "Would viewing your firm as a potential ME result in any changes that would make it more efficient and effective in the way it operates?" In contemplating an answer to this question, it will be useful to review the discussion of the nature of multinationalism, give attention to the benefits which might accrue to your firm from global integration and coordination, and then consider the kinds of managerial systems necessary to convert your firm into a multinational enterprise.

Accountants have much or all of the expertise required to assist the ME with respect to the problems addressed in this paper. Specifically, we accountants will be remiss if we do not play a significant role in the development of the following areas in MEs.

1. *Control systems:* This is a traditional province of accountants, who can help design control systems with the flexibility to adapt to the changing "game plan" of dynamic MEs, thus accounting for and controlling interactions among foreign affiliates.
2. *Performance evaluation:* This is another traditional realm of accountants. Performance evaluation systems for MEs must be developed to distinguish between entity and manager performance and to provide for the evaluation of managers based on their contributions to their own entity, other affiliates, and the activities at headquarters. The blurred lines of responsibility and authority in MEs make this an especially demanding assignment.
3. *Resource management systems:* Accountants should help develop systems that enable MEs to coordinate cash management, taxation, logistics, risk evaluation and hedging, and other managerial activities globally.
4. *Information systems:* Accountants have always been in charge of one information system—financial information reporting. In MEs, accountants should not only raise these reports to higher levels of sophistication but should also participate in the design and development of the global management information system.
5. *Coordination tools:* Accountants have no initial disadvantage in this area

since no participants in international operations have a thorough grasp of "how to coordinate." Accountants have every opportunity to participate fully with other groups in the development, implementation, and even the utilization of coordination tools. Accountants' opportunities are amplified, since many of the coordination tools will be used in conjunction with the control system, a system managed by accountants.

Accountants who are in the forefront in these activities can expect to be full-fledged members of the "management team" and participants in the coordination processes in MEs. In this way, they will continuously be in touch with the progressive ideas associated with MEs and will play a part in the future evolution of management processes.

While the primary purpose of describing the mode of operations of MEs and how they differ from non-MEs has been to portray the role accountants can play in MEs, the secondary purpose is to suggest some implications for external financial reporting from the perspective of an ME. The major point to make regarding the latter purpose is that it is possible that finding the appropriate solutions to certain external reporting problems in international operations may depend upon an understanding of the nature of the ME as an integrated and coordinated global network, rather than as a U.S. firm with foreign operations. Accounting rule-making bodies, such as the FASB, as well as individual accountants, such as ourselves, who influence those bodies, might well reach different conclusions about what constitutes proper external reporting for companies in international operations if the perspective is that of the non-ME as opposed to that of the ME.

Currency translation is an example. When viewed from the perspective of the ME, which regards its foreign operations in the same way as its domestic operations, it appears to make little sense to adjust for inflation in the U.S. after translation to the U.S. dollar. This so-called "translate first, then adjust for inflation" approach results in reporting foreign activities in terms of the U.S. economy as if they had taken place in the U.S. and been subject to U.S. inflation. From the viewpoint of the ME, foreign-held resources should be stated in terms of the foreign economy, because (with certain exceptions) that is where the resources will be retained and used to produce an income stream. This analysis suggests that the "restate first for local country inflation, then translate" approach is preferable.

In a similar fashion, the wisdom of alternative financial reporting solutions in the areas of consolidation, disclosure, and resource valuation may be pondered and debated from the perspective of the ME. These and others are left to the reader for consideration.

SUMMARY

This paper has examined a great many complex and interrelated ideas and concepts. It is useful to review and summarize these point by point in a logical progression manner.

1. The ME is defined as a company in international operations that is highly integrated and coordinated on a global basis.
2. Multinationalism—the idea that international companies should operate like MEs—is portrayed as increasing in appeal, with more and more companies striving to emulate MEs.
3. Environment-related problems and opportunities are shown to elicit the mode of operations characteristic of the ME. That is, the greater uncertainties in international operations can be dealt with effectively, and the greater opportunities presented by multiple environments can be capitalized upon with a coordinative form of management.
4. The management style, control systems, performance evaluation systems, resource management systems, and information systems of MEs and non-MEs are examined, and the kinds of coordination methods used in MEs are considered.
5. The opportunities for accountants to particpate in the development of the systems required by MEs, as well as in the development of coordination tools, are represented as excellent.
6. Finally, it is postulated that when accountants view international operations from the perspective of an ME, the solutions to certain external financial reporting problems may be perceived differently from the solutions otherwise proposed.

It is hoped that this paper has stimulated readers to investigate the problems and opportunities of MEs. They represent a tremendous challenge to accountants.

NOTES

1. *Wall Street Journal,* 18 April, 1973, p. 1.
2. *Business Week,* 12 April, 1976.
3. *Wall Street Journal, op. cit.*
4. *Business Week, op. cit.*
5. Paul Hoffman, "Designing the Multinational Information System," in *International Management Information Systems* (New York: American Management Association, 1967), p. 6.

Financial Control and Reporting

in Multinational Enterprises

J. Frank Drapalik

Partner
Ernst & Ernst

Much of what I have to say is the result of insights gained through personal experience and in discussions with my associates and clients whose companies have significant foreign operations.* Professor Scott has indicated that many opportunities are available to enterprising accountants in the operations of multinational enterprises. In general, I agree with his assertion; however, I feel there are opportunities that Professor Scott has mentioned only tangentially, namely, those that are available to the management services personnel in the international public accounting firms.

For the most part, I agree with Professor Scott's position that multinational enterprises are here to stay and are going to continue to grow and become even more important to our economy than they are today. However, I feel that while certain sectors of the economy will be receptive to the growth of multinational enterprises, other sectors of the economy will not. For example, I think that the service sector is likely to be less multinational than the manu-

*The author gratefully acknowledges the helpful comments of Professors George M. Scott, University of Texas at Austin, and Dhia D. AlHashim, California State University at Northridge, with regard to an earlier draft.

facturing sector, and within manufacturing some industries will be more multinational than will others, at least, in the sense in which Professor Scott speaks. This is significant, because I believe that analyses of attributes of various industries and sectors could be done now, enabling us to predict accurately the extent to which industries are amenable to multinationalization. This information, in turn, would promote orderly and rapid economic growth.

Further, I think that multinationalism will flourish in some parts of the world but will atrophy in other parts. In particular, I think that there are many countries of the Third World that, at least for the foreseeable future, will be adopting policies and practices having the effect of excluding multinational enterprises, which will either have to extract themselves from these Third World countries or adapt to their requirements. Peter Gabriel, in an article called "Adaption: The Name of the MNCs' Game," has noted that multinational enterprises may not be permitted to continue to own the facilities in some developing countries, but instead will provide only managerial services to those facilities.[1] In effect, MEs would run the companies for their true owners, who are likely to be the governments of the Third World countries. To do this, of course, multinational enterprises will need a surplus of high-level managerial ability, which they may have. However, one problem from the perspective of the multinational enterprises is that the ME may be unable to integrate these Third World operations, which they manage but do not own, into their global operations as thoroughly as if full ownership and control of these foreign operations were vested with the ME.

Moving more directly into the content of Professor Scott's position, I will discuss the points in approximately the sequence in which he presents them—covering only those that are of particular interest.

Professor Scott began by expressing his opinion that "Multinational enterprises are widely viewed as the most efficient organizational vehicles that have ever existed for mobilizing the world's scarce resources." I think we should note that certainly there is room for some dissent on this point—and while I personally agree with Professor Scott, and some writings of which I am aware also tend in this direction, I don't think we should be so dogmatic as to assume that even if they are so "widely viewed" that it is necessarily universally true. His view is rapidly becoming the conventional wisdom, but I, for one, would like to see some statistical facts; I think it is still an open question and one that requires research rather than just reiteration.

But while that point may be simply a quibble, following from it is a much more important related matter, and that is that, even if multinational enterprises are the most efficient organizations ever, it is not inconceivable—

indeed it is even likely—that as time moves along some other form of organization may evolve which becomes even more efficient. It is important to
keep in mind that we should continuously be alert to this possibility and we
should not place all of our marbles, so to speak, with multinational enterprises
in the expectation that they will necessarily continue to be the most efficient
organizational vehicles.

In discussing Dr. Scott's presentation of some impressive statistics on the
growth and the changing nature of international business, two important
points should be made here. First, I would like to see a breakdown of these
statistics that indicate which industries are developing more rapidly in international operations, and whether or not the rate of growth of international
operations among industries is remaining stable through time. I acknowledge
that Professor Scott did not have time to give this breakdown of the statistics
but I do think that it would be worthwhile.

We did have a slowdown in the growth of international operations during
the worldwide recession that started about two years ago and from which the
world now seems to be only somewhat tentatively recovering. During that
period, foreign investments by United States companies in particular, as well
as the foreign countries to a lesser extent, decreased or at least had a slower
rate of increase. We cannot yet be certain what the implications of this are for
the future of the multinational enterprise; certainly multinational enterprises
are again expanding at a rapid rate. But it is important to note that the
slowdown demonstrated that this is not necessarily a continuous process, in
that certain events—such as the recession of the past two years—can have a
devastating impact upon multinational enterprises. Accordingly, it is by no
means assured that multinational enterprises will continue to grow at a rapid
rate. Having said this, however, I must concede that, even if multinational enterprises grow no more at all but simply remain stable in terms of their total
foreign investments, they will nevertheless remain a force to be reckoned with
in the world and deserving of every bit of the attention accorded them by Professor Scott and others.

In his comments defining the nature of multinational enterprises, Professor
Scott emphasizes the many dimensions of the multinational enterprises, yet
noting that no one dimension is all important, and that no one dimension is
either totally necessary or self-sufficient. He correctly pinpoints the importance of the idea of integration, I believe, and I support his concept of
coordination, which I have seen in literature only within the context of his
writings. I do not disagree with this idea in the slightest—emphasizing what
Professor Scott has already noted—that no two enterprises are the same. The

diversity of attitudes within companies, of motivations in entering international operations, and of the many other characteristics of companies is astounding. No two companies are the same even with respect to just two of the several criteria that Professor Scott puts forward as essential for determining whether or not a company is a multinational enterprise.

The important concept in this regard that Professor Scott does not address is that—while his stereotype of multinational enterprises is interesting from an academic and conceptual point of view—in the practical world, we accountants must deal with each enterprise on an individual basis. This is partly because we, as accountants, do not necessarily interact with all of the dimensions of the multinational enterprise; indeed, we deal primarily with the controllers' group, and to a lesser extent with the treasurers' group, in multinational enterprises. The controllers' area is less likely than most to be multinational with respect to attitudes and the translation of these attitudes into daily operations. Therefore, we accountants are probably even less likely to identify a company as a multinational enterprise, than are other professional groups that interact with other parts of the multinational enterprise which are more multinational than is the typical controllers' group. This suggests that we should pause to consider from time to time whether a company with which we are dealing and which does not appear to be multinational may, in fact, be multinational. If it is, perhaps we are providing the wrong services to that company, services that are appropriate for a domestic enterprise but not as well suited to a multinational enterprise.

Continuing in this general vein, Professor Scott notes that, "Literally thousands of companies are following in the footsteps of the leaders in multinationalism, by incorporating into their own organizational designs and long-range plans those ingredients of multinationalism which they perceive as relevant to their company." While I cannot disagree with this statement, he does seem to suggest that there might be literally a stampede in process, and that we had better get out of the way quickly or we'll be run over. I don't think he intends this, but I think that it is worth noting that for most companies among his thousands, this evolution is not rapid. It cannot be seen each day, nor is the CPA likely to perceive many changes between his visits. It is usually a glacial process that has to take into account the slowness of personnel in adapting to new processes, as well as the fact that even the managers who are leading this charge toward multinationalism are only gradually becoming multinational in their own attitudes, and so cannot lead any faster than they themselves can proceed along this path. So while I agree that these processes are taking place, I don't think that we can take a look at a company and conclude that, because we don't see rapid change in the direction of multinationalism, it isn't becoming multinational, or that it doesn't need the services that we accountants can potentially provide to companies that are enroute toward multinationalism.

In Professor Scott's very brief summary of the various environments which influence a company and its international operations, he delineates the implications of these environments, but when these are set down so briefly, it is difficult to give environmental differences the emphasis they deserve. And it is too easy for the listener or reader simply to gloss over these differences. But let me emphasize that the differences in these environments are very real and pervasive: they affect not only financial control from a manager's perspective, but they also affect external financial reporting in its every dimension. For example, the standards for reporting in each country are different: various legal requirements for reporting exist and the groups within society that impose these requirements are diverse. In some countries, it is the government, which imposes the requirements, in others it is professional associations of accountants (with which we in the United States and other Anglo-Saxon countries are familiar), and in other countries still, it is a combination of these that determine the reporting requirements.

These differences in environments—not just in accounting but in the social, cultural, and other environments—are monumental. They are greater than we are likely to perceive when working with these companies on a day-to-day basis. We tend to think that, once we learn to function at all with a local environment, we understand environments. But in fact, those of you who have worked abroad probably recognize that old saying: "When I first went abroad, I was totally confused. After a few weeks, I thought I knew everything. After six months, I realized I actually knew very little, because it was only then that I began to realize the full extent of the differences in the environments of the foreign country."

I think that this is true in accounting and for accounting and accountants in multinational enterprises as well. There is a tendency in dealing with international operations to panic at first because of the differences. The second step appears to be overcoming these differences at a superficial level, for example, by being able to restate foreign accounting statements in terms of United States accounting principles. After you have been into this for a longer period of time, you realize that you must have a very good command of the deeper differences in the environments, beyond being able even to convert into the equivalents of United States generally accepted accounting principles, to explain how the equivalents are formulated, and how the trends within the society that lead to changes in these principles. To operate effectively in foreign environments, those of us within multinational enterprises, as well as public accountants who provide services to multinational enterprises, must strive to achieve a greater depth of knowledge about the foreign environments. You cannot do this simply by listening to Professor Scott or myself expound upon these differences. You have to experience them by direct contact over a long period of time.

I am intrigued with Professor Scott's idea about coordinative management, which he dubs "a new form of management." He suggests that coordinative management is required in multinational enterprises, because the joint participation of both the local managers and the headquarters managers is required to enable multinational enterprises to coordinate their operations on a global basis. I will readily admit that I am not too familiar with this concept, having seen it only in Professor Scott's writings. It does have a certain element of appeal, but I might suggest that—while the particular way in which Professor Scott describes it does seem to set it apart from other forms of management with which I am acquainted—it does have ingredients in common with a number of approaches to management, and, therefore, it appears to be not entirely unique. For example, it embodies certain elements of the idea of management by consensus utilized by Japanese managers. It also contains ingredients of collegial management, a form of management that has been discussed in the literature for many, many years. And the idea of cooperative management appears to be not entirely dissimilar to Professor Scott's coordinative management. It seems to me that the particular contribution Professor Scott has made is the melding of various ingredients of several forms of management and combining them eclectically into a package he deems most suitable to the management of multinational enterprises in a coordinated fashion. If this is so, it does not detract from the merit of his ideas. What it perhaps does do is provide us with a means of understanding them better, for we can go to the literature that describes collegial management, consensus management, cooperative management, et cetera, and satisfy ourselves from an examination of that literature that what Professor Scott has merged into coordinative management is indeed appropriate for multinational enterprises. I understand from personal conversation with Professor Scott that he has developed a working paper called "Management Style in Multinational Enterprises," which discusses some of these approaches that I have just mentioned and shows their relationship to coordinative management.

Professor Scott indicates that one of the major tenets of his coordinative management style is interactive management, that is, managers interacting to make decisions by communicating extensively among themselves. Is it possible that this is more a matter of degree than of absolute difference from other forms of management? Isn't it true that even with a hierarchical arrangement, where authority and responsibility are specifically delegated at each level in the hierarchy, there is nevertheless a degree of interaction between the different levels and among the managers at a particular level? This interaction enables managers to know that the decisions they promulgate as their own are, in fact, acceptable to other managers above, below, and lateral to them. No manager would care to have a track record of making decisions that are rarely palatable to other concerned parties, and therefore, every manager does, in fact, pay attention to what these other parties think and their attitudes toward the probable decisions that he will make. Accordingly, he is likely to discuss a matter with these managers, at least to some limited degree, before he makes an important decision. This suggests that, at least in some sense, almost every decision is jointly made, in that the decision maker is influenced by the attitudes and the opinions of persons other than himself. This is not intended to detract from Professor Scott's concept. As presented, the idea of interactive management is important. I also think that it is a natural extension of some processes that are already at work in most companies. And, indeed, by giving attention to these processes, I believe it will be more feasible to understand Professor Scott's interactive form of management and to see that it is not really such a radical departure from what we have, but, in fact, the difference is primarily one of degree. This, in turn, makes it more palatable to those persons who might be interested in implementing interactive management, or who should be interested in doing so.

Professor Scott alluded to the problem of differential rates of inflation and to how accounting control systems must account for this inflation in different countries. As a slight digression, let me elaborate on the matter of inflation in international operations. Accountants throughout the world are trying to recognize the effects of the changing value of a currency in financial statements. In fact, there are approaches and variations of approaches to inflation accounting that are already in use or being considered for use in different countries. In South America for many years, certain of the governments have required revaluation of property for tax or book purposes or both. In the United Kingdom and in Australia, inflation accounting is in the process of being adopted, but the approaches are significantly different from each other and from those that we are probably going to be using in the United States.

These different approaches to inflation accounting create a problem for the corporate financial officer when making a consolidation, or for the CPA who expresses his opinion on consolidated statements that include revalued statements of these foreign subsidiaries. It also poses a problem—and this is more related to Professor Scott's concerns—in developing the accounting control systems that facilitate accounting for inflation. The control systems which he envisions are primarily for managerial analysis, and yet, given the different approaches to inflation of the different countries, this means that the control systems—if they are based on the local approach to inflation—will each be different from the others in the multinational enterprise system. This lack of standardization will cause problems. How would inflation adjusted financial statements, for example, in a Latin American country, be compared with inflation adjusted statements in Japan?

Nevertheless, there are some alternatives. It may well be that for external financial reporting purposes in each country, a different form of inflation adjustments will be needed. However, it may well be appropriate to have a standardized inflation adjustment approach for all of the subsidiaries of a multinational enterprise to provide comparability among these for managerial purposes. It is likely that this latter version will be used by the ME for its consolidated financial reporting as well, if this is permitted. Thus once again, we see the specter of multiple sets of accounting systems to permit conformance with local requirements, as well as to fulfill the standardized global managerial needs of the multinational enterprise. This is a somewhat disconcerting prospect, and I hope that it can be avoided in one way or another.

I can cite here the example of Philips N. V., the well-known Netherlands-based electronics firm, which uses replacement value accounting throughout its operations in some one hundred and thirty countries of the world. What I cannot tell you, however, is the extent to which this company and others will also be required to conform—for external reporting purposes—to the different requirements for current value accounting in these respective countries. It is possible that Philips may have to develop several different current value accounting approaches for use in the different countries to supplement the standard approach it now uses on a global basis. The Philips case will bear careful scrutiny in the future, and U.S. multinational enterprises may well receive some good tips about which direction they should go with respect to inflation accounting.

Professor Scott devotes some attention to the problems of performance evaluation in multinational enterprises. Certainly, while these evaluations may be greatly exasperated by international operations and made even more difficult by the management structure of multinational enterprises, it is nevertheless worth noting that performance evaluation is a managerial problem that has not been resolved in an entirely satisfactory manner within domestic enterprises. In my duties as a CPA and as an advisor to management, I rarely encounter a domestic company that is entirely satisfied with performance evaluation in its own operation. And here I am referring both to the evaluation of the managers themselves and to the evaluation of the utilization of the resources put at the managers' disposal.

I add these comments only to give special emphasis to Professor Scott's statements. If we cannot solve—at least have not yet solved—the performance evaluation problems satisfactorily in domestic enterprises, how then do we hope to do justice to them in international operations and, to go the next step, in the operations of multinational enterprises? I tend to be rather pessimistic with respect to the prospects for resolution of this problem.

Professor Scott gives some small notice in passing to the pooling of cash resources within multinational enterprises. To me, this is a most interesting topic. I'm aware that several international banks based in the United States have been participating in the development of these cash pool systems for the last five to seven years. It seems quite clear that multinational enterprises cannot go, and are unlikely to go, very far along the road toward fully rationalizing cash movements within their global network without the assistance of a comprehensive global banking system, one that juxtaposes bank subsidiaries with company subsidiaries in the same countries.

Unfortunately, countries tend toward nationalism when it comes to banking activities within their borders, and "multinational banks" are encountering local banking laws and customs that inhibit a full rationalization of their global operations. While these banks have made great strides, there is still a long way to go before cash management systems in international operations can be nearly as fully rationalized as is possible in the United States. Until that time, there will always be delays in the transmission of currency between countries, and there will be added expenses because of exchange requirements, various exchange fees, and more complicated transactions. It is in this area where we see one of the most obvious ways in which multinational operations are inherently less efficient than are domestic operations, and these inefficiencies cost the ME and the world dearly.

Professor Scott has thrown a challenge to the international CPA firms by asking, "Would viewing your firm as a potential ME result in any changes that would make it more efficient and effective in the way it operates?" As a member of the kind of international CPA firms to which Professor Scott directs this question, I feel compelled to respond at least as well as I am able. I will not pretend to be able to make a full and learned response to this question. I think that it is the kind of query that one must store in the back of his mind and bring forth on many occasions in the ensuing years, when it may seem more relevant in the context of the problems in international accounting firm management that we will face at that time. Nevertheless, let me briefly comment on this issue.

Following Professor Scott's suggestion in reviewing the nature of multinationalism, let us first consider the difference between the type of services we render and the type of services which Scott seems to set up as provided by his archetypal multinational enterprise; that is, the difference between a service-oriented company, such as a CPA firm, and a manufacturing-oriented company. We can then see that some of the types of coordination which Scott addresses slip through the boards when we begin speaking of a service company. For example, the logistics and logistics information systems problems about which he is concerned are largely irrelevant in the context of the service company. On the other hand, the financial policies and financial integration and coordination that he suggests for multinational enterprises may be equally as important for CPA firms. Certainly the performance evaluation problems have some relevance to CPA firms. For example, we expect our foreign offices to provide services to subsidiaries of our stateside clients, whether or not this is the kind of activity to which they would devote their professional personnel, given the choice. Accordingly, they should be evaluated in consideration of this.

Taking a slightly different tack, one might suggest that, while the primary product provided by multinational enterprises is physical in nature, the primary product provided by CPAs is human services—the services of our partners, managers, and staff accountants around the world. This suggests that the most important aspects of coordination for a service-oriented firm, such as our CPA firm, relate to the personnel policies that might be appropriate to the multinational enterprise. A particularly important aspect of this may be the cross-training that is possible within the CPA firm to insure that it provides uniformly good services around the globe.

I am convinced that a permanent solution to many of the accounting profession's problems, such as lack of standardization of generally accepted accounting principles, is greatly facilitated by a continuous program of mutual exchange of personnel between overseas and domestic operations. Face-to-face discussions of mutual problems improve communications in a number of ways that all of us have experienced. Further, by this exchange of personnel, I believe that we will all come to understand each other's systems a good bit better. Most optimistically, the result could be that we take the best from each country for merger into one accounting approach that ultimately will become more or less standard. In this sense, at least, I think there is something to what Professor Scott has said about applying the concepts of multinationalism to CPA firms.

In his discussion of currency translation, Professor Scott has gone from a general question to a more specific problem. While the problem has been given extensive attention by persons more expert on currency translation than I am, I might suggest that this does tie in with my previous comments about cross-fertilization of accounting thought. We accountants in the United States have in the past, I think, been a bit too provincial in our outlook. We have tended to develop solutions to our own accounting problems, which are unique to our own circumstances, and have paid scant attention to accounting thought in other countries. It might well be that, if we were to give more attention to what accountants in other countries have done about currency translation, we would find that almost none of the accountants in the world are satisfied with the translation techniques they use. This might suggest, then, that we are indeed on the wrong approach, as Professor Scott hints when he mentions the possibility of using purchasing power parity indices for translation purposes. I'm not suggesting that, as a consequence, we would embrace Scott's ideas on the topic, but if we discovered that everyone was basically dissatisfied with current translation techniques, we might be somewhat more inclined to question the basic validity of these, as well as our own, and perhaps be more motivated to search for a radically different approach. It is possible also that, in some obscure place in the world, there is a translation approach that we would acknowledge to be superior to our own, if we only knew about it.

At the beginning of this paper, I indicated that I would examine some areas where accounting firms—in particular the management services divisions of these firms—could provide additional services to multinational enterprises. I will comment on these areas very briefly. The first is that of designing and developing management accounting systems. To ensure that there is efficient integration between the tax accounting system, local financial reporting, and statutory compliance, CPAs could be deeply involved in installing tax accounting systems and other types of accounting systems so that global standardization is accomplished where useful while incorporating systems features to provide for unique local reporting requirements.

The second area is that of advance planning for new foreign installations and acquisitions, including helping the MEs establish goals, evaluate investment alternatives, project probable results, and plan from a tax viewpoint.

The third area involves assisting in the evaluation of economic and accounting risks for making foreign exchange hedging decisions. This area has become particularly important since the issuance of FASB Statement No. 8 on currency translation.

International managers often need the help of independent financial consultants when they face questions of cost and revenue allocations, transfer pricing, budgeting, and integration of local management goals with the goals of the worldwide organization, to mention just a few more possibilities. Some CPAs are already providing these and a great many other services for their clients. But too many management decisions in multinational enterprises are still being made without adequate input from accountants, and I think we have an exciting opportunity to provide the additional input that is needed.

I would like to conclude with some advice on how we should approach these international accounting problems and opportunities. We should do it like two porcupines making love: optimistically, enthusiastically, but *very* carefully!

NOTES

1. Peter P. Gabriel, "Adaption: the Name of the MNCs' Game," *Columbia Journal of World Business*, November-December 1972.

SIX

Harmonization of Accounting

A detailed analysis of the often divergent priorities and responsibilities of accounting firms and regulatory agencies in their quest to standardize world accounting and auditing practices.

Hanns-Martin W. Schoenfeld

Weldon Powell
Professor of Accountancy
University of Illinois
at Urbana-Champaign

Seymour M. Bohrer

Managing Partner
Los Angeles Office
Peat, Marwick, Mitchell & Co.

Dr. Schoenfeld holds both an M.B.A. and a D.B.A. degree from the University of Hamburg, Germany. He also holds a Ph.D. degree from Technical University of Braunschweig, Germany. He has taught throughout the world and has published various articles and books dealing with different aspects of accounting. Dr. Schoenfeld is chairman of the AAA International Accounting Section.

Mr. Bohrer holds a B.S. degree from the Ohio State University. He joined the firm in 1947 and was admitted to partnership in 1957. He is chairman of the AICPA Entertainment Industries Task Force and is a frequent speaker at various professional societies and meetings.

Harmonization of Accounting

Hanns-Martin W. Schoenfeld

Weldon Powell Professor of Accountancy
University of Illinois at Urbana-Champaign

Accounting represents the major tool for control, analysis, and decision-making in an industrial environment; today it is undergoing rapid changes. Unfortunately, the state of the art in several industrialized countries has not reached the same stage of development, has not attained the same rate of change, has not emphasized similar solutions. In spite of the fact that accounting as practiced today can be traced to a common source in Italy, national developments—particularly in the late nineteenth and the first half of the twentieth century—have contributed more differences than they have resolved problems. Initially such differences were of little importance to individual firms or even entire national economies. This situation changed with worldwide economic integration and the advent of multinational enterprises; today all firms operating across national boundaries have no choice but to deal with existing accounting differences. Companies are forced to generate accounting records compatible with the headquarters' requirements without violating national principles—a sometimes very difficult and always costly task.

The problem is further aggravated by dissimilar states of development in auditing and the accounting profession. As a consequence, in addition to some duplication of records, often duplication of audits—to comply with national requirements—are unavoidable. More recently, the emergence of worldwide auditing firms partially helped to cope with such problems. Presently, only these specialists are able to deal with the complexities of the status quo. With their assistance, a client at least receives information which is adjusted to his

173

frame of reference. Nevertheless, the situation urgently demands a resolution through harmonization of accounting and auditing principles. This is, at best, a difficult and, at worst, an almost impossible task; many reasons contribute to this pessimistic assessment. The international auditing firms, however, are a first step toward an improvement of the situation.

DIVERGENT ACCOUNTING PRINCIPLES—THE PRESENT STATE

In assessing the status quo, a distinction has to be made between at least three groups of countries with different accounting problems. These include the following.

1. *Industrialized Western Countries.* These countries generally have highly developed accounting principles and procedures; historical developments, compounded by different economic policies and different approaches toward the development of accounting have resulted in noncompatible solutions. These differences, however, are fully understood, can be analyzed and transposed and there is hope for reaching a harmonized solution eventually.

2. *Socialist Countries.* These countries adhere to a basically different economic policy which—since all means of production are state owned—requires a rigid, formalized control and places even more emphasis on accounting including the budgeting and planning process. Accounting principles (dominated by the Russian approach) are uniform on a nationwide basis,[1] are strictly enforced, and change only as economic policies change. Existing principles differ—in many instances substantially—from western solutions. These differences presently appear to be of less importance, because ownership of operations in socialist countries by western corporations is either not allowed or not very widespread, except in Yugoslavia.

3. *Developing Countries.* These countries often have no accounting standards or only fragmentary accounting standards. Many existing regulations and pronouncements represent verbatim copies of the U.S., British, French, or Russian systems. Frequently, standards lack practical substance, and the accounting profession is neither well trained nor organized. Therefore, a comparison with accounting in industrialized countries is almost meaningless.

In view of this situation, the following analysis will be limited to western industrialized countries because these are the only areas in which meaningful progress towards harmonization can be expected. To realize the magnitude of the problems fully, some examples will serve as illustrations.

Accounting data disclosed in financial statements of most nations are based traditionally on historic cost; usually, decreases in values are recognized through the lower of cost or market principle. This approach does not necessarily produce comparable outcomes, because price changes and turnover rates for equipment influence results—even in periods with mild inflation. How large the difference might be becomes apparent when considering some of the applicable principles. In Switzerland, for example, no limitations on the write-downs of assets exist: the directors of a company are even permitted to create ". . . hidden reserves, if desirable to assure continued prosperity or equalization of dividends."[2] This blanket permission to apply overly conservative principles is only mitigated by a requirement to disclose the insurance value of permanent assets (if these are insured).[3] A similar undervaluation is legal in Sweden: machinery and equipment are depreciated over time periods substantially shorter than economic life; inventories are valued at the lower cost or market, less a reserve of up to 60% of the inventory value. Occasionally, this procedure results in negative inventories.[4]

The noncomparability of data is particularly obvious in the case of inventory valuation. Legally applicable methods abound. Some examples are:[5]

1. FIFO—most prevalent;
2. LIFO—permitted in some countries; not permitted in Australia, Bahamas, Colombia, Fiji, Greece, India, Malaysia, New Zealand, Pakistan, and Panama;
3. Weighted-average—practiced by majority in Argentina, Bolivia, Brazil, Greece, India, Iran, Japan, Mexico, Paraguay, Uruguay; not permitted in the United Kingdom;
4. Base-stock—practiced by majority in Bolivia, Canada, Netherlands, Republic of Ireland, South Africa, Spain, Sweden, Trinidad, and Zaire; and
5. Other methods—flat cost, retail method, current value.

Furthermore, it must be noted that *cost of market* is not interpreted in the same manner. Market is measured in some countries as net realizable value (selling price less reasonable predictable cost) and in others in terms of replacement cost (Greece, Brazil, Switzerland, Venezuela).

Depreciation practices also vary considerably between countries; however, depreciation tends to exceed economic value decline (France, Germany, Greece, Italy, Japan, Sweden, and Switzerland).[6] A wide range of depreciation methods including single-item depreciation, various types of accelerated depreciation (sum-of-the-years-digit, double-declining balance method, and sinking funds method), composite depreciation, and immediate write-off of small items can be found.

To conclude that conservatism in valuation prevails is entirely justified. There are, however, some strange exceptions. In Belgium, Greece and Spain,—although fast write-offs prevail, depreciation is regarded to be optional depending on whether or not sufficient income is available to absorb the charge.[7] On the other hand, there are economically oriented—and thus less conservative—approaches in the Netherlands. Some major companies—notably Philips NV and Eindhoven—revalue their assets on the basis of current replacement costs. Resulting changes are charged directly to a revaluation surplus account; if losses arise, these will be absorbed into the revaluation surplus. Philips even goes so far as to distinguish between inflation-induced price changes—generally value increases—and technology-induced value declines, which are of particular importance for a technology-oriented company.[8] Presently, it seems to be the least conservative position which approximates best the measurement of changes in "true" economic values.

Inflation adjustments are customary in many countries which have had a history of major inflation problems in recent decades. Frequently, the effects are disclosed in financial statements. This is illustrated by practices in several Latin American countries: Chile has probably enforced the policy more rigidly than others, but Argentina and Brazil are also examples for this policy.[9] All financial statement values are adjusted annually for inflation, using an index for a general increase of all values. In Brazil, for example, these data must be disclosed in addition to historical cost values. All such monetary correction computed on the basis of government coefficients are charged annually to reserves; they may eventually be transferred to equity capital through the issue of stock dividends. This practice, nevertheless, does not generate "true" values, because any application of coefficients changes the level of all values but does not reflect specific value changes of individual financial statement items.

Aside from procedural differences, different financing approaches are reflected in accounting data. In Germany, for example, pension reserves represent a major form of capital, often exceeding equity capital. Companies are allowed to accumulate such reserves tax-exempt and invest the capital at their discretion, provided future pensions are guaranteed by insurance. These amounts are regarded as "social capital," which for analysis purposes should be treated as the equivalent of equity. Swedish investment reserves, on the other hand, are generated by voluntary excessive depreciation; amounts are not usable by the company at its discretion and 46% of the total even has to be deposited in a blocked bank account.

Discrepancies in income statements are equally disturbing. Sales revenues often are not disclosed. In Austria and Switzerland, for example, items such as "net revenues from sales" are shown; these are the result of gross sales revenues less deductions for all items which are not required to be shown separately. Obviously such figures are meaningless. For consolidations the situation is again nonuniform: consolidations are completely missing in many Latin American countries and Spain; they are rarely practiced in Greece, Italy, and the Philippines; and in Germany only domestic subsidiaries are included.

Another important problem is created by the auditor's certificate. The certification of a "fair" presentation of the financial situation exists in Anglo-Saxon countries, whereas in continental Europe the certificate states that "the financial statements are in accordance with legal requirements and company statutes." Whether both certificates imply a similar meaning is highly arguable. If strict regulations apply—as is the case in Germany—the implications are relatively close to a U.S. or British certificate; in Switzerland and Italy the meaning is entirely different. Furthermore, the discovery of events requiring a qualified certificate are dependent on auditing standards, which in some countries are almost nonexistent and are not enforced in others.

These examples, which unfortunately represent only a small selection, clearly demonstrate the desirability and need for harmonization and standardization. They also convey an understanding of the difficulties which will have to be overcome with every step in this direction.

OBSTACLES TO HARMONIZATION

To assess problems encountered when attempting to harmonize accounting, the origin of principles or standards has to be traced. Basically, there are two different systems, none of which, however, exists in its pure form.

1. *Professional self-regulation.* This approach prevails in the United States, in the United Kingdom, and in countries influenced by the Anglo-American tradition. It has resulted in a high degree of flexibility—compared to the second system—because adaptation to changing needs is relatively fast due to the fact that specialists deal directly with arising questions. Such systems, on the other hand, have some undesirable features. Decisions are based on a consensus or a majority, consequently

certain dominating (or one-sided) interests have slowed down progress. Furthermore, there seems to be a propensity towards *ad hoc* solutions which are not necessarily coherent and integrated. The fact that additional inputs by the SEC and other regulatory agencies were needed suggest the existence of such deficiencies.

2. *Legislation of accounting principles.* This approach, which represents the other extreme of what appears to be a continuum, prevails on the European continent and in Latin America. Legislation ranges from a few nonspecific sections in commercial codes (Switzerland) all the way to detailed requirements in corporate codes, which are often accompanied by decrees of ministries of economic affairs (Germany, Sweden, France). Sometimes, elaborate uniform systems of accounts exist, which are either voluntary (Germany, Switzerland) or required by law (France). All law-based systems tend to be less responsive to change as is clearly demonstrated by past experience. In spite of the fact that a high degree of uniformity seems to exist, the amount of information disclosed tends to be low, since most laws have not been revised recently. Most of these laws were enacted in the 1930s, which explains their emphasis on creditor protection. In this context, conservatism is completely acceptable because it does not jeopardize the creditor's position.

In recent years, some changes in approach and attitude have occurred. In Germany, for example, legal regulations have been modernized, and their applicability has been extended considerably. The "publicity law" postulates a public interest in accounting data and requires publication of audited financial statements—initially applicable to corporations only—from other business entities or groups of firms.[10] This law applies if two of the following three criteria are met: (1) assets of more than 125 million Deutsche-mark (DM), (2) sales of more than 250 million DM, or (3) more than 5,000 employees. This at least indicates more widespread acceptance of disclosure requirements. The shift in attitude is further underlined by the fact that the accounting profession was consulted before passing the law. Other differences in the sources of accounting principles also tend to fade. In the United States, greater emphasis on government regulation seems to emerge through the recent activities of the SEC. The creation of the FASB removes the development of accounting principles at least one step further from the profession and closer to a neutral source. In Europe, the accounting profession, represented by their institutes, plays an increasingly larger role in the development and interpretation of the legal accounting framework. Both trends suggest a future convergence of approaches balancing governmental and professional influence.

There are, however, some major obstacles which pose problems for harmonization. First of all, there are basic philosophical differences. Oldham assesses these different attitudes by submitting that in the U.K.—using the Anglo-Saxon approach as an example—initially society's attitude is assessed, then a law is passed.[11] On the Continent goals are developed and then laws are passed to change society's attitude. This—although an overgeneralization— nevertheless seems to be a partially valid characterization of the basic approaches. In addition, chauvinistic beliefs in the superiority of one's own system prevail.[12] This attitude has its roots in genuine conviction, but also has components of adherence to familiar traditions, lack of knowledge concerning other systems, and resistance to change. This problem is further aggravated by the absence of an agreement on accounting objectives: in some countries, the emphasis is on creditor protection only, whereas in others (Netherlands) disclosure of the true economic position takes precedence. The U.S. and British attitudes may lie somewhere in between concentrating on certain important economic information items, still permitting compromises to meet auditing evidence requirements and yet not entirely unsympathetic towards companies' needs to avoid excessive disclosure.

Another obstacle arises from the relationship between accounting and the national economic and tax system. In most countries, tax collection is based on accounting data; although valuation and income determination rules may differ for tax and commercial accounting, both are frequently tied together. In Germany, for example, the minimum tax valuation is not allowed to be lower than the values stated in published financial statements. As a consequence, the lowest permissible tax valuation will be used for all financial statements. Since tax measures often are designed to stimulate economic development in certain sectors or regions, a harmonization of accounting standards will require rewriting of tax legislation. In other countries, such as Sweden and France, strong emphasis is placed on macroeconomic planning which utilizes accounting data. Any adjustment of standards will again require major changes reaching far beyond the individual firm. Such changes will meet major resistance; however, since these are technical obstacles, they might be overcome more easily than psychological barriers.

Finally, accounting data are serving as information tools for investors and other parties external to the firm. These groups, therefore, must be reeducated to overcome resistance against accounting changes. If such changes are major, their willingness to adjust is not necessarily high, in spite of the fact that more information may be disclosed. Particularly in countries with limited numbers of stockholders, these groups are not at all interested in disclosure.

Given all the above reasons for adherence to traditional systems, it seems reasonable to predict that harmonization will be a very slow process.

CURRENT ATTEMPTS TO HARMONIZE ACCOUNTING AND AUDITING PRINCIPLES

Because of existing differences in accounting principles, procedures, and auditing practices, demands for harmonization or even complete standardization have become widespread. Due to the initially different approaches in development of accounting principles, it should be expected that steps towards harmonization will have similar origins. Attempts are under way presently by (1) the accounting profession, (2) legislative bodies, and (3) individual firms.

Harmonization, as understood today, is different from standardization. "The term harmonizations as opposed to standardization implies a reconciliation of different points of view. This is a more practical and concilatory approach than standardization, particularly when standardization means that the procedures of one country should be adopted by all others. Harmonization becomes a matter of better communication, of information in a form that can be interpreted and understood internationally."[13] This seems to be a realistic approach, which is more likely to succeed than rigid standardization.

Harmonization Attempts by the Accounting Profession

Regional Activities. During the last decade, several regional organizations have been started by the profession. Usually their goals are limited to the creation of better understanding among professionals and do not include standardization or harmonization of accounting principles. Several regional groups need to be mentioned.

The Inter-American Accounting Conference (IAAC) was initiated by the Puerto Rican Institute of Accountants in 1949. Western hemisphere countries are represented through their professional institutes and organizations. The IAAC meets every two to three years. Its basic goals are:

> To encourage among the professional accountants of two continents a mutual understanding of and a cooperative approach to common problems of the profession.

> To encourage the study and discussion of these problems to the ends that we might unify the principles, methods and programs and thus work together towards a better coordination of all the diverse aspects of the profession.

To disseminate technical information and to foster the change of ideas concerning accounting principles and procedures in all their various applications.

To raise the standards and to maintain the dignity of the professions of accounting.[14]

The IAAC is organized in several committees which have concentrated on auditing standards, accounting principles, preparation and training of the accountant, and the development of the profession. These efforts have been relatively productive, especially in the areas of terminology, education, auditing standards, and professional development. IAAC has aided the Latin American countries, where uniform accounting standards have been adopted and more precise accounting terminology is used now.[15] The results can be regarded as an orientation towards the U.S. profession.

The Conference of Asian and Pacific Accountants (CAPA) was organized in 1957 and meets biannually. Nineteen countries participate: Australia, Burma, Canada, Ceylon, Republic of China, Hong Kong, India, Indonesia, Japan, Lebanon, South Korea, New Zealand, Pakistan, Malaysia, Philippines, Singapore, Thailand, Samoa, and the United States. Each country is represented by its major accounting institutes and organizations. CAPA is mainly designed for an exchange of information. Discussion topics have included the development of international terminology, uniform accounting practices, impact of tax policies on economic development and international investments, and managerial accounting. However, no direct steps to influence accounting in specific countries have been taken.[16]

The Accountants International Study Group (AISG) was organized in 1967; its members are Great Britain, the United States, and Canada, represented by their institutes. AISG analyzes and summarizes practices in three countries and offers recommendations for changes. The following studies have been published:

1. Accounting and Auditing Approaches to Inventories in Three Nations (sponsored by Britain);
2. The Independent Auditors Reporting Standards in Three Nations (sponsored by U.S.A.);
3. Using the Working Report of an Auditor (sponsored by Canada);
4. Diverse Activities of Conglomerates (sponsored by U.S.A.);
5. Consolidated Financial Statements (sponsored by U.S.A.);
6. Accounting for Corporate Income Tax (sponsored by Canada);
7. Profit Forecasts (sponsored by Britain);

8. Fund Statements (sponsored by Canada); and
9. Extraordinary and Prior Period Items (sponsored by U.S.A.).

These studies serve the purpose of information exchange and may be regarded as forerunners of future international studies on a broader basis.[17]

The Anglo-German Liaison Committee is an example of a smaller regional organization. Founded in 1970, it serves the purpose to study topics of mutual interest by the members of the Institutes of Britain and Germany. Seminars are held annually; issues discussed have included inflationary price level accounting, problems of consolidated balance sheets, auditing principles and practices, presentation of stock, and work in process, et cetera. The main function of this committee is the improvement of understanding between the major exponents of two differing views (professional versus legislative principles) within the EC.[18]

One of the most active organizations is the Union Européenne des Experts Comptables, Économiques et Financiers (UEC). Founded in 1951 in Paris, its members include representatives of twelve professional associations from Austria, Belgium, France, Germany, Italy, Luxembourg, the Netherlands, Portugal, Spain, and Switzerland, representing approximately 150,000 professional accountants.[19] Yugoslavia is a corresponding member. Its objectives according to article II of the UEC statutes include the following:

Facilitate the exchange of views of all problems within their competence between auditors in the fields of accounting, economics and finance.

Promote progress in corporate management techniques and, in particular, in the fields of accounting and auditing by instituting the most rational and effective practices.

Compare the different methods followed in the training for and the entry into the ranks of the profession in each nation with a view to European cooperation.

Study the circumstances under which a member of the profession may be allowed to exercise his duties in a European country other than his own either on a permanent or temporary basis.

Examine the rules of professional conduct to be respected by European financial and economic experts.

Create and maintain relations with all supernational bodies whose activites are of interest to the profession.

Take steps to foster a spirit of unity among economic and financial accountants in Europe and work towards the improvement of conditions and methods of work.

Bi- or triannual Congresses and committees which meet frequently concentrate largely on the underlying differences between countries' practices. Guidance statements which are not mandatory are published, but they are regarded as authoritative guidelines on principles and practices desirable for the profession in Europe.[20] To reduce the existing language barriers the UEC has produced a "lexicon;" first published in 1961 in five languages; two more languages were added in 1964. UEC's major contributions can be seen in the attempt to create understanding for procedures in other countries and to lay the groundwork for concerted professional and legislative actions.

Worldwide Activities. The International Congress of Accountants was convened for the first time in St. Louis in 1904. Subsequent Congresses were held at Amsterdam (1926), New York (1929), London (1933), Berlin (1938), London (1952), Amsterdam (1957), New York (1962), Paris (1967), and Sydney (1972); the next Congress meets in Munich (1977).

The Congresses have several important purposes:

1. The Congresses serve as a vital channel for the exchange of professional information and ideas.

2. They encourage study concerning the structure of professional organizations and of professional education plans.

3. They facilitate social and cultural activities and encourage new friendship.

4. The Congresses provide opportunities to study and discuss policies, practices, and methods of accounting, auditing and reporting from various countries.

5. In every country it is important to develop the image of the profession . . . The International Congresses give us opportunities to face, frankly, our difficulties and our differences. They give a little time for reflection. They emphasize the importance of the accountant and give us better recognition of our role in the economic world of today.[21]

Congresses have greatly enhanced the understanding of accounting problems in other countries and have created the climate for future steps towards harmonization.

As a result of the International Congresses, the International Working Party was created in 1967. Its task was to consider the part played by the International Congress in the development of accounting thought and understanding. Following the recommendations of its final report, the International Co-ordination Committee for the Accountancy Profession (ICCAP) was created in 1971. Its stated purpose is "to examine the scope and frequency of future Congresses and their objectives and to give consideration to the views of other accounting bodies."[22] ICCAP continues to harmonize efforts between congresses, i.e., it attempts to develop a coordinated, worldwide accountancy profession with uniform professional standards.

As the immediate result of the work of ICCAP, the International Accounting Standards Committee (IASC) was organized in June 1973. IASC, headquartered in London and initially supported by the founding members including Australia, Canada, France, Germany, Japan, Mexico, the Netherlands, the United Kingdom, and the United States, has since been joined by a large number of countries (see Appendix I). Its objective is "to formulate and publish in the public interest, basic standards to be observed in the presentation of audited accounts and financial statements and to promote their worldwide acceptance and observance."[23] Members of IASC agree to support its objectives and any standards issued, to promote compliance with such standards in their country's financial statements, and to disclose and explain cases of non-compliance. The AICPA has strongly encouraged its members to comply with international standards.

International accounting standards are promulgated by a steering committee which conducts research and issues exposure drafts. A two-thirds vote is required to pass an exposure draft; a three-fourths vote is needed to issue a statement of international accounting standards. Dissenting opinions are not allowed in the exposure draft or in the final opinion.

As of October 1976, the following standards and exposure drafts have been issued by IASC: (Standards and Exposure Drafts are shown in Appendix II.)
International Accounting Standards Issued

IAS 1. "Disclosure of Accounting Policies," January 1975.

IAS 2. "Valuation and Presentation of Inventories in the Context of the Historical Cost System," October 1975.

IAS 3. "Consolidated Financial Statements," June 1976.

IAS 4. "Depreciation Accounting," October 1976.

IAS 5. "Information to be Disclosed in Financial Statements," October 1976.

Exposure Drafts Issued
    E6. "Accounting Treatment of Changing Prices," January 1976.
    E7. "Statement of Source and Application of Funds," June 1976.
    E8. "The Treatment in the Income Statement of Unusual Items and Changes in Accounting Estimates and Accounting Policies," October 1976.

Scheduled Exposure Drafts
    Events Occurring After the Balance Sheet Date.
    Accounting for Long-term Contracts.
    Accounting for Diversified Operations.
    The Treatment of Leases in Financial Statements.

The meaning of the term *accounting standards* in the new international context is described by the first chairman of IASC, Sir Henry Benson: "An accounting standard is a clear definite directive as to how financial statements should be presented; what should be contained in them; and how the multifarious items which go to make up financial statements should be dealt with."[24] In his opinion, "Standards are based on a consensus of informed opinion as to what is most appropriate having regard to the normal conduct of business by management, the needs of users of financial statements, comprising creditors, employees, investors and governments, and the rights and obligations of shareholders. It does not mean that they are merely the lowest common denominator of what happens in practice . . . . Standards are not absolute and immutable, they change, sometimes quite quickly, because circumstances and opinion change."[25]

The standards issued by IASC raise a number of questions. The first concerns quality: since standards are based on consensus, it is apparent that sometimes too much rigidity is avoided. However, it can be assumed that future amendments will eventually clarify and tighten these rules. The second question concerns the relationship between international standards and national laws or standards set by national (professional) bodies. This problem is of particular importance because international standards, in some instances, may be contrary to national law or standards. For example, the use of the equity method in consolidated statements (IASC Standard No. 3) is clearly illegal in Germany. The position which should be taken by the profession in such a situation has been outlined by Sir Henry Benson:

A question which can fairly be asked at this point is how can international standards be applied when the local laws (either company laws or taxation regulations) require accounts to be produced in a way which differs from the international standards. This is a practical difficulty but not one which is by any means insuperable. In such cases the local laws must of course prevail but what can and should be done is for the financial statements to disclose the extent to which the adoption of the local laws or local regulations has required divergence from international standards. This will have the salutary effect of drawing to the attention of the users of the financial statements those areas where an international standard has not been observed; it will put the users on notice to make appropriate allowances and adjustments before arriving at their business judgements or making comparisons. In course of time, as international standards grow in stature, the number of such divergences can be expected to be reduced.[26]

Since general accounting policies to be followed are stated in the international accounting standards, only deviations have to be reported. International standards thus will at least provide users of financial statements with basic points of reference on which they can base their evaluations; every major deviation will be noted. Of course, the reliability of such judgment will directly depend on the quality of available standards and compliance by the local professional accountants.

In evaluating the work of the IASC, it must be noted that these are the first international standards which have been developed. At the very least, the issuing of these new standards has brought out differences of approaches in various countries. For the first time, a common basis for comparison of national practice with "worldwide standard practice" has been created. This in itself represents a major improvement over the past situation. However, it would be overly optimistic to expect that IASC standards will immediately result in more uniform financial statements. Undoubtedly, if international standards are followed, then deficiencies in information contained in published financial statements will come to light. Whether this is sufficient to allow users of financial statements to make valid comparisons without difficulties remains to be seen, because while deviations from standards must be mentioned, inclusion of adjusted data are not demanded. Nevertheless, all major divergences will be noted and users will not entirely depend on their sometimes limited knowledge of accounting practice in other countries.

Harmonization Attempts by Legislative Bodies

Attempts to harmonize or even standardize accounting practice by legislative bodies can only occur in regions where supranational organizations exist. This is the case in the European Community (EC). Harmonization attempts in the EC deal with corporate structures and accounting requirements as included in corporation laws. However, these attempts will contribute to the goal of a uniform market only if unified. An additional attempt is the development of a new corporation, the Société Européenne (SE), which can be incorporated in all member countries. Pronouncements concerning both matters take the form of "directives" by the High Commission of the EC in Brussels. These instruct member countries to change their legislation to achieve uniformity. Only the major directives concerning accounting will be considered.

Harmonization of Company Laws by the EC. Presently, several directives have been issued. The first directive (March 1968) requires that "limited companies" and "partnerships limited by shares" must publish annual balance sheets and profit and loss accounts. The second directive specifies rules governing maintenance and alteration of equity capital as well as minimum paid-up share capital, and restricts both the payment of dividends and the right of the company to purchase its own shares. The third directive applies to mergers: it requires management to publish specific data concerning the contemplated merger, and to issue an independent accountant's report attesting to the fairness of the share exchanges. The fourth directive (see Appendix III) specifies details to be disclosed in annual financial statements—consisting of balance sheet, profit and loss account, and explanatory notes—by all companies whose liability is limited through share capital. Excluded are banks and insurance companies for which separate directives are forthcoming. The fifth directive and a proposed professional law deal with the auditor's responsibilities, his liabilities for inaccuracies in reports and prospectuses, and his right to practice in all countries of the EC. Additional directives are in the planning stage; these will address issues of consolidated accounts, transnational mergers, insurance companies, credit institutions, and minimal educational requirements for statutory auditors.

Most important for harmonization of accounting is Directive No. 4. It follows the German practice of specifying all important details of balance sheets and profit and loss statements. Instead of using a materiality concept, companies are required to disclose certain items regardless of their size. The balance sheet requires presentation of (1) unpaid subscribed capital, (2) formation expenses, (3) fixed assets, and (4) current assets. This "inverted liquidity" principle is replicated on the liability side, where the groups are (1) equity capital, (2) reserves and value adjustments, (3) provisions for contingencies,

(4) creditors, (5) accruals, and (6) profits (see articles 8–11). All movements of fixed assets throughout the period shall be disclosed either in the balance sheet or in the notes to the accounts.

A similar standardized approach is prescribed for the profit and loss statement. Net sales must be disclosed, certain operating costs must be shown, and financial and exceptional items have to be separated from operational expenses (see articles 19–23).

Valuation rules adopted are based on acquisition cost. However, since some countries—particularly the Netherlands—permit replacement valuation, this, also, is considered to be legal. In this case all reserves which are generated through revaluation shall be shown in a separate "revaluation account." Valuation methods used must be disclosed in the notes to the annual accounts.

Some other items are noteworthy. For example, all payments made throughout the year to members of the administrative, managerial, and supervisory bodies must be disclosed separately. The annual report shall, furthermore, contain a detailed review of the developments of the company's business and should give particulars of important events and expected future developments. However, specific auditing requirements are not mentioned, since these are still under discussion and will appear in Directive No. 5.

It is apparent throughout Directive No. 4 that there is no intent to interfere with specific national regulations which differ from the approach prescribed. Therefore, many articles of Directive No. 4 expressly permit the application of differing accounting principles. Consequently, an immediate impact can only be expected through the standardization of formats of financial statements; the valuation of the items presented will remain as diversified as before.

Another similar attempt needs to be mentioned. In 1969 and 1970, the governments of Denmark, Finland, Norway, and Sweden agreed to harmonize their company laws. The proposed Nordic Company Act specifies rules for accounting in articles 96–108. It is noteworthy that the Nordic Company Act differs from the Continental approach by requiring a legal reserve, which is based on the amount of liabilities and not on equity capital. In almost all other respects it follows the Continental approach; statement format, details to be disclosed in the balance sheet, the profit and loss statement, and the explanatory notes are specified. The prevailing conservatism, i.e., the trend to permit undervaluation, has been maintained in view of the existing tax legislation. It also has been decided that the Nordic Company Act should not include all special accounting requirements, but that these shall be regulated later in a separate Bookkeeping Law similar to the Swedish practice.[27]

Development of Accounting Rules for the Société Européenne (SE). To speed up European integration, the High Commission issued Directive No. 4 on the European Corporation, which represents a corporate code for entities which can be incorporated in all member countries directly under the jurisdiction of the EC.[28] This proposed code contains all accounting requirements. Basically, it is similar in intent and detail to the regulations for the harmonization of accounting for other corporations which remain under national jurisdiction. Therefore, it is not contained in the Appendix; only parts which differ from the general regulations are shown in Appendix IV.

The European Corporation requires that so-called group accounts, i.e., consolidated financial statements, must be prepared. It also requires audits, specifying that auditors have to be independent and must meet professional requirements (to be regulated later). The auditor, in carrying out his duty, shall be completely free to examine and check any documents and assets of the SE, can demand all necessary explanations, is allowed to check all documents of associated undertakings, and can employ other auditors and specialists to assist in his audit. If not satisfied, he is entitled to give a qualified certificate. Any qualification or the withholding of a certificate shall be expressly explained.

Assessment of Harmonization Attempts

All harmonization and standardization attempts discussed do not seem to go very far. This holds true for the international standards as well as for the supranational legislations. Frequently, it has been argued that worldwide standards or harmonization rules will bring down accounting practice to the lowest common denominator, i.e., will result in rules with which everybody will be able to live. This certainly seems to be true for certain aspects of the legislations recommended within the EC, since for all practical purposes, national regulations have remained intact.

Undoubtedly, it would be advantageous if accounting standards in all major industrial nations of the world were similar. Since no such similarity can be expected in the near future, the IASC approach to disclose departures at least from a theoretical standard (which may not be used by anybody) has considerable appeal. If such a code of disclosure is adhered to, a higher degree of understandibility of financial reports for this user can be assured. Therefore, the international accounting standards issued by the IASC present a first, major step towards increasing uniformity on a regional or even worldwide basis. This seems to be particularly true because the accounting profession is supporting these attempts strongly.

In the case of the proposed European legislation, the participation of the profession has become much stronger. A working group (Group d'Études) of the institutes representing the EC member countries has cooperated in formulating the accounting principles. This group has attempted to incorporate the views of the various professional organizations into the legislation and has tried to maintain a high level of accounting standards. Even if this has resulted in the permission to maintain national regulations for the moment, leading members of the profession maintain that the increased exchange of ideas and the discussion of specific accounting principles will eventually lead to a convergence of attitudes. This positive effect can be expected in particular, whenever new standards, or legal regulations, which are not applied in some participating countries, will be passed. The validity of this argument can be demonstrated in the case of inflationary adjustments, which are presently much debated in industrialized countries. Although complete agreement may not be reached, present thinking in the U.S., Britain, and on the Continent have moved much closer. It is regrettable, however, that present efforts concerning new legislation in the EC countries and standardization efforts by the IASC are not fully coordinated. Conclusions which might be reached by the SEC or the FASB also seem to differ at least in procedural matters. Since the issue of liability of auditors is not unified, the various institutes may also be inclined to settle for other solutions. Harmonization is, therefore, not to be expected soon—and may still be several decades away.

INTERIM COMPANY SOLUTIONS

Since presently neither of the above-mentioned laws nor most of the IASC standards are in effect, it is unavoidable for multinational firms to solve their accounting problems internally and even for external purposes, should such needs arise. For externally used data, while the situation is difficult, however, the solution is clear. For example, whenever access to the New York or some other stock exchange is sought, the company must provide financial statements which convert all data to the principles applicable at the exchange in question. This creates the necessity for additional explanatory footnotes or an adjustment of the entire set of financial statements. The Philips annual report is an example of this approach: it contains a section explaining the change in values which occur if adjusted to U.S. accounting principles.[29] Unfortunately, this need to issue differing financial reports in various countries neither improves the credibility in financial statements nor the objectivity of accounting principles.

Given the present situation, multinational firms have no choice but to provide financial statements which satisfy several requirements. These requirements are:

1. Provide financial statements for information, comparison, and decision purposes which are understandable in the country (or countries) in which
   a. a particular subsidiary is operating,
   b. a holding company has to make worldwide financial decisions, and
   c. the stockholders and major users of the financial statement reside.
2. Provide financial statements for consolidation for one or more domiciles.[30]

The major requirements which have to be met are (1) compliance and, (2) understandability. Since taxation, legal matters, governmental aid, government subsidized loans, et cetera are limited to the realm of one economic system, and privileges depend on the use of accepted procedures, compliance is required. Furthermore, understandability has to be guaranteed within the national environment to use efficiently local employees who have been trained for the national system. Adherence to national accounting standards also facilitates—within certain limits—performance comparisons with local competitors. Such an evaluation is indispensable because a comparison with subsidiaries operating in countries with different environmental conditions does not always give satisfactory results—particularly since with growing nationalism a large number of managerial decisions (pricing, financing, et cetera) must be made on a decentralized national basis. A survey has shown that, for these reasons, most multinational corporations are forced to keep several sets of accounting records to comply with local and international requirements.[31] These different sets of financial statements are the following:

1. *National financial statements* on the basis of nationally accepted accounting principles; these guarantee understandability within the national economy and do not require additional employee education. Statements are sufficient to inform the public as well as stockholders in the respective countries. Also, a comparison with competitors operating under the same environmental conditions is thereby facilitated, and management receives information which is relevant within the national economic system.
2. *Translated financial statements for consolidation.* Compliance with accounting principles and translation methods accepted in the country

of the home office are necessary. Frequently, several of these statements have to be provided using the generally accepted accounting
principles of all countries in which a large number of stockholders reside. Their main purpose consists in consolidation and publication;
therefore, compliance with accepted accounting principles takes
precedence over adjustments reflecting the true economic situation
of the multinational enterprises.

3. *Tax statements* wherever required by national regulations.
4. *Financial statements reflecting the economic situation of the enterprise.*
   These are for internal use only; therefore, uniform contents of accounts, uniform valuation methods for assets of all subsidiaries are
   used (LIFO, FIFO, and other valuations have to be readjusted).
   Moreover, accelerated depreciation adopted solely for tax purposes
   must be converted to write downs reflecting the true consumption of
   assets. To neutralize inflation-caused national financing policies, separation of corresponding assets and liabilities might be advisable. For
   translation, methods best suited for the particular multinational enterprises can be developed. If market or replacement values are
   utilized, major changes in financial ratios result since revaluation increases equities, whereas period profits are less affected; in this case,
   comparisons with typical national financial ratios become impossible.
   These financial statements, however, appear to be the only acceptable data basis for decisions involving the entire multinational enterprise.[32]

Accounting problems in connection with external reporting require all
financial statements mentioned in items 1–3. However, these do not solve the
internal control and decision-making problems of multinational enterprises.
These areas require the statements mentioned under item 4 and a further development of managerial accounting.

It seems worthwhile to explore the control and performance evaluation
issue further, because this area seems to represent the future direction in international accounting—and, consequently, an area which must be dealt with by
the profession. Also, harmonization of financial accounting data may never
become sufficient to solve all arising problems. To appreciate the scope of the
problem fully, attention must be given to the differences which will influence
accounting data. Some of them are:

1. Specific local capital structures (for example, less equity capital in many
   countries);

2. Typical financing patterns which arise from the membership in multinational business organizations (for example, utilization of overall goodwill and foreign assets as collateral);

3. Lower working capital needs as the results of overall cash-budgeting;

4. Differing cost structures due to differences in local wage, social overhead, tax, et cetera;

5. Revenue differentials due to varying prices in local markets;

6. Cost differentials due to imposed transfer prices and typical internal charges such as know-how fees, license fees, and assessments for centrally executed services;

7. Differences in local productivity caused by education, tradition, climate, and other factors;

8. Differences in profit potential, which arise from the particular development stage of subsidiaries (such as new versus well-established operations, full function subsidiaries versus limited function subsidiaries) and development stages of countries.

In view of these differences it becomes apparent that the quantity of data required for accounting systems of multinationals is much larger than for domestic operations. This need arises, because "known facts" which every manager takes for granted in a national environment (due to similar education, day-to-day exposure, and frequent contacts with each other) are unknown to other participants in a multinational evaluation and decision process. Without incorporating specific details of unavoidable deviations into the data basis, it is impossible to develop sufficient information for effective control. Even if such data are included, elements of subjectivity will remain, because a large number of the activities to be monitored can only be evaluated in terms of management control.[33]

To assess the range of data needed for a decision and performance evaluation oriented accounting system, a distinction between two types of multinational enterprises has to be made: (1) financial conglomerates developed to maximize profits on a worldwide basis, and (2) enterprises which carry out operating activities in several countries.

For financial conglomerates and for the financial sector of operating multinationals, financial accounting data appear adequate for decisions such as cash planning, allocation of funds in fluctuating money markets, and other short-term decisions involving foreign currencies. In this case, realistic exchange rates must be determined on an *ad hoc* basis. However, for medium-term cash budgeting the exchange rate problem already arises. Data must be supported by overall economic and monetary indicators or projections, which usually are not part of the financial accounting system. The scope of this activity should not be underestimated because transfer restrictions, cost of money exchange, inflation rates, credits cost, as well as future profit potentials, vary considerably.

For performance evaluation, particularly profitability, modified financial accounting data remain useful. However, it already becomes apparent that a straightforward return-on investment evaluation of subsidiary performance— already questionable in a domestic environment—cannot be applied.[34] As a substitute, the residual-income-method has been suggested.[35] It calls for the adjustment of target profit rates and elimination of nontypical influences, which prevent a direct comparison between subsidiaries around the world. Since adjustments to a large extent are subjective, company internal guidelines for supporting evidence must be developed to assure a common approach.

In most cases, performance measurement and evaluation of operating multinationals require specific methods of analysis. These should distinguish between *efficiency* and *effectiveness*. Most multinationals emphasize innovation, because such activities have provided their major competitive edge over local operations. This involves technology and know-how transfers, which need continuous adaptation to local conditions. Under these circumstances, efficiency comparisons are unlikely to measure actual accomplishments. Rather, the quality of execution of certain activities, i.e., their effectiveness, ought to be analyzed. For this type of analysis, methods are either not available or have not been researched sufficiently.

Measurements of efficiency should also be utilized; these are relative and largely based on comparisons—with other time periods, target values, or similar operations in other plants during the same time period. Two types of such measurements prevail, namely: (1) overall measures, evaluating the entire operation, and (2) individual measures, analyzing specific activities, business functions, or parts of such functions.

In both cases a uniform measurement of cost in terms of resource consumption must be developed because differences in historical cost from various regions and systems result in erroneous assessments. For this purpose the European approach to cost measurement seems to hold considerable promise for multinationals.[36] *Overall measurements,* unfortunately, seldom yield useful results in multinational settings because of the differences in the development of subsidiaries, their goals, and their limited activities. This necessitates *comparison of smaller segments* for which statistical measurements must be introduced, which allow a prior assessment of typical or expected deviations for each country, thus reducing the analyst's work to a much smaller set of extraordinary or nonrandom changes. Some of these methods are already utilized in domestic managerial accounting; however, they have not been applied widely to multinational operations.

The measurement of effectiveness poses an extremely difficult problem. Experience suggests that a thorough on-the-spot analysis, combined with full understanding of local constraints, permits a satisfactory performance evaluation. Such procedures have yielded limited results in the area of internal auditing, drawing on so-called operational or management auditing procedures.[37] However, internal auditing in multinationals will only serve its purpose when it encompasses an independent appraisal of all activities within the organization. Every audit should utilize a systems approach, analyzing local subsystems (or parts thereof) with respect to their proper functioning in the framework of the goals of the overall system. This in itself represents a creative activity, because today's financial auditing procedures cannot be sufficiently defined or standardized.[38] If internal auditing is regarded as part of a management-oriented control system which facilitates the flow of control information upwards, then it will eventually become part of the professional activities of auditors who attempt to serve their clients in a multinational environment which lacks harmonization and at the same time requires a thorough performance analysis.

The preceding discussion—although largely normative—suggests that a promising development of international accounting can be expected if managerial accounting will be included. This conclusion is based on the fact that financial accounting has failed so far and may not be able in the future—due to its built-in constraints—to generate solutions for the in-depth evaluation of multinational companies. Harmonization of international accounting—although helpful—does not seem to provide satisfactory answers to control problems; therefore the profession must anticipate other developments and prepare for these.

NOTES

1. A listing of all relevant East German titles of laws and decrees to implement uniform valuation and accounting procedures can be found in *Kontenrahnen 1974, Industrie*, (Berlin 1974), pp. 201–20.

2. See Section 663, *Swiss Code of Obligations* (Code d'Obligatons).

3. See Section 665, *Swiss Code of Obligations.*

4. Swedish regulations require a FIFO valuation basis which can be reduced by as much as 60%. This percentage may be applied to the averages of the two preceding years which occasionally result in negative inventory values. Furthermore, for all materials and staple goods the lowest price of any one of the nine preceding periods may be used, which in turn can be reduced by 30%. See AICPA, *Professional Accounting in 30 Countries* (New York, 1975), pp. 559–60.

5. See Price, Waterhouse, *Accounting Principles and Reporting Practices, A Survey in 46 Countries* (1975), pp. 77–102.

6. See Arthur Andersen & Co., *Accounting Standards for Business Enterprises Throughout the World* (1974), p. 57.

7. *Ibid.,* p. 57.

8. For the description of details, see Report of American Accounting Association Committee on International Accounting, 1974–75, *The Accounting Review,* Supplement to Volume XLXI, pp. 107–33.

9. For details, see AICPA, *Professional Accounting in 30 Countries.*

10. H. M. Schoenfeld, "New German Regulations for the Publication of Financial Statements," *The International Journal of Accounting* 5: no. 2, (Spring 1970), 69–88.

11. K. Michael Oldham, *Accounting Systems and Practice in Europe* (Epping-Essex, 1975), pp. 8–9.

12. *Ibid.,* p. 35.

13. John A. Wilson, "The Need for Standardization of International Accounting," *Touche Ross Tempo* (Winter 1969), p. 40.

14. K. A. Abdullah and D. L. Kyle "Inter-American Accounting Conferences," *Canadian Chartered Accountant* (October 1972), p. 45.

15. *Ibid.,* pp. 47–50.

16. For details see Fifth Conference of Asian and Pacific Accountants—1968, *Accountants Journal* (March 1968), p. 271.

17. R. Douglas Thomas, "The Accountants International Study Group—The First Three Years," *Canadian Chartered Accountant* (September 1971), p. 224.

18. First Anglo-American Seminar, Wiesbaden, *Journal UEC* (October 1972), p. 240.

19. "Business and Accountants in Modern Society," *The Accountant* (October 23, 1975), p. 479.

20. For example, UEC, *The Audit Report* (April 1975).

21. Arthur B. Foye, "Why International Congresses of Accountants?" *Haskins & Sells Selected Papers* (1962), p. 21.

22. "The Accounting World," *The Accountant* (July 6, 1972), pp. 1–2.

23. Joseph Cummings, "The International Accounting Standards Committee—Its Purpose and Status," *CPA Journal* 44 (September 1974), 51.

24. Sir Henry Benson, Address at the Accountantsdag, Amsterdam, July 1976, *IASC News,* 4: no. 5 (August 2, 1976), p. 3.

25. *Ibid.,* p. 3.

26. *Ibid.,* p. 4.

27. Per V. A. Hanner, "Towards a Nordic Companies Act: A Report on the Company Law Reform in Denmark, Finland, Norway and Sweden," *Journal UEC* no. 1 (January 1971), pp. 19–25.

28. Directive No. 4, Supplement to Bulletin 8–1970 of the European Communities.

29. See Report of the AAA Committee on International Accounting, 1974–75, *Ibid.,* pp. 107–133.

30. For a discussion of the determination of a domicile, see G. G. Mueller, *International Accounting* (New York, 1967), p. 160.

31. *Business International Corporation Solving International Accounting Problems* (New York, 1969).

32. For more details, see H. M. Schoenfeld, "Some Special Accounting Problems of Multinational Enterprises Management," *International Review,* no. 4/5 (1969), pp. 3–11.

33. This term is used as developed by R. N. Anthony, *Planning and Control Systems: A Framework for Analysis* (Cambridge, Mass.: Harvard University Press, 1965).

34. For a detailed discussion see J. J. Mauriel and R. N. Anthony, "Misevaluation of Investment Center Performance," *Harvard Business Review* (March-April 1966), p. 100.

35. E. C. Bursk, J. Dearden, D. F. Hawkins, and V. M. Longstreet, *Financial Control of Multinationals Operations* (New York: Research Foundation of the Financial Executives, 1971).

36. For an analysis of this approach see H. M. Schoenfeld, *Cost Terminology and Cost Theory: A Study of Its Development and Present State in Central Europe* (Urbana, Illinois: Center for International Education and Research in Accounting, 1974), pp. 5–43.

37. The only summary treatment available on internal auditing for multinationals incorporating the limited information available in English, German, and French is by A. Zund, *Kontrolle und Revision in der Multinationalen Unternehmung* (Bern, 1973).

38. D. E. Wilson, "Dynamic Auditing in A Changing World," *The Internal Auditor* 27: no. 5 (1970), pp. 10–17.

Harmonization of Accounting

Seymour M. Bohrer

Managing Partner, Los Angeles Office
Peat, Marwick, Mitchell & Co.

Let me begin by saying I appreciate this opportunity to discuss the very important and timely topic of harmonization of accounting, and to share the topic with Professor Schoenfeld, a most distinguished member of academia.

Before going on to discuss some of the practical aspects of implementing this concept, I feel it is necessary first to conceptually define the term *harmonization* and contrast it with the principle of *standardization*.

Harmonization, as defined by Webster's dictionary, is: "an interweaving of different accounts into a single narrative." As defined in Professor Schoenfeld's paper, harmonization is "a reconcilement of different points of view." Both definitions are quite similar. Harmonization differs from standardization since the latter implies adherence to a rigid code and is not in concert with the concept of a profession. No profession could ultimately endure in an environment of rigid rules nor would it serve the public interest. Accounting itself is evolutionary and not conducive to rigidity or strict uniformity.

As a practical matter, uniformity does not exist nationally, let alone internationally. Consequently, the concept of harmonization is a more realistic approach and has a greater likelihood of prevailing over standardization. However, as pointed out in Professor Schoenfeld's paper, *meaningful* harmonization will generally by necessity be limited to the Western industrialized nations.

Let us now discuss *briefly* some of the additional dimensions that arise as a result of the political and cultural differences faced by every multinational organization. Over and above the obvious dimension of having to understand

198

and function under many sets of "rules," there exists a basic philosophical conflict of interests at the national level, the conflict being that the guest nation's objective is to exercise control over resources allocated abroad while the host nation seeks to control foreign investments to advance its national interests and goals. This concept of nationalism is by no means new, but the point here is that it generally results in rules or measures being imposed by the host nation which affect the day-to-day business practices and the accounting and information systems of the guest company and, to some extent, the profession of accounting. This situation has no solution; however, we must all understand that it exists—and be ready to react in spite of it—in order to achieve any degree of meaningful harmonization.

Another of the realities of accounting and auditing for global business is that accounting principles as well as auditing standards vary significantly from country to country. For instance, it is not usual practice in all countries for the auditor to review internal control, confirm accounts, or observe the taking of a physical inventory, all of which are customary in this country. Variances from the Anglo-Saxon audit approach with which we are familiar result from many of the factors I previously mentioned, for example, a different set of governing rules resulting in part from the concept of nationalism and differing needs of the users of financial statements, et cetera.

In many countries statutory audits are required; however, from country to country the primary objective of a statutory audit ranges from a detail review to detect fraud to the evaluation of management's ability to conform with the national financial reporting requirement. Most international auditing firms have adopted the posture of performing only a single type of audit which adheres to standards recognized and accepted in the United States and United Kingdom, our firm included. Statutory audits that are of a lesser scope are generally left to the local auditors.

Before discussing the tasks ahead of us as a profession and particularly those facing international accounting firms, I am going to describe to you an interesting analogy about the world of international sports used in a paper by one of my partners, Joseph Cummings, who is chairman of the International Accounting Standards Committee. Picture for a moment a soccer match being played between West Germany and Brazil in Brazil for the world championship. The score is tied and the match is in the final seconds. Suddenly a Brazil forward—in total disregard of the rigid rules governing international soccer—seizes the ball, and clutching it in his arms, runs 10 yards, and hurls himself into the goal net. Brazil is awarded a score and pandemonium breaks loose.

The international repercussions would be immense. Ultimately, the international governing body of soccer would be called upon to resolve the issue and enforce a well-defined, agreed-upon set of rules. Perhaps the game would be called a tie or Brazil required to forfeit due to the infraction of the rules. The substance of the matter is that international rules, which may not conform to local rules, would be enforced and prevail.

The sad story is that, with all of our multinational sophistication, there has been far more attention given over the past twenty-five years to establishing international rules for soccer than for governing international accounting and reporting. The accounting profession has begun to do something about this deplorable condition, but needs a great deal more recognition and support if the effort is to be acceptable, enforceable, and successful.

The serious need to move forward in the area of harmonization can be illustrated by focusing on the following statistics from the August 1976 publication of the U.S. Department of Commerce entitled *Survey of Current Business*:

		Billions
U. S. Assets Abroad—	1972	$ 50
	1975	304

U. S. direct investment abroad (defined as equity in and loans to subsidiaries and divisions abroad)

	Billions
1966	$ 52
1974	119
1975	133

Foreign direct investment position in the U.S.

	Billions
1960	$ 7
1974	24
1975	27

In addition, the New York Stock Exchange is listing an ever-increasing number of foreign securities. *The NYSE 1975 Fact Book* indicates 182 foreign securities were listed with an aggregate market value of approximately $15 billion and there are numerous U.S. corporations listed on foreign stock exchanges. The trend indicated by the statistics illustrates the need for us to take appropriate measures to assure ourselves that the accounting profession can help provide management with the financial tools with which to evaluate and monitor the expanding overseas investment.

Prudent investment decisions must be predicated upon understandable and more uniform financial data. The availability of such management tools will only become a reality when a meaningful degree of harmonization is achieved. An interesting example is the following situation which involved inadequate financial information. Assume you are the banker handling Company B's borrowing activities.

> Company B manufactures and sells its products to a wholly owned subsidiary, Company A, which along with B's other subsidiaries is not consolidated because the local accounting standards do not require consolidation. B accounts for its investments on the cost basis. A is experiencing severe difficulty in selling the product and reduces the inventory carried in its accounts to estimated net realizable value. Since B does not consolidate with its subsidiaries, it has recognized a profit on the sales to A *and* has not recognized the impairment of its investment equal to the loss incurred by A's inventory write-down.

> Upon consolidation, two things become painfully apparent: (1) B cannot sell A any more of the goods it has been producing all year, and (2) the consolidated entity is in severe financial difficulty.

The International Accounting Standards Committee focused on the fact of life that countries are not willing to relinquish their nationalistic rights to establish accounting and reporting standards. The approach adopted by IASC is the most plausible because the international standards promulgated by the body do not take precedence over established policies within a nation, but rather require disclosure of variances from the international standards.

One inherent problem in this approach is that each country, even though in agreement with the concept of harmonization, may attempt to have its national accounting and reporting standards serve as the prescribed international model because of nationalistic tendencies. For an international standard to be accepted in the United States, it will have to be specifically adopted by the Financial Accounting Standards Board. If a standard is at great variance with United States generally accepted accounting principles, the Financial Accounting Standards Board will be urged by the AICPA to give early consideration to such variances with the thought in mind to achieve harmonization.

In his work, Professor Schoenfeld has set forth a summary of the activities, philosophies, and pronouncements of the numerous regional bodies and the International Congress of Accountants, ICCAP and IASC. Therefore, I will not reiterate these matters. As Professor Schoenfeld points out in his writings, " . . . it would be overly optimistic to expect that IASC standards will *im-*

mediately result in more uniform financial statements" [italics added]. I share this feeling. In my view, the ultimate success of pronouncements issued by IASC or any such body depends upon the ability and willingness of the member nations to enforce such pronouncements.

A related comment on the subject that appeared in the January 16, 1975 edition of the British publication *The Accountant* was as follows, "Commendable as are the aims of IASC, a word of caution must be sounded. The acceptance and implementation of accounting standards on an international scale has not passed the formative stage of development; worldwide enforcement is likely to take years, rather than months and the level of enforcement is expected to be uneven." In spite of this view, disclosing variances from international standards is a significant improvement over prior "nonharmonized" practices.

The approach to the matter of harmonization in our firm—and I'm sure that every other major international accounting firm has taken a comparable approach—was to form an international committee charged with the responsibility of being the formal coordinating body within the firm to promote uniformity internationally.

Its first step was to perform a detailed worldwide study on the application of accounting principles, including reports and financial statement disclosures. The study was conducted through the use of a detail questionnaire that considered the following matters: (1) types of business entities, (2) company law and the accounting and auditing profession, (3) reporting and audit requirements, (4) generally accepted accounting standards, (5) Stock Exchange and Securities Commission, (6) accountants' report, (7) financial statement disclosure, (8) translated financial statements and accountants' report, and (9) recommendations.

The questionnaire was sent to a total of 43 countries in the following geographic areas: Africa, Asia, Australasia, Continental Europe, Latin America, Republic of Ireland, South Africa, United Kingdom, and North America. The recommendations of the International Committee were adopted as firm policy in March 1976. Our present plan is to survey the practice again in two years to determine the extent and magnitude of the implementation problems being encountered.

Many of the committee's recommendations that were set forth are, of course, now paralleled by IASC standards issued. The following are some of our firm's internal recommendations that still are not specifically contained in IASC pronouncements.

1. Amounts due to and from related parties should be disclosed. The nature and volume of such transactions must also be disclosed.
2. In situations where the parent is dependent upon cash remittances from subsidiaries, consideration must be given to issuing parent only financial statements as well as consolidated financial statements.
3. When financial statements and auditors' reports are in currencies or languages different from the origin, accounting standards used in the original presentation shall be disclosed along with a reconciliation with differences in amounts.

The following fundamental auditing standards to be applied on all multinational audit engagements have been established by our firm and others. Some of these, while implied in authoritative literature of numerous countries, may not be specifically set forth therein.

1. The examination is to be performed by a person or persons having adequate technical training and proficiency in auditing, with due care and with an objective state of mind.
2. The work is to be adequately planned and properly executed. If assistants are employed, they are to be adequately supervised.
3. There is to be an organized study and evaluation of internal control to determine the degree of reliance to be placed thereon in determining the nature, extent, and timing of audit procedures.
4. Sufficient appropriate evidential matter is to be obtained through analysis, inspection, observation, inquiry, confirmation, and computation to afford a reasonable basis for expressing an opinion on the financial statements.

We have also established "Recommended Principal Auditing Procedures" which are intended for use on multinational engagements. Such procedures are, of course, not all inclusive but deal with procedures considered to be of utmost importance. The principal procedures address themselves to the following areas: (1) preparation and preaudit planning; (2) evaluation of internal control; (3) tests of detailed transactions; (4) accounts receivable; (5) inventories; (6) property, plant, and equipment; (7) income and expense accounts; (8) review of workpapers; and (9) preissuance review. The specific detailed procedures used are ultimately left to the judgment of the local personnel, based upon their evaluation of existing conditions.

In addition, a comprehensive set of guidelines and procedures were established to attempt to harmonize standards of independence and integrity, particularly with respect to publicly listed companies.

Personnel is another problem faced by most major international accounting firms. This is overcome to a degree by the interchange of personnel between offices. This approach has proved to be an outstanding means to develop uniformity in the conduct and development of a firm's worldwide audit and accounting practice. It is our view that such interchanges not only help the professional development of the respective offices, but also are very enriching experiences for the personnel involved. We feel an individual should usually be with a firm at least four years before being considered for such a transfer; we select only our most outstanding individuals for these exchanges. In the past two years, our Los Angeles office has sent personnel to Milan, Frankfurt, Sydney, and Paris. During the same period, we received individuals from Dusseldorf, London, and Tokyo. We feel these interchanges will help promote the cross-fertilization of our practice and will ultimately minimize communications problems and aid in training overseas and U.S. personnel. Also, in the interest of uniformity of training, we provide our international offices with training courses used in the domestic practice.

Another item in the personnel area that our firm and others are attempting to do is develop our international practice so as to maximize the number of national partners in our respective foreign offices. This development will, by its nature, be done over a relatively long period of time. The approach has the advantage of permitting the accountant to have the closest *touch and feel* for the local national matters.

One of the tasks all international auditing firms must face is that of effective communication with and between international offices. The communication process is even more important when the work requested of a foreign office is less than a full-scope examination. The originating U.S. office cannot presume the foreign office will know the needs of the U.S. office. Clear instructions must be given regarding the work to be performed as well as the accounting information required. Audit management personnel handling clients with multinational operations are encouraged to visit major foreign segments for the purposes of obtaining first hand knowledge of local conditions and to discuss appropriate accounting matter with the local engagement personnel.

It is anticipated that international accounting will be influenced by the forthcoming 11th International Congress of Accountants to be held in Munich in October 1977. On its agenda is the project of creating a new and permanent global accounting organization whose member bodies will represent accountants in public practice, industry, government, and education throughout the world. If established, this organization will be called the International Federation of Accountants (IFAC) and will replace the International Commission for the Coordination of the Accounting Profession (ICCAP). Approximately 130 accounting bodies from 83 countries will be eligible to join IFAC. It is expected that IASC will become the accounting standard setting committee for IFAC, and separate committees of IFAC will be established to study auditing, independency ethics, and technical communications.

It is my view that international accounting principles have come a long way since the establishment of ICCAP in 1967. We have seen the IASC issue five standards since its creation in June 1973. IASC's work is becoming more visible each day. In fact, the International Federation of Stock Exchanges recommended to its member exchanges situated in IASC countries to require as part of the listing requirements reference to the adherence to international standards of accounting.

In summary, many obstacles to harmonization of accounting continue to exist. These include nationalism, communication barriers, varying levels of trained personnel, and the like. Much has already been accomplished in an attempt to achieve harmonization. Still more will be accomplished through organizations such as IASC and ICCAP.

With the advent of supersonic flight, changing international markets, and evolving financial centers, we find that the world truly is a smaller place. If we do not keep pace, we will find ourselves viewing the accounting and financial affairs of the world from rather varied sets of national accounting standards which, to date, have not adequately met the challenges of our vastly more complex world of international finances and accounting. A uniform set of international accounting and reporting standards would seem to be the ideal solution. However, it should be noted that even in a relatively simple case of making a dress or suit of clothes, it is difficult—if not impossible—to have the final product void of cultural differences. Harmonization is the first step in an evolutionary process that will lead to more uniformity.

SEVEN

Multinational Enterprises and Taxation

A pragmatic discussion of basic areas of complexity and conflict in the application of national rules of taxation to multinational corporations.

Robert J. Patrick, Jr.

Formerly, International Tax Director, Office of International Tax Affairs of the U.S. Treasury Department

Samuel M. Frohlich

Director International Tax Practice Arthur Young & Co.

Mr. Patrick holds both a B.A. and an LL.B degree from Stanford University and a Master of International Affairs degree from Columbia University. Formerly an associate with Cleary, Gottlieb, Steen and Hamilton in New York City and Paris, France. Mr. Patrick is a member of the Council of the United States Branch of the International Fiscal Association. He is currently an associate with Delaney & Patrick.

Mr. Frohlich holds a B.S. degree from Lehigh University and an M.B.A. degree from New York University. Mr. Frohlich is chairman of AICPA's international Tax Committee and is a member of AICPA Federal Tax Division Executive Committee, Council of the United States Branch of the International Fiscal Association, and a member of the Advisory Board of Tax Management.

Multinational Enterprises and Taxation

Robert J. Patrick, Jr.

Formerly, International Tax Counsel &
Director, Office of International Tax
Affairs of the U.S. Treasury Department

For more than fifteen years, the major Congressional debates in the United States on taxation of foreign source income have concerned the question of whether the earnings of U.S.-controlled foreign subsidiaries should be taxed as their income is earned rather than upon dividend repatriation—the issue of "tax deferral." This issue, which raises such considerations as whether we want foreign investment by United States corporations—or at least whether such investment is "good" or "bad"—has exhausted enormous amounts of time and talent. Further, it has diverted attention and resources from certain fundamental tax problems that will be with us as long as business enterprises conduct their business in more than one jurisdiction, whether or not we have "tax deferral."

The fact is that a group of related enterprises operating in a number of countries, each having different tax laws and tax rates, can lead to tax avoidance and administrative difficulties in determining whether or not appropriate prices are charged in intercompany transactions, and to a risk of double taxation of the same profits. These factors—and tax rules adopted to deal with them—can distort trade and investment decisions just as much as tariff barriers, exchange controls, and the like.

When the taxing country has determined that it has taxing jurisdiction, it generally seeks a tax upon what it considers to be a fair share of the income attributable to that country, whether by reason or residence, nationality, or source of income. The multinational enterprise is primarily concerned with the efficient conduct of its business and with maximizing its profits. At a minimum, it must attempt to avoid double taxation and where possible, it will conduct its operations to minimize its tax burden. The ground rules for determining the amount of taxes to be paid by the multinational are set out in the source of income and tax accounting rules for each jurisdiction, e.g., what is income, what income is from sources within the jurisdiction, when and to what extent is foreign source income exempt or entitled to a foreign tax credit?

A basic question is whether or not there are sensible rules for determining the source of income, allocating income and expenses, and imposing a reasonable total tax burden on international business income. Business profits traditionally have been subject to a corporate tax at the company level plus an income tax or final witholding tax when distributed to the shareholders. A growing tendency among developed countries is to alter this traditional approach in order to provide for at least partial integration of corporate and shareholder taxes. If it is not merely a passing fad, this development will also have major influence on international investment patterns.

It is not my intention to discuss the merits of deferral or the foreign tax of credit, but to discuss certain basic areas of complexity and conflict in the application of national rules of taxation to multinational corporations, to outline the choices that the United States has made or is considering in approaching these issues, and to indicate the limits of the solutions that we now have.

Specifically, I would like to discuss what I consider to be the following major areas of uncertainty and conflict in substantive rules, each of which has an important impact upon business decisions.

1. What rules are applied by a country to determine the source of income of a multinational enterprise?
2. When income is earned in transactions between related corporations in two different countries, what tests should be applied to determine how much each corporation earned (or lost) in each country?
3. When expenses are incurred by operations of a single corporate entity, how should those expenses be allocated between domestic and foreign source income of the corporation?
4. Assuming that the preceding determinations have been made, what should a country's tax take be with respect to the business profits of a multinational enterprise and its foreign shareholders?

BASIC UNITED STATES RULES

Let us begin with some basic tax rules applicable to international business income. From an international classification, our federal corporate tax structure is a classic one: profits are taxed at the corporate level and again at the shareholder level when earnings are distributed. When a domestic United States corporation is owned by foreign shareholders, except where modified by treaty, we impose a 30% withholding tax on payments of dividends to the foreign shareholders as a final tax liability.

With respect to our assertion of tax jurisdiction, the United States claims the right to tax U.S. corporations on their worldwide income, and to tax foreign corporations on their United States source income and on a limited amount of foreign source income that we consider to be connected with their United States business. Our tax code also provides that in the case of some U.S.-controlled foreign corporations earning certain defined types of "tax haven" income, the earnings are taxable to United States shareholders—in effect as a dividend—even though undistributed by the foreign corporation.

Our tax structure attempts to avoid double taxation of the same income by the United States and foreign countries by allowing a U.S. taxpayer a credit against United States tax on his foreign source income for foreign income taxes imposed on that income.

All determinations as to what is the taxable income base, including deductions to be taken into account and the determination of earnings and profits of foreign subsidiaries, are made for U.S. tax purposes under U.S. tax accounting rules. This presupposes the abilities of taxpayers and administrators to make accurate and timely adjustments from foreign income statements and tax returns—including foreign exchange translations—to adjust them to U.S. standards. Debate continues as to whether this is a realistic assumption.

Where business is conducted by a multinational through foreign subsidiaries, the United States asserts the right to adjust accounts to produce the taxable income that would have been earned by independent entities. This includes transactions among wholly foreign affiliates that are United States controlled, since there can be United States tax consequences arising in wholly foreign transactions. For example, there might be a constructive dividend to the parent from one subsidiary and a constructive contribution to capital by the parent to another subsidiary if the two subsidiaries do not deal at arm's length with each other.

Finally, it is by comparison with U.S. income tax law that we determine whether a levy imposed by a foreign government is an income tax that can be credited against United States income tax or is merely to be deducted as a royalty, excise tax, fee, and the like in computing net income. This examination involves comparison of the tax base, i.e., is the tax imposed on "net income," whether or not income has been "realized" under United States concepts, and whether or not the tax is part of a general income tax, and the like.

Stating these general principles creates a deceptive sense of certainty. Let us now look at some of the problems encountered in their application.

SOURCE OF INCOME RULES

Source of income rules are of importance in determining when the United States imposes tax on foreign corporations, since foreign corporations are subject to tax only on U.S. source income and on certain limited categories of foreign source income connected with a U.S. business. For U.S. corporate taxpayers, the source of income is critical in determining their foreign tax credit, which is limited to a credit against U.S. income tax for foreign income taxes imposed upon foreign source income. Thus, if there are high foreign taxes but little foreign source income under U.S. rules, excess credits will be generated that cannot be claimed by the taxpayer against United States tax. This may lead the taxpayer to enter into activities designed to produce low tax foreign source income which can be repatriated, in effect, tax free.

The Internal Revenue Code classifies and assigns income to specific sources. Some source rules arise out of tradition. For example, most countries consider that income from real property has its source in the country in which the property is located. Most rules are clearly arbitrary—developed over time to accomplish a particular result—and may depend upon whether the jurisdiction is an exporter or importer of capital or services. Under United States rules, income from the sale of personal property generally has its source where title passes and income from services has a source where the services are physically performed. Under Brazilian or Indian rules, income from the sale of stock has its source in the country in which the company whose shares are sold is incorporated, and income from services has its source in the country of residence of the person paying for the services. The U.S. Congress has just reenacted a rule to the effect that foreign corporations receiving interest on U.S. bank deposits must classify that interest as foreign source income. What is intended is simply that we will not tax such income, i.e., it should be exempt. In the case of other interest income paid by U.S. persons, the U.S. generally does intend to tax it and provides that it is from U.S. sources if paid by a United States payer.

Our present source rules create a series of problems and opportunities and are a major factor in international tax planning:

1. *Ease of manipulation.* The artificiality of certain rules permits taxpayers to maximize tax advantages by structuring transactions to produce domestic or foreign source income or losses depending upon their tax position. For example, the rule that the source of income on the sale of personal property depends on the place where title is passed can be used to generate either domestic or foreign source income. One result is increased complexity through piecemeal antiavoidance rules. For example, special source rules for capital gains were adopted in the Tax Reform Act of 1976 which attempted to relate the source for foreign tax credit purposes to whether "substantial" foreign tax was imposed on the gain from the sale of personal property or not.

2. *Characterization.* The characterization that is given for tax purposes to a particular activity will affect the source of income rule that is applicable to the income generated by the activity. This may lead to designing contracts allocating compensation to activities generating a particular source of income. If a corporation in Country B desires to have a particular machine to use in its production, it may purchase the machine from the United States manufacturer who exports, with title passing abroad, to Country B. In that case, under our tax code and regulations, the export income will be partially United States source income and partially foreign source income, since it is generated by property manufactured in the U.S. and sold abroad with title passing abroad. If title passed in the United States, all of the sales income would be U.S. source income. Alternatively, the corporation in Country B may license the machine for use in its assembly line and the royalty income paid to the United States licensor is treated as wholly foreign source income. If, instead, the Country B corporation requested that the supplier design a new machine to be used in B's assembly line, the fee generated by the design services performed by the supplier will be United States source income, assuming that the design services are performed in the U.S. To complete the picture, if corporation B is a subsidiary of the U.S. supplier, the machine could be contributed tax free by the United States parent company with no income being generated on the transaction. However, dividend income subsequently received from the subsidiary on its profits from manufacturing in Country B will be foreign source income when received by the parent company.

3. *Tracing.* A great deal of debate has involved the question of whether in avoiding double taxation we should have a foreign tax credit on an overall basis (aggregating all foreign income and taxes) or a per-country

basis (crediting foreign taxes only on income from sources within each foreign country). The 1976 Tax Reform Act provides that in the future only the overall computation is to be used (with separate rules for oil income). This is unlikely to end the debate that has seen a per-country limitation used between 1918 and 1921, an overall limitation between 1921 and 1932, the lesser of the per-country or overall between 1932 and 1954, the per-country between 1954 and 1961, and a choice of either the per-country or the overall limitation at the taxpayer's election from 1960 through 1976.

The important question is why we say income is from one source and not another. For example, we treat dividend payments out of foreign earnings as having their source in the country of the incorporation of a foreign subsidiary. This means that regardless of where the activities producing earnings in a foreign subsidiary occurred or where taxes were imposed, those earnings, when distributed from the first-tier foreign subsidiary to the U.S. parent company, will be deemed to have their source in the country in which that first-tier subsidiary is incorporated and all income taxes on such earnings treated as if paid to that country. This means that a foreign holding company can be utilized to hold stock in lower-tier subsidiaries and to receive a mix of dividend interest and royalty income in order to average out high and low foreign taxes and, in effect, achieve an "overall" averaging of the foreign tax credit at that level. This is one of several factors that has just led the congressional tax writing committees to choose the so-called "overall" limitation for the tax credit—permitting such averaging at the parent company level—rather than the arguably purer concept of computing the credit on a country-by-country basis and attempting the difficult task of tracing income to its ultimate "source."

4. *Conflicts in source rules.* A major area of confrontation today in accommodating source rules in bilateral income tax conventions is the tendency of some developing countries to find the source of income on all payments for services to be in the country in which the payer is a resident, regardless of where the services are performed, and to impose significant income tax on the payments. The result is that the U.S. taxpayer performing the service in the United States had domestic source income on the transaction under U.S. source rules and therefore cannot claim a foreign tax credit for the foreign country's tax on that income. Imposition of a withholding tax on gross payments of fees for services may also raise questions as to whether there is, in fact, a creditable "income tax" under United States concepts.

We can conclude in general that our source rules (1) are arbitrary, (2) may lead to artificial arrangements to affect the source of income or losses, and (3) frequently lead to conflict between the United States and other jurisdictions as to the source of income, which will affect either the right to impose tax or determine which country should give a credit for a tax imposed by the other country. There has been relatively little careful analysis of our source rules, yet they remain a touchstone of most of our other rules for imposing tax in the international area. There is little question that the source rules themselves and the extent of harmonization could be improved.

INTERCOMPANY PRICING UNDER SECTION 482

The Organization for Economic Cooperation and Development (OECD) in its recent "Guideline for Multinationals" stresses that multinationals are to: "refrain from making use of the particular facilities available to them, such as transfer pricing, which does not conform to an arms-length standard, for modifying in ways contrary to national laws the tax base on which members of the group are assessed."

Section 482 of the Internal Revenue Code authorizes the Internal Revenue Service to "distribute, apportion, or allocate gross income, deductions, credits, or allowances between or among. . . . organizations, trades, or businesses" in the case of any two or more organizations, trades, or businesses owned or controlled directly or indirectly by the same interests, if the Internal Revenue Service determines that such distribution, apportionment or allocation is necessary to prevent evasion of taxes or clearly to reflect the income. Detailed regulations under this section were promulgated in 1968, covering intercompany charges for interest, services, licensing of intangibles, leasing of tangible property, and the pricing of products. In several of these areas the regulations contain safe-haven perimeters within which taxpayers may structure their transactions to avoid IRS adjustments. While there are problems with each of the these subjects, the greatest controversy lies with the pricing regulations where there are no "safe-haven" rules.

The basic standard of Section 482 is that transactions should be carried on between related parties on an arm's length basis. The Treasury's interest is to avoid the shifting of income from a United States taxpayer to a foreign entity. The regulations for pricing set forth three specified methods for establishing acceptable prices: the comparable uncontrolled price method, the resale price method (employing the use of a markup on resale), and the cost plus method (using a gross profit percentage). It is important to note that all three methods are based upon the concept of a "comparable uncontrolled transaction," i.e., what would unrelated parties have done? When that test cannot reasonably be applied, the regulations suggest that some other method of pricing might be used, but offer no guidance as to what other methods are acceptable.

If comparable uncontrolled prices were generally ascertainable there would be little difficulty with the proposed regulations. Where there are sales under comparable circumstances to controlled parties as well as to unrelated parties, there is a ready basis for comparison subject to adjustments for transportation and similar expenses. Perhaps 40% or more of all U.S. exports from United States producers are to related entities abroad. Among these transactions are a number of sales in which comparable prices would be difficult to ascertain. Indeed, in some industries the only sales that occur at certain stages of production are between affiliates. Studies by the Industrial Conference board and by the Internal Revenue Service itself have indicated that comparable uncontrolled prices are not ascertained in a large volume of cases and that agents make price adjustments using a wide variety of methods not described in the regulations.

Taxpayers have proposed a number of safe-haven intercompany pricing rules on the sale of products to related entities. One tendency on audit has been to find an allocation supported on the basis of a reasonable profit split. The Treasury Department advocated such a method in an arbitrary fashion in proposing the Domestic International Sales corporation (DISC) export tax incentive by the terms of which 50% of the combined taxable income of the manufacturer and a related export company is allocated as export profit and the remaining one-half is allocated to the manufacturer. This is also the practical effect of United States source of income rule relating to the manufacturing of a product in the United States and its sale abroad.

The fact is that an arbitrary allocation of profit between two entities does not necessarily take into account the relative economic contribution of each of the entities. Thus, DISC corporations have generally been established as shell companies in which 50% of the combined export profit is automatically allocated to a virtually nonexistent shell corporation. If a test dividing profits is to be offered as an alternative method, weight must be given to the relative elements of the business, i.e., there must be a requirement of substance for all entities entitled to an allocation of profits. Such rules become more complex when applied to the export sale of components to be incorporated in a second country in a manufacturing process for further resale.

Other suggested alternatives have included:

1. The IRS should accept transfer prices based on incremental costs in ap-

propriate circumstances. It is argued that recognition should be given to the fact that the United States market is the principal market for most domestic companies and that the existence of foreign activities should not be presumed to justify allocations of general management or similar expenses. The major question is: When are circumstances appropriate for incremental costing? The regulations under Section 482 suggest the possible use of an incremental method of pricing where there is an effort to "establish or maintain" a foreign market. There has been little elucidation of this subject. The traditional IRS approach has been to deny that United States companies with substantial foreign operations and sales relative to domestic sales can continue to operate at a profit if their claim is that the foreign sales are priced on a incremental basis.

2. A safe haven should be provided for situations where tax avoidance is presumptively not a major objective, aswhen United States and foreign tax rates are comparable, and generally should be accorded more liberal treatment for cases where transactions are not arranged for tax avoidance purposes, but for good faith business reasons, or to reflect good accounting practice. To the extent that this approach does not beg the question, the contrary position is that it does not answer the fact that although the taxpayer is not avoiding taxes, the foreign government is collecting taxes to which it is not entitled and, in so doing, at the expense of the United States Treasury.

3. A policy should be adopted of not proposing minor adjustments in formulas for transfer prices, royalties, or cost allocations which have been accepted in an audit for a previous year, if the facts in that year were not substantially different from those in the current year. There is certainly little basis for objecting to this suggestion. It is basically a judgment to be made at the audit level but overall policy could be announced.

4. The Internal Revenue Service should give advance rulings in pricing cases. The usual reply is that these questions are inherently "factual," with factors varying from year to year. Traditionally the Service does not rule on "factual" questions and to do so would be misleading. There is also a problem in coordinating a ruling procedure at the national and district levels. Yet, the fact is that in the mineral and other areas where it is difficult to find transactions occurring between uncontrolled parties, the Service and taxpayer have been working out formulas for prospective transactions.

United States intercompany pricing rules have been amplified by more detailed regulations than are found in the laws of any other developed country. To what extent should we attempt to spell out pricing rules in intricate detail? Empirical evidence dictates that the Internal Revenue Service often does not apply these rules in the manner contemplated. Taxpayers and some in the administration seek simple solutions and guidelines. To date, such simplification has not been forthcoming. Others suggest that such simplification and certainty is a quixotic goal, and the most that we can expect in intercompany pricing is to enunciate a basic standard that taxpayers should make a reasonable effort to approximate an uncontrolled price.

ALLOCATION OF EXPENSES TO FOREIGN SOURCE INCOME

If we assume that we have agreed on the source of income produced from a particular activity, and that the activity is being conducted at arm's length with a related foreign corporation, or is in fact being conducted with a wholly independent party, we still have a potential problem with respect as to whether deductions permitted under domestic law should be allocable in whole or in part to domestic or foreign source income. This is true for countries exempting foreign source income and for countries like the United States that grant a foreign tax credit for foreign taxes imposed on foreign source income. The question is how much of the taypayer's income is foreign source income and how much is domestic? If the U.S. does not allocate proper expenses to foreign source income, the expenses simply reduce United States tax on domestic source income. On the other hand, when expenses are allocated to foreign source income on which foreign taxes have been imposed, the effect is to produce a higher effective foreign tax rate. At some point this effective rate exceeds the United States tax rate on the foreign income and excess tax credits are generated. This can be looked at as a high foreign tax rate or as double taxation, depending upon whether you think there was a proper expense allocation.

What deductions claimed by a United States taxpayer—such as interest expense, administrative overhead, state taxes, charitable contributions, and the like—should be taken against foreign source income? To what extent, if any, should this rule take into account whether or not a foreign jurisdiction will permit a deduction if these allocated expenses are charged by the United States taxpayer to that foreign affiliate? Most countries have not thought very much about this; some believe that the United States tax authorities recently have given it overly theoretical consideration. After years of preparation, sweeping and highly controversial rules were proposed by the Treasury Department in 1973 with respect to the allocation of expenses to foreign source income; the 1973 proposals have been withdrawn, and new proposals were published on November 8, 1976.

The most difficult area—and the one that has generated the greatest concern—is in the allocation of expenses deducted currently for research and development between foreign and domestic source income. The proposed regulations contemplate that expenses clearly identifiable with domestic or foreign income will be so allocated, as well as the vast amount of research that is not clearly related to one source or the other. The 1976 proposed regulations start with the approach that the apportionment should be on the basis of reasonable expectations as to where the income would be earned on the basis of broad product lines.

The statutory framework of the Internal Revenue Code of 1954 permits research and development expenses as a current deduction at the election of the taxpayer instead of as an amount to be capitalized. With this rule, we combine a provision that has been in our tax laws since the 1920s that all expenses must be allocated or apportioned to items or classes of gross income from foreign and domestic sources. A major problem is thus created by the fact that current research and development expenses—whether successful or wasted—may not produce income that is received in the same tax accounting year in which the expenses are incurred. There is likely to be a mismatching of expenses and revenues.

An additional factor that makes the allocation of research expense critical is the fact that payments for technology in the form of royalties usually attract significant foreign withholding taxes on the gross payment, creating a high effective rate if deductions are allocated to the royalties. The U.S. domestic tax law itself provides for a statutory 30% rate on the gross payment of royalties to a foreigner. Under treaty policy, the United States is prepared to eliminate this withholding tax in bilateral conventions. The model convention of the OECD also calls for elimination of withholding tax. However, because of revenue considerations, most developing countries may reduce but continue to impose some withholding tax in their treaties. Data compiled by the U.S. Treasury indicates that in 1972 United States parent corporations received some $825 million in rents and royalties from their foreign subsidiaries, and that foreign withholding taxes paid—even with substantial tax treaty reductions in many instances—were 13% of the gross royalties.

With this background, what is the situation for a fairly typical high technology company in the United States? The taxpayer is probably increasing research and development expenses each year; most of this research is not successful in generating new products or improvements. The taxpayer engaged in the export of products has one or more foreign manufacturing subsidiaries that manufacture under patent and know-how licenses or through contributions of such technology previously developed in the United States; the taxpayer also licenses unrelated foreign manufacturers to use his previously developed technology. The royalties paid by related companies are received on an arm's length basis to meet the standards of Section 482. Note, however, that such transferred technology represents the product of successful research; we may question whether the royalty rates typically reflect payment for a proportionate share of unsuccessful research. After all, the test is that of licensing an unrelated entity and the taxpayer is prepared to license both related and unrelated entities on the same terms. Should the cost of unsuccessful research (or expanding research) be built into the expense allocation rules?

As indicated, some of the technology was previously transferred in a tax-free contribution to capital to a manufacturing subsidiary; a ruling was received from the Internal Revenue Service, under Sections 351 and 367, that tax avoidance was not a principal purpose of the transfer, since the property is to be used in manufacturing in the country in which the subsidiary is incorporated. Under published ruling guidelines, a transfer in such a case does not have "tax avoidance" as a principal purpose. The transferee country imposes a substantial corporate tax on the profits of the subsidiary. When those after-tax profits are repatriated by way of dividends to the parent company in the United States, domestic tax on the dividends is offset by a foreign tax credit for the foreign income and withholding taxes. In effect, the expense of developing the technology has been deducted against earlier United States source income. The technology is now used to produce profits in a foreign country which generate tax revenues solely for that country.

Each year the taxpayer receives dividends from his foreign affiliates, export income, and royalties from overseas licenses to related and unrelated parties. The foreign earnings—including undistributed earnings of wholly owned foreign subsidiaries—may constitute some 50% of the consolidated earnings reported in financial statements of the enterprise. The other one-half of the taxpayer's consolidated earnings is from domestic sources from the manufacture and sale of products generated by successful technology. What portion of the amount spent on research and development income by the United States parent company should be allocated to foreign or domestic income, and on what basis? Assuming that only a small portion can be definitely attributed to domestic income or foreign source income, what of the vast amount of other research expenses including that which was unsuccessful? A basic question that must be answered is whether expenses for unsuccessful research that may have worldwide application should be allocated solely to domestic income or to domestic and to worldwide income.

Let us select from among a few of the possible alternatives for allocating or not allocating the research expense.

1. *Gross-to-gross allocation.* It can be argued under the statute that if an expense cannot be definitely allocated to some item or class of gross income, such expense is to be apportioned between domestic and foreign income on a ratable basis. Historically, the term *ratable* has been viewed as a fraction in which the numerator is gross income from foreign sources and the denominator is worldwide gross income. This fraction, if interpreted in such fashion, has the mechanical defect of allocating the research and development expense to such disparate types of income as royalties, export income, dividends and interest—some of which are net items, as in the case of dividend income. Moreover, the gross-to-gross allocation has only a tenuous relationship between certain types of expenses such as research and development expense and unrelated types of income. For example, a dividend may be paid out of the earnings of a foreign subsidiary that has made minimal use of transferred technology and has generated its earnings out of the rendering of services. Because of the "apples and oranges" mix in the gross-to-gross formula, there has been a reluctance to propose rules using this mix, and the proposed Treasury regulations reject it as the starting point for an allocation. The November 1976 proposals would, however, permit a gross-to-gross rule as a safe-haven allocation provided that it met a minimum level of allocation, ascertained by a more complex computation determined by comparing domestic and foreign sales as described in alternative (3) below.

2. *Capitalization approach.* Theoretically, it might be possible, at least by statute, to require that for purposes of allocation to foreign source income, a taxpayer must keep an account of research and development expense that would be amortized between foreign and domestic source income over a period of time. The intention would be to relate current research expenses to future earnings. Ideally, the formula would be based upon historical patterns for the company concerned. It is clear that this is basically a theoretical approach to the issue; major administrative problems would be involved in finding appropriate guidelines for determining the useful life of technology or for amortizing unsuccessful research for a company or for an industry.

3. *Reasonable expectation test.* The regulations proposed in 1973, and again, underlying those proposed in 1976, adopt the approach that research and development expenses should be allocated to foreign income when there is a reasonable expectation that the fruits of successful research

and development will be used to produce the foreign income. This expectation would be based on prior performance and on expected utilization of successful research within broad product lines. Thus, if the parent company and a foreign subsidiary are manufacturing the same type of product, then the dividend income from the subsidiary is reduced by an allocable portion of research and developments expense. The regulations adopt a look-through approach to determine the basis for the allocation. The allocation to foreign earnings is based on the sales of the foreign affiliates and licensees compared with worldwide sales of the affiliates, licensees, and parent company.

Ascertaining the sales of a foreign unrelated licensee raises substantial practical problems. This approach also contains the inherent problem in which only a portion of a dividend represents earnings on transferred technology—whether such technology has been transferred in the past or may be transferred in the future—and any dividend received represents, in most cases, only a portion of the total subsidiary earnings for the year. The mechanics of the allocation, however, produce the same amount of expense regardless of the amount of earnings distributed. Thus, $1 million in expense may be allocated to $100 or $10 million of dividends being repatriated in a taxable year.

4. *Limiting allocations to income produced by research and development.* Consideration has also been given to limiting the expense allocation to those types of income clearly producing profits attributable to research and development expense. This type of income is clearly produced in domestic and export sales of products produced with technology, to license fees for the use of technology, and to income received on sales of technology. But what should be done about dividend income generated by technology transferred abroad tax free? A proposed solution would be to require that all transfers of technology be for consideration whether by way of payment for technology in a sale or by a license. The allocation is thus limited to income generated by transfers of research and development. Under this proposal, the taxpayer would have to value his technology and transfer it at an arm's-length price to an affiliate or to an independent purchaser, or he would have to license the affiliate or purchaser. If the transfer is for a lump sum, the determination of allocable expenses is made in the year of the transfer. If the arrangement is through a royalty license, allocations would be made annually. Subsequent dividends distributed by the foreign affiliate should bear no further allocation since those earnings are, in effect, being generated out of the operations and assets of the affiliate, which has paid for them either by way of purchase price or by royalty.

Establishing this theoretical framework still leaves the question of the basis for allocation. One could maintain a look-through test to determine the volume of domestic and foreign sales. It would be possible to measure this in the case of royalties on the comparability of product lines manufactured through domestic and foreign sales by use of the same technology. It is entirely possible, however, that the threshold determination for allocation of expenses may exceed the net royalty income that is received. This is a fact of life with respect to licensing arrangements today. It appears appropriate to deem a percentage of royalty income received over time on an arm's-length basis under Section 482 as representing a profit element that would delineate in all cases a ceiling on the amount of allocation. For example, all arm's-length royalties could be deemed to carry a 20% profit. The tentative allocation would be made against this profit, and if the allocation of expense exceeded 80% of the royalty income, it would be reduced to 80%.

Export income allocations could be made on the basis of current rules on the source of income so that 50% of expense would be deemed to U.S. source and 50% to foreign source. This would have little deterrent effect on export production by U.S. taxpayers.

The objections to this approach include questions as to the regulatory authority to require transfers for value under Sections 351 and 367. If this procedure were allowed as an optional approach by the taxpayer, the question remains as to what rule would apply in the absence of this election to treat all transfers as taxable. Obviously, there must be consideration received on the transfer or else the thrust of the allocations could always be avoided in tax-free transfer. Questions have been raised as to the ability of the Internal Revenue Service to determine arm's-length prices on the sale of technology to an affiliate. Industry expressed concern that requiring taxation on transfers of technology abroad would inhibit the present techniques for foreign joint ventures, whereby United States taxpayers transfer technology to a joint venture and the foreign partner puts up the cash contribution. Recognition of income would substantially alter these arrangements.

5. *Deemed allocations to foreign income.* The deemed profit approach might be adopted in another form. For example, when a multinational enterprise reaches some threshold level of foreign source income through its domestic and foreign operations, an arbitrary percentage of research and development expense might be made allocable to the foreign source income.

6. *Incremental approach.* United States taxpayers have argued that the United States is the primary market for products developed through domestic research and development, and any advantages obtained by foreign licensing or transfers abroad is purely incremental to this market

and no expenses for past development should be allocated to current income. This argument is similar to the argument by developing countries that they need not allow expense deductions or cost-sharing for research conducted in the United States. But when more than half of the consolidated income of the enterprises is from abroad, can it possibly be said to be incremental? The 1976 proposed regulations have given some weight to such arguments. They permit an arbitrary percentage of total research and development expense to be allocated to the geographic location in which the research is carried on (this would be 50% in 1977). A taxpayer may show by historical data that the percentage should be increased by showing limited production of a product abroad or a significant lag in the transfer of technology abroad.

Many of the practical difficulties in making allocations to foreign source income arise from the desire, on one hand, to obtain a theoretically pure concept and maximize the accuracy with which a determination is made between domestic and foreign source income. On the other hand, there is a desire to produce an administrable rule permitting the computation of costs and foreign tax credits. It is clear that some of these objectives must be sacrificed to have a workable system. Any final resolution of this issue, perhaps by legislation, must consider the degree to which the United States tax system should provide a tax incentive to domestic research.

TAKING STOCK

We have now reviewed a series of complicated rules and options on source of income, intercompany pricing, and allocations of deductions and should pause to see where we are. We can readily see the situation of the United States taxpayer. He is likely to have some serious tax problems.

1. The tax administration in developing Country A tells the taxpayer that he is not entitled to a 6% royalty on the technology he has previously transferred to a subsidiary in that country. The reasons given are as follows:
   a. The last transfer of technology was eight years ago, and there is no evidence that there has been a flow of new technology into the subsidiary;
   b. The taxpayer has previously recovered all of his expenses through sale of the product in the United States where his primary market has been; and
   c. Any payments flowing out for the supposed technology represent

      dividend income to the taypayer and, in addition to denying any deduction for the payment, a 25% withholding tax will be imposed.

2. A portion of his royalty income from an unrelated licensee in Country B is being treated by the United States as being from the performance of services in the U.S., and Country B is imposing a 30% withholding tax on the full amount of the payment for the technology and services; hence, a portion of the Country B tax is not going to be creditable against his U.S. tax on that income

3. Foreign Country C is contending that the taxpayer's sale of components to his manufacturing subsidiary in Country C was in excess of an arm's length price and is proposing a pricing adjustment. The taxpayer has already paid domestic taxes on what he assumed to be his profit in the U.S.

4. The Internal Revenue Service is preparing to allocate additional domestic research expenses against the royalties from Countries A and B and dividend income received from a subsidiary in Country D. These allocations will generate excess foreign tax credits. With respect to the research allocations, the taxpayer argues that there is a substantial lag in the time in which any technology is transferred abroad, that the research is primarily intended for the United States market, and that the research is primarily of value to the parent company; thus the expenses were properly allocated to the United States. Indeed these arguments sound very similar to those being made by the tax administration of Country A.

The interaction of these conflicting source of income, pricing, and allocation rules threaten to make one or more of these investments uneconomic. The question arises as to why it is necessary to develop intricate rules on source of income, intercompany pricing, and allocation of expenses. The answer from the Treasury standpoint is simply that failure to do so permits the erosion of the United States corporate tax base to other taxing jurisdictions. In addition, failure to identify net foreign source income encourages U.S. taxpayers to give little resistance to foreign tax claims if the foreign taxes merely offset domestic tax under the credit mechanism. One important question is the extent to which seeking precision in such areas as intercompany pricing under Section 482 is unproductive if United States adjustments, themselves, are, in turn, offset by foreign tax credits for foreign taxes. For example, the United States may claim that a domestic company selling to a foreign subsidiary should have charged a higher price and reported more net profit in the U.S. However, the adjustment—if treated as foreign source income—may not produce additional United States tax if the foreign subsidiary has paid a foreign tax on reported profits, which are then distributed as a dividend to the U.S. parent, carrying with the dividend a credit for the foreign tax. In such a case, if after the United States adjustment, the taxpayer fails to seek a corresponding adjustment and reduction of tax in the foreign country, has he made a voluntary tax payment to that country that is not creditable? This area is under current development.

If source of income and allocation rules are to be applied unilaterally by the tax jurisdictions, where does this leave the taxpayer? Is he merely an inter-pleader between two or more taxing jurisdictions? What protection does he have, and what are the potential pathways out of the maze?

Cooperation today between different taxing jurisdictions is found primarily in the development of bilateral tax conventions.

1. *Source Rules.* The Model Income Tax Convention of the Organization for Economic Cooperation and Development (OECD), through the provision of common treaty source rules, seeks to avoid conflicts between treaty partners. Under the terms of these tax conventions, which the United States follows, industrial and commercial profits from the active conduct of a trade or business are taxable in the country in which a permanent establishment is located. If attributed to the permanent establishment in one country, the income will, in effect, be given a source in that country. The other treaty country will either exempt the income or give a tax credit for its treaty partner's tax on such income. In the case of other income, the treaties provide a source and reduce or eliminate withholding taxes, thus reducing the potential for double taxation. To the extent that some international harmonization of source rules is occurring through this approach, conflict is being reduced.

2. *Intercompany Pricing and Deduction Allocation Rules.* In general the existing model treaties provide only limited guidance for intercompany pricing and virtually no specific guidance for allocation of deductions, other than in the case of branches. The standard treaty model of the OECD provides rules for the deduction of overhead and other expenses in the case of branch operations carried out in one treaty country by an enterprise of the other treaty country. The treaties also provide that the tax authorities are entitled to adjust intercompany pricing between separately incorporated affiliates to an arm's length arrangement, but do not assure taxpayers of the right to charge intercompany expenses. The newer model conventions do provide that an affiliate, operating in one country and owned by an enterprise of the other country, is to be entitled to all of the deductions and expense allocations to which domestic enterprises of the first country would be entitled in dealing with

one another, i.e., "national treatment." These rules provide a rudimentary groundwork for more comprehensive treaty statements of the right to claim deductions for benefits conferred on an entity in one country by expenditures of a related entity in another treaty country.

3. *Competent authority.* Of major significance—yet limited to date in application and acceptance—are competent authority proceedings under treaties to permit the tax authorities to meet together to resolve issues of source of income, characterization of activities, intercompany pricing, and elimination of double taxation. A number of treaties permit the reopening of statutes of limitation to allow correlative adjustments where an adjustment is made in the other country. But the procedures in most countries have not been spelled out. To what extent, for example, is the taxpayer intimidated by the prospect that some countries will reopen closed years to examine other issues if a competent authority proceeding is commenced?

4. *Other Approaches.* The treaty process is a slow one and uncertain. Being bilateral in nature, treaties do not cover third country problems and are subject to variation in their terms. The United States has only made a start toward obtaining treaties with developing countries, where many of these issues are most serious. Treaties seem to offer the most likely promise for harmonization, however. It might be possible, for example, that agreement could be reached between treaty countries with more sophisticated tax administrations as to advance rulings on certain types of transactions—such as royalty rates—just as the tax authorities themselves are eager to seek exchange of information between the tax administrations. Recent statements from government officials have predicted closer cooperation by treaty partners in audit programs, perhaps taking the form of joint audits. While taxpayers may be alarmed at the prospect of such increased activity, one salutary effect could be efficiency and certainty, since intercompany transactions would be reviewed at the same time by the competent authorities and adjustments made on a current basis.

To what extent should we try an entirely different concept? It is interesting to observe that little attention has been paid at the international level to the use of formulas for calculating allocable income to separately incorporated, but related, entities operating in different countries, such as an allocation based on payroll, property, and sales. This approach is utilized by individual states in the U.S. and has far-reaching consequences for international operations of companies doing business in states employing a "unitary" method of taxation. The fact that little serious consideration has been given to these rules by foreign countries is probably a proper result. While allocation formulas have the appearance of certainty in allocating income and expenses, formulary methods assume comparable rates of return from the mix of labor and capital employed in the business. It is unrealistic to assume this return to be the same in different areas of the world. Thus, a formula that might give a reasonable allocation of income to units of an enterprise operating in New York and California is unlikely to give a reasonable allocation to an enterprise operating in California and in Botswana. Attempts to make adjustments in the formula for different countries, companies, or industries would result in a maze of administrative regulations; nor would one be likely to find that all countries would agree on the same formula or its application. A major problem is simply determining what is a "unitary" business.

How important is it that harmonization be developed in these areas? Are these merely problems to be shrugged off as involving business judgment as to whether or not the cost of doing business warrants the foreign investment? It is rather difficult to see, for example, on what basis the Treasury Department can justify foregoing its standard (and generally accepted) intercompany pricing rules because less developed Country A has now decided that it will not permit royalties to be paid in any form.

On the other hand, there is a point that should be borne in mind by government policy makers. As each country steps up its intercompany pricing allocations and raises issues of allocation of expenses between foreign and domestic source income, there will be a tax constraint on conducting intercompany transactions that could lead to a preferred practice of manufacturing locally in each country to supply consumers in that country and avoid the burden of multiple tax audits and adjustments that occur in the case of intercompany transactions. This will affect decisions concerning exporting and the location of manufacturing facilities. The tax factor would be in addition to the fact that multinationals are generally under pressure to move technology abroad and that nationalistic pressures call for local production in countries throughout the world.

TAX BURDEN ON MULTINATIONAL BUSINESS INCOME

If we assume that issues as to the source of income, pricing, and allocations of deductions have been resolved, we are still faced with a major policy question as to the tax burden that a country should impose upon business profits earned by a multinational corporation and its shareholders. For illustration, we can take the case of a company incorporated in the taxing jurisdiction and owned both by domestic residents and foreign corporate and individual share-holders.

The taxation of business income under a classic tax structure is said to produce economic double taxation. That is, business income is taxed at the corporate level which in the United States is at a statutory 48% rate. The income remaining after taxes that is distributed to the shareholders is then taxed to the shareholders at their individual tax rates, or in the case of a foreign share-holder by withholding, perhaps at a 30% rate as in the United States.

The organization of the multinational corporation with investors from, and investments in, other countries may substantially pyramid the total tax burden. For example, assuming that there are no applicable tax treaties, if a Dutch investor invests in a United States corporation which has a Nether-lands subsidiary, taxes are imposed at the corporate level of the subsidiary in the Netherlands and upon dividend payments (by way of a Dutch withhold-ing tax) on distributions from the Dutch subsidiary to the U.S. parent. The dividend is then taxed at the United States corporate tax level (subject to a domestic tax credit for Dutch corporate and withholding taxes, which may be reduced by allocable deductions), followed by a 30% U.S. withholding tax on the net profits distributed by the domestic parent corporation to its Dutch shareholder who, if an individual, is subject to personal income tax in the Netherlands. Internal tax laws which provide credits for foreign source in-come or treaty arrangements (as is the case with the United States and the Netherlands whereby withholding taxes are reduced) provide credits for tax reductions or exemption for foreign source income and help mitigate, but fre-quently do not eliminate, multiple taxation of the income. For a number of years, this cascade effect of taxation has been thought to be an important area for future harmonization. A new development has emerged, however.

In reviewing the question of sovereign countries obtaining a fair share of profits from the operation of multinational enterprises, the issue of immediate significance is the international impact of domestic integrated corporate-shareholder tax structures. These systems have been designed to integrate partially the domestic corporate and shareholder tax on business profits in order to reduce—to a greater or lesser extent—economic double taxation of profits earned by corporate enterprises. These rules now apply to or are con-templated for Belgium, Canada, France, Germany, and the United Kingdom and have been recommended for adoption throughout the European Eco-nomic Community in a draft directive of the EEC Commission.

Mitigation of taxation may be given at the company level (i.e., a split rate system as under present German law), or at the shareholder level (an imputation system as in France or the United Kingdom), or in some combination of the two. Total integration to prevent so-called "economic double taxation" could be achieved by a split rate system with a zero rate for distributed profits or by an imputation system with a full credit for the corporation tax. In practice no developed country has adopted a system of full integration.

Under the British-French imputation system, the credit against the shareholders' income tax is for company tax withheld, and where the company tax exceeds the taxpayer's liability, a refund is made to the taxpayer. Under the Canadian-Belgian version, the credit is for a domestic tax deemed to have been paid and any excess paid by the corporation over the tax required to be paid by the taxpayer is not refunded to the taxpayer.

International problems are presented under both the split rate form of tax in which a higher tax is imposed on retained earnings than on distributed profits and under an imputation system in which shareholders are treated as having paid a portion of the corporate tax. In the case of a split rate system the questions include whether a distribution by a foreign owned subsidiary should have the full benefit of the lower tax rate on distributed income, whether distributions by domestic branches of foreign corporations should have the benefit of the lower tax rate; and whether reciprocal withholding tax rates will apply in double taxation conventions between countries having split rate systems and countries not having such systems. In the case of imputation credit systems, the international issues include whether or not the tax credit given to domestic residents is also to be given to foreign portfolio investors, direct investors, and branches and whether or not the credit should be given to domestic shareholders on their income from foreign investments.

The systems integrating corporate and shareholder taxes have generally been adopted for domestic tax purposes and without granting an imputation to domestic investors with respect to their foreign source investments and without extending the credit for imputation to foreign investors. This latter step has been modified in a number of French and United Kingdom treaties with respect to portfolio investments by foreign shareholders and, in the case of the pending treaty between the United States and the U.K., the United Kingdom imputation credit would be extended to U.S. corporations with investments in subsidiaries in the United Kingdom.

The treatment of United States shareholders in United Kingdom corporations under the U.K. tax integration system for shareholder and corporate taxes represents a major policy development in U.S. tax treaties. Discussions about a basic revision of our existing treaty began in 1973 in connection with the adoption of an integrated corporate-shareholder tax system by the United

Kingdom. The system adopted provides that a portion of a tax collected at the corporate level will, on the distribution of dividends by a United Kingdom corporation, be treated not only as an advance payment of a portion of the corporate income tax—designated an Advance Corporation Tax or ACT— but also as a payment by the shareholder if he is a U.K. resident to satisfy his personal tax liabilities. British resident shareholders include the ACT in income and claim a credit or refund for the ACT payment.

A report by the Chancellor of the Exchequer to Parliament in 1971 stated that the object of corporate and shareholder tax integration could be achieved either by an imputation type of system—which France had adopted in 1965— or by a split rate system—such as that in effect in Germany—in which a higher tax is imposed on retained earnings than on distributed earnings. The United Kingdom elected an imputation system which came into force in 1973, basing the choice on, among other stated reasons, the fact that this system could present some advantage in tax treaty negotiations with countries having classical tax systems, such as the United States.

The Treasury Department negotiated a treaty with France that was signed in 1967 and reserved its position on the treatment of United States investors by France under their imputation system. The United Kingdom adoption of an imputation system clearly marked an emerging trend in European taxation. In the interim, the Commission of the European Economic Community (EEC) having rejected the earlier advice of its experts that Community income tax harmonization could best be achieved by a classical tax system, recommended an imputation system for all member countries. The commission's public recommendations have not spelled out mechanics for the tax treatment of investors from nonmember countries. In announcing in July 1975 a proposed directive for the harmonization of company taxation within the Community under an imputation system, the commission proposed that, in order to avoid discrimination, each Community shareholder of a Community corporation should be treated in the same fashion—whether or not a resident of the same EEC country as the paying corporation—and that tax imputation benefits are to flow through subsidiary-parent distributions to ultimate individual shareholders. The proposals contemplate an intercountry clearinghouse to distribute revenues equitably among the taxing jurisdictions.

With respect to shareholders who are not EEC residents, the proposed directive states that tax credits may be granted in whole or part to third country residents, but does not provide guidelines for negotiation of such arrangements. The accompanying press release merely said: "Insofar as the possibility of a tax credit for nationals of third countries is concerned, the Commission believes that Member States, with the Commission's assistance, should adopt a common position in negotiating double taxation treaties with third countries."

The Treasury Department review of integrated tax systems attempted to take a long-range approach based upon United States adherence to the principles of freedom of capital movements and nondiscrimination. Consistent with the approach of the EEC Commission, it was concluded that at least two tendencies of integration systems are inconsistent with these principles, unless appropriate adjustments are made. First, investment by residents of imputation countries will be withdrawn gradually from countries having a classical system of taxation and new flows of capital will be reduced, as after-tax returns on investments would be greater in home countries having imputation systems. So long as the United States retains a classical tax structure, a U.S. corporation will have to pay out higher dividends than a European corporation to make the yield on the U.S. shares as attractive to Europeans in EEC countries as shares in EEC corporations. This is a direct consequence of the refund of a substantial part of the corporate tax as in France and the United Kingdom.

Second, American investors will be subject to substantially higher taxes on income from their operations in countries with imputation systems as compared with competing locally and other "preferred shareholder" owned enterprises operating in those countries. As a consequence, shares of EEC corporations in the hands of local owners will be worth more in the hands of Americans.

Whether the United States acts to counteract the first tendency or not obviously depends upon the relative level of tax on capital we wish to maintain. Our unilateral decision will thus determine the extent to which we remain competitive. With respect to the second tendency, the Treasury position was that the principles of free movement of capital and nondiscrimination require countries that have adopted imputation systems to grant foreign shareholders a credit with respect to distributed profits to mitigate the discriminatory benefits given to domestic shareholders. While this principle was voluntarily accepted by France and the United Kingdom in treaty agreements with respect to foreign portfolio investors, the Treasury position has been that credits should be given to direct investors as well.

An integrated tax system splits the tax on capital which is invested in corporate form between a corporation and its shareholders, with the extent of the split depending upon whether profits are retained or distributed. There is no easy or clearly acceptable solution to adapting such a system to foreign corporate investors, and it is not particularly helpful to argue about whether or not the imputed tax is a corporate or shareholder tax. But the imputation system focuses attention on the principle that discrimination against foreign investors, whether at the corporate or the shareholder level, is undesirable and inconsistent with treaty objectives. It may be consistent with the principles of an imputation system not to grant a credit on domestic intercompany distributions, but to grant it only when there is a final distribution to individual shareholders. But when distributions leave the country—including distributions to corporate shareholders—the tax credit has to be determined at the border, since the source country cannot (except with difficulty) make a final reckoning beyond that point. For various reasons, including potential escape from tax in all countries, compromises may have to be made between the treatment of foreign shareholders and domestic shareholders and this is likely to involve treaty bargaining. A major objective, however, should be to minimize discriminatory treatment.

The United Kingdom treaty, which is presently pending before the United States Senate, represents an effort to reduce the degree of discrimination between U.S. and British investors in United Kingdom corporations and gives notice that the United States has embarked on a program of negotiation and renegotiation of treaties to achieve results in keeping with the principles of nondiscrimination and free capital movements.

Under the proposed new treaty, the United Kingdom will grant a tax credit to all United States investors in British corporations with respect to the Advance Corporation Tax collected in the U.K. In the case of dividends paid by a corporation resident in the U.K. to a United States corporation which controls 10% or more of the voting stock of the United Kingdom corporation, the payment by the U.K. will equal one-half of the credit which would be payable to an individual resident in the United Kingdom, less 5% of the aggregate amount of the dividend and tax credit. In the case of other United States shareholders, the payment will equal the full credit payable to an individual resident in the United Kingdom less 15% of the aggregate amount of the dividend and the tax credit.

On the other side, beginning with 1975, the United States reduced its withholding tax on dividend income to 5% in the case of corporate direct investors—which is a change from 15% under the existing treaty—and will retain the 15% rate in the case of United Kingdom portfolio investors.

The treaty spells out in some detail the implications of the Advance Corporation Tax for United States tax credit purposes. A U.S. shareholder, whether portfolio or direct, will be considered to have received dividends consisting of cash payments from the distributing company and of the amount of the credit refunded by the government of the United Kingdom. The 5% or 15% tax withheld from such aggregate amount, as the case may be, will be treated as a withholding tax under section 901 of the Internal Revenue Code. In the case of the corporate direct investor that receives a refund of only one-half of the Advance Corporation Tax, the one-half of the tax collected and not refunded by the United Kingdom will be treated as a section 902 indirect credit. The "taxes covered" and "foreign tax credit" provision of the treaty insure a foreign tax credit on this basis.

There is increasing agreement today in the United States that it may be desirable to integrate corporate and shareholder taxation. What are the implications of such integration for United States taxation or foreign source income? How will the United States tax foreign shareholders investing in U.S. companies? What level of tax will be imposed on the foreign shareholder if there is taxation at only one level? The administration in July 1976 proposed a combination deduction for distributions to shareholders by the corporation and a partial credit for shareholders. The accompanying material stated that the foreign shareholders would automatically benefit from the deduction on distributed income but would not necessarily receive the credit against income tax liability in the form of a refund.

How would the United States tax the foreign source income of U.S. corporate investors abroad? Will the degree of integration be controlling? For example, full integration of domestic corporate and individual taxes would seem inconsistent with maintaining tax deferral on foreign earnings in foreign companies, since U.S. shareholders would not be taxed currently on the earnings of those subsidiaries. How would foreign taxes be treated? Would foreign corporate taxes be permitted as a credit against domestic personal income taxes imposed on U.S. shareholders? At present, only U.S. corporate investors are entitled to a foreign tax credit for foreign corporate taxes.

We have seen that in such fundamental areas as source of income, intercompany pricing, and allocation of deductions—which have been inherent parts of our tax laws for decades—we have only a start toward harmonization and certainty. In the case of tax integration, we are merely at the point of identifying the issues.

Multinational Enterprises and Taxation

Samuel M. Frohlich

Director of International Tax Practice
Arthur Young & Co.

I find myself in the very unusual position at the moment of having been asked to provide a rebuttal to points raised by Robert Patrick, which in large part involves views he had or shared with others in the Treasury Department during his period of government service. Over the years I have found myself more times in agreement with him than in opposition to the positions he has taken. But naturally, there were significant points of disagreement, since at the time we were viewing the same problem from very different prospectives. Therefore, on some of the issues, we will be in sharp disagreement, but for many of the other items that Mr. Patrick has referred to you, you can assume an implied agreement if I do not comment further.

As Mr. Patrick has indicated, a key area for our consideration is how the tax system of the United States meshes with the systems of other countries. Of course, no tax systems can be exactly alike. However, when the tax systems in two or more countries properly complement each other—or are made to do so by treaties—transactions involving more than one country are taxed in an equitable fashion from the standpoint of the revenues of the countries and the cost to the taxpayers involved. When the systems are not in step, considerable problems arise and double taxation frequently results.

Unfortunately, it is often the U.S. tax system, not the foreign tax system, that is out of step. In this regard, for example, the U.S. is certainly one of the very few countries in the world that taxes its incorporated entities and citizens on a worldwide basis. Further, the U.S. considers foreign corporations taxable to a considerably greater degree than most other countries. For example, the Subpart F rules tax certain types of income of controlled foreign corporations prior to repatriation of the income to the United States. Also, the "effectively connected" rules are quite extensive in their application to foreign corporations doing business in the U.S.

In addition, the requirements throughout our tax system that everything has to be converted to a U.S. tax accounting basis cause untold problems in coordinating the tax system of the U.S. with those of foreign jurisdictions. Problems arise in this regard both in terms of timing and in the absolute amount of income to be taxed in each of the jurisdictions.

The crucial way in which the U.S. tax system deals with the taxation of U.S. entities and individuals receiving foreign income to assure that only a fair amount of total tax is paid—keeping in mind the U.S. tax system's overall philosophy of worldwide taxation of its entities and individuals—is the foreign tax credit structure. I must say that in large part the foreign tax credit system has proved to be a very effective method of doing just that. The system is sophisticated but workable. In particular, through the recognition of carryovers—both two years back and five years forward—it is designed to cover long-term business developments in the international area, rather than only year-to-year results.

I must admit some concern, however, that the foreign tax credit philosophy that has existed over the last twenty-five years is changing dramatically and not for the better. Congress, in the last two years and in discussions over a longer period than that, has been taking quick, and sharp shots at the foreign tax credit. For example, we see the recent changes (1) affecting individuals stationed abroad which requires allocation of some of the foreign tax credit away; (2) limiting the use of certain amounts of foreign taxes paid by oil companies; (3) limiting the method of computing the foreign tax credit limitation from the two methods—per country and overall—to using only overall; and (4) that took place last year in Congress concerning the total elimination of the foreign tax credit, providing an unfortunate trend.

If this continues it will be even more difficult, and perhaps impossible, for U.S. corporations to operate economically outside the United States. It would not be uncommon—if the foreign tax credit were to be disallowed—to see the overall tax rate on operations in developed countries to reach or exceed 75%.

Hopefully, good business sense will prevail and the foreign tax credit will continue to be available in a meaningful form.

Another foreign tax credit matter that should receive attention is the question of what foreign taxes ere considered to be foreign *income taxes* for purposes of credit. Mr. Patrick referred to this briefly in the early portion of his discussion. There seems to be a trend to limiting the taxes that will qualify as credits. This is already a problem for a number of major international companies, but with the Tax on Value Added (TVA) representing a greater and greater slice of the total tax collections of many developed countries, its unavailability as a credit in those situations where the company bears the cost, is pushing up the overall cost of doing business around the world. Up to now this has not caused a level of taxation that would require discontinuing operations in those jurisdictions. However, the continued emphasis on TVA type of taxation, the attack on the qualification of other foreign taxes as income taxes, and the changing systems around the world will have to be reviewed carefully to assure that the U.S. foreign tax credit system continues to operate effectively.

SOURCE OF INCOME

Mr. Patrick indicated that because of the piecemeal development of the source of income rules, they are somewhat arbitrary and can cause tax inequities. While I agree that the rules are not totally tied together, I believe that they operate relatively effectively and are the most sophisticated rules of this type in any tax law with which I am familiar.

It is my view that this is an area in which tax planning, in the highest sense of this concept, is required for U.S. corporations to obtain an equitable result. For example, as mentioned by Mr. Patrick, when fees are charged for services performed in the U.S. to a foreign company—whether related or unrelated—the foreign jurisdiction will normally impose a withholding tax on the gross fee paid. However, the source of the income will be U.S. under our source rules. Some way has to be found by the U.S. corporate recipient to absorb these credits, or an overall business loss or serious double taxation would result. Utilizing these excess credits against low tax foreign source income becomes a necessary, meaningful, and appropriate accomplishment for the taxpayer and his advisors.

Further on this subject, I must admit to some concern that the IRS is trying to develop source of income rules of their own without benefit of legislation or new case law. For example, in the recently issued 1.861—8 proposed regulations, which follow, in this particular instance, the approach in the 1973 version of the proposed regulations, the source of income treatment of losses on sales of capital assets represents a new wrinkle. Under case law and the source of income regulations generally, it had been accepted by the international business community for many years that the source of income on the sale of personal property is where title passes, assuming that an artificial arrangement had not been established to obtain a specific tax benefit.

Now under the proposed 1.861—8 regulations, losses on such transactions will be allocated to the assets that gave rise to income from the property sold. Therefore, for example, on the sale of shares of a foreign corporation operating wholly abroad, a loss would be allocated foreign regardless of where the sale took place and to whom the sale was made. If there had been a gain, the source of the gain would be determined on a totally different basis—where title passed. For example, if the sale were consummated in the U.S., the gain would represent U.S. source income.

Is this a reasonable way to administer the U.S. tax law, developing one rule for the treatment of gains and a totally different rule for the treatment of losses? Whatever the rule should be, it should be the same regardless of whether a profit or loss is derived. Our tax principles should certainly not result in piecemeal rules in an attempt to prevent so-called "excessive tax planning."

A final comment on the question of source of income and the foreign tax credit limitation. Mr. Patrick implied that the per-country system is the preferable approach. Due to the worldwide nature of the operations of the companies that we are discussing here, and the different states of activities that may exist from one country to the next, I submit that our Congress in the Tax Reform Act of 1976 chose the right foreign tax credit limitation (per country) to eliminate, if one had to go. By the continued use of the overall limitation some parity and balance can be obtained for most major international companies, which would not be the case if only the per country limitation were available.

INTERCOMPANY PRICING AND SECTION 482

I agree with Mr. Patrick that safe-haven rules would be a major step forward in dealing with intercompany pricing problems. This is the aspect of the Section 482 regulations that has involved controversies of the largest dollar amounts. However, it has been my experience that the IRS agents are more likely to attack those other portions of Section 482 that can be more easily analyzed. This includes interest charges, licensing arrangements, and intercompany services.

Because of the steady attack by the IRS on these transactions in the course of examinations, I submit that they are of equal importance in terms of developing some type of safe haven recognition. Such recognition has already been given to interest.

In the case of royalties and fees, if the IRS does not allow any real latitude in charging royalties or service fees, and the foreign jurisdiction either makes it difficult to remit or does not allow a deduction locally, the taxpayer is caught in the middle. In many cases a blocked income election is not possible on technical grounds, and no treaties are in force between the U.S. and the other country. The taxpayer is then left in an impossible position. At present there are no safe havens at all for these transactions, and I think they are clearly needed particularly in dealing with developing countries.

On the general topic of intercompany allocations, it is interesting to note that more and more countries are utilizing this tax approach. Many of the countries had laws involving intercompany allocations on the books for many years but never implemented them. The United Kingdom is a good case in point. Recently they have been paying a great deal more attention to intercompany pricing transactions and have made major industry studies. The U.K. is continuing their review of these transactions to assure that reasonable pricing arrangements exist between related entities.

Mr. Patrick mentioned the incremental basis of intercompany pricing. I wholly agree with him that the incremental basis is a reasonable pricing alternative if the facts fit the use to which the taxpayer plans to employ this method. It certainly is a much used internal costing arrangement which is designed by companies to test the profitability of each of its operations. If the taxpayer uses the method fairly and properly, the IRS should administer its use accordingly.

Further, I totally agree with Patrick's comments that IRS agents should test the overall method of intercompany dealings rather than looking for unintended minor infractions. If the method employed is substantially fair, detailed analyses of accounts should not be required. Tracking down small amounts of unimportant issues can be a major administrative burden and is not an effective use of time by either party. Good faith is the keynote to the Section 482 area and must be exercised fully or arguments leading nowhere develop.

I should also note that the reference to intercompany transactions in recent treaties is a good trend; Mr. Patrick can be thanked for this development.

This should prove to be an effective way of handling cases in their later stages where there are reasonable positions in two taxing jurisdictions but a compromise has to be reached.

ALLOCATION OF EXPENSES TO FOREIGN SOURCE INCOME

This is a particularly good time to talk about this subject since the newly proposed regulations have just been issued. They were published in the November 4 Federal Register, and comments on these regulations are due December 7 with hearings to be held December 16. Clearly, the timing is such that the administration is hoping to finalize these regulations prior to the inauguration date.

The fact that these regulations are being reissued in proposed form gives recognition to the fact that the 1973 regulations were met with a great deal of strong adverse comment. The Treasury Department and Internal Revenue Service has been wrestling with these very difficult allocation rules for some time, and they seem to be making every effort to develop a sensible approach. While the effort has been great, it is the view of many that even the newly proposed regulations do not recognize the business needs and operating methods of the business community that functions on a worldwide basis.

Also, let me mention that sometimes it is a very close question as to where the Section 482 allocation rules leave off and where Section 861 concepts begin. Clearly, when a company is already in foreign tax credit limitation, it does not make a great deal of difference (from an immediate U.S. tax standpoint) which rules are brought into play, because in either case the effect is the loss of the tax benefit of a deduction. A real problem in this basic area— whether it be Section 482 or 861—is that many of the direct or indirect expenses that would ordinarily be charged or allocated to a foreign subsidiary or branch will not be accepted as deductions in the foreign country. Where the tax rate is comparable in the two countries, the overall tax effect of both jurisdictions not accepting the expenditure as an offset to income is disastrous.

On a positive note the newly proposed regulations have been made prospective for years beginning after December 31, 1976. This is a major concession by the Treasury and it cures an important problem that existed under the 1973 proposed regulations. The potential effect of the previously proposed regulations on companies with a number of open years was significant. This was particularly unfair to those companies that had made a reasonable effort to comply fully with the principles of allocating expenses to foreign source income but were not in a position to comply with specific rules that were not even issued when they made their determinations. Due to the change in the overall concept in the 1973 proposed regulations—which has been followed through to a major extent in the 1976 proposal—their prospective nature is certainly the proper approach.

However, in my view, the proposed regulations are still trying to do too much. They call for exactitude in an area where only reasonableness is possible. When taxpayers can demonstrate that they have made a realistic effort to arrive at foreign source income, that should be sufficient. If, on the other hand, the taxpayer has disregarded the clear intention of the statute, the IRS should examine the situation vigorously and take strong measures to assure that the taxpayer complies with the law.

One of the major problems with the two sets of proposed regulations is the disregard of the taxable year concept for allocation and apportionment purposes. The taxable year concept is one of the cardinal principles of the tax law and should not be disturbed in a limited situation such as this. Rather than requiring allocation on the basis of prior income, prospective income, or even to a category of income which may never arise, the results of operations for the taxable year itself should be utilized except in very rare circumstances. The basic rule of allocation should certainly be to allocate deductions, first to income to which it clearly relates, and where such relationship does not exist, the remaining pool of expenses should normally be allocated on a gross income basis. If this is done evenhandedly and consistently, serious distortions are not likely to arise.

Further, in the new proposals—despite the advantage to taxpayers—it seems somewhat unrealistic to call for a series of optional calculations for interest and research and development allocations. For large companies in particular, the development of the information necessary to make the calculations called for will be extremely difficult. It is recognized that these are designed to be safe-haven options but it also may have the effect of representing the only escape valve that the IRS will accept from a too harsh application of the regular allocation rules. The administrative burden of developing all of the information required to make computations on a number of different bases may be too great. Rather, an overall approach, such as described in the previous paragraph, should develop reasonable results while recognizing the serious drawbacks of a major information-gathering effort that would have to be instituted to make computations for both interest and research and development under two or even three methods.

Mr. Patrick has summarized the present state of the rules and referred to the various options that relate to allocation of research and development expenses—the portion of the regulations that has received by far the most interest of the business community. I'll try not to repeat the points made but rather comment on some of the issues that were raised and refer briefly to a few others.

The research and development allocation approach that would seem to have broad application to a number of international companies is the incremental method. This method should certainly be included in the regulations for use when the R&D effort is specifically entered into for the development of products for the U.S. market, and overseas use is at the second stage of development. If this is not the company's business method, for example when overseas involvement is as heavy as U.S. involvement from the very beginning, then this method would not apply. But, since it fits the pattern of so many companies, it should not be disregarded totally in the regulations, as is the case at present. In fact, this is often the way that these companies handle the allocations operationally in determining their own profit pools.

Another method of spreading R&D costs that I have always felt generated very fair results is a cost-sharing arrangement such as the one included in the regulations under Section 482. If, in fact, new developments in one location, say in the U.S., are shared with related companies around the world on a current and regular basis, what better way to spread those costs than to spread the initial costs to all of the affiliates that benefit from the R&D? It is surprising that more companies, with affiliates in high tax countries have not entered into this type of arrangement.

Of course, a major problem in utilizing this method is whether the foreign jurisdiction will accept the charge. I would think that most developed countries would be much more likely to accept properly evidenced charges as deductions at the stage that the expenditure is incurred, than they would be if the charge represented an allocation or apportionment in a later year of overall costs which cannot be as closely related to the operation in the country as a cost-sharing charge would be.

It should be noted that the 50% allocation on the basis of the geographical location of the R&D activity, which is now included in the regulations, was a major concession made by the IRS and should be applauded. However, again this approach needs careful review and is too all encompassing. Since the methods of operation of companies vary so greatly, some latitude should be given to choose a method which, if it can be defended, should be acceptable to the Internal Revenue Service.

While I agree that the previously described allocation of research and development expenditures will often be the most important item to a large group of taxpayers, the effect of the excessive attention given to this subject has been that some of the other areas—such as overhead, the treatment of losses, the treatment of state taxes, and even the allocation of interest—have not received the required consideration. Particularly the allocation of overhead and the treatment of losses should have been modified in the development of new proposed regulations. For overhead, it is my view that the system referred to previously—direct allocation—in which a clear relationship between income and expenses exists, and everything else in the pot to be allocated to all income would be the most preferable method. Again, consistency and fairness is the important consideration.

As to the allocation of losses on sale of capital assets, I have referred in the "source of income" section of this paper to the unfortunate precedent that would be set in treating losses in one fashion and gains on similar transactions in another. The title passage rule on sale of personal property, except in artificially arranged transactions, has been established by the courts as a reasonable rule in a number of well thought out decisions. It is inappropriate to tamper with this rule for such a limited purpose.

Just one final comment on the allocation rules. In my view one major problem is that the administration in writing these rules starts with a very defensive attitude. They start with the premise that there are widespread unwarranted violations of the allocation rules and that, unless all avenues of possible benefits are closed, the violations will continue in the future.

In my view, a more positive attitude should be demonstrated by the IRS and it is likely to be infectious. There should be general rules that provide that reasonable, consistent, realistic allocations will be accepted. If, however, the taxpayer takes a "greedy" approach or shows disregard of the principles of the statute involved, the Internal Revenue Service should have the authority to crack down hard.

SOME FINAL REMARKS

Mr. Patrick has covered many of the major points of interest concerning recent developments in the treaty area; he was very involved with treaty matters during his years in Treasury and I am in basic agreement with his view on this subject.

One point that I would like to cover briefly is the Competent Authority procedure to which he referred. It has been my experience recently that the procedure is working much more effectively than in the past. This is due to the substantial effort that has been made by the Internal Revenue Service to attract companies to utilize this procedure. In prior years the procedure took so long to develop to a conclusion that companies could not afford the time and expenditure of waiting out the period of settlement. Now the Service has developed close ties with the Competent Authority personnel of our treaty partners and has been able to settle a large number of cases in a relatively short period of time. The credibility that has been developed should add further impetus to this procedure designed to prevent double taxation.

Unfortunately, double taxation problems do not end with treaty countries. Similar problems arise in transactions involving operations in nontreaty countries. These situations have to be handled fairly with the realistic recognition that it is unlikely that treaties will be negotiated and signed with these countries in the near future. The U.S. may have to bend a bit for the benefit of their own taxpayers without giving taxpayers the impression that the U.S. will automatically absorb the tax liability. The taxpayer should be able to demonstrate a full effort to obtain the proper tax result in the foreign jurisdiction.

On another matter, as Mr. Patrick indicated, the clear trend in developed countries is away from the classic tax system to an integrated corporate-shareholder tax system. This would involve either a split rate tax system, such as in Germany, or an imputation system, such as exists in France and the U.K. I do not believe the U.S. has any choice but to give careful study to these systems and seriously consider adopting one of the methods. Otherwise, the overall tax results to U.S. companies operating internationally may be so out of step with the tax cost to foreign companies that it will be impossible for the U.S. to compete effectively. It should be noted that despite the differing systems, a reasonable tax result has been obtained with the U.K., for example, under the revised treaty. I do not believe though that we can bank on a forceful negotiator such as Mr. Patrick to lead us continually through the many problems that might have arisen if the treaty had not been developed with a view to coordinating the two tax systems.

One final shot: in my view there has been too great a concern in the recent past by the administration and the Congress on the tax contest between the government and its U.S. corporate taxpayers and too little concern as to the worldwide income that will be given up if international ventures become unprofitable to the potential U.S. participant.

Other countries such as Germany will gladly take the business and will be able to do so if their profit line benefits significantly from a lower tax bite in their home country.

The competitive aspects of international business must get a greater emphasis in our tax legislation. It is my understanding that over the last ten years the balance of remittances by U.S. corporations to the United States has far exceeded the outflow of investment. This was the case during the period of the Foreign Direct Investment Program which was the first time that exchange controls were instituted to affect the international operations of U.S. companies seriously. Even though the international companies involved were already carrying their share in terms of being on the plus side of the balance of payments, these companies were asked to stretch even further and met these additional commitments.

The recent changes in the Tax Reform Act of 1976 and previous international tax changes in the spring of 1975 indicate that international companies are still an easy target. For example, the changes in the "earned income exclusion" affecting employees of U.S. companies working abroad is a major negative step in the international competitive arena. These changes involve reducing the amount of the exclusion, computing the tax at higher effective tax rates, and loss of a portion of the foreign tax credits. For employers having a number of employees abroad—such as those in the contracting business—the economics of their prior arrangements change significantly. There will be cases in which to bid on contracts, a U.S. contractor will have to employ more lower cost foreign employees, local or third country nationals, or may not even be able to bid on the contract at all because its costs will far exceed those of its foreign competitors. How can this help to bring about a reduction of unemployment in the U.S.? In some cases, U.S. individuals will have to come back to the United States and add to the already high unemployment rate in the construction business. This is just one example of what can happen in an unwarranted attack on multinationals.

It should be noted that a Ways and Means Task Force is presently studying certain international tax issues, including the question of deferral. The long-range aspects should be made known to this group as well as to other groups in Washington involved in international business issues. We should try to help them develop reasonable rules to the benefit of the U.S. economy.

The international company has a strong role to play. It should not be made to fight in the international arena with both hands tied behind its back. A combination of high tax rates and heavy administrative burdens will have this result. The goal of developing the U.S. and world economy should be kept constantly in mind and then the international company will retain its position as a major economic force for the United States.

Appendixes

The materials within these appendixes are presented as they were at the time this lecture series took place in September-December 1976.

APPENDIX I

Founder and Associate Members of

IASC

COUNTRY   ACCOUNTANCY BODY

Founder Members:

Australia   The Institute of Chartered Accountants in Australia
                 Australian Society of Accountants

Canada   The Canadian Institute of Chartered Accountants in conjunc-
                     tion with the General Accountants' Association and The
                     Society of Industrial Accountants of Canada

France   Ordre des Experts Comptables et des Comptables Agréés
Germany   Institut der Wirtschaftsprüfer in Deutschland e.V.
                 Wirtschaftsprüferkammer

Japan   The Japanese Institute of Certified Public Accountants

Mexico   Instituto Mexicano de Contadores Públicos, A.C.

Netherlands   Nederlands Instituut van Registeraccountants

UK & Ireland   The Institute of Chartered Accountants in England and Wales
                 The Institute of Chartered Accountants of Scotland
                 The Institute of Chartered Accountants in Ireland
                 The Association of Certified Accountants

International Accounting Standards Committee, News release, August 1976,
pp. 3, 4.

The Institute of Cost and Management Accountants

The Chartered Institute of Public Finance and Accountancy

USA   American Institute of Certified Public Accountants

Associate Members:

Bangladesh   The Institute of Chartered Accountants of Bangladesh

Belgium   Collège National des Experts Comptables de Belgique

Institut des Reviseurs d'Entreprises

Institut Belge des Reviseurs de Banques

Denmark   Foreningen Af Statsautoriserede Revisorer

Fiji   The Fiji Institute of Accountants

Ghana   The Institute of Chartered Accountants (Ghana)

Greece   Institute of Certified Public Accountants of Greece

Hong Kong   Hong Kong Society of Accountants

India   The Institute of Chartered Accountants of India

The Institute of Cost and Works Accountants of India

Israel   The Institute of Certified Public Accountants in Israel

Jamaica   The Institute of Chartered Accountants of Jamaica

Korea   Korean Institute of Certified Public Accountants

Luxembourg   Ordre des Experts Comptables Luxembourgeois

Malaysia   The Malaysian Association of Certified Public Accountants

Malta   The Malta Institute of Accountants

New Zealand   New Zealand Society of Accountants

Nigeria   The Institute of Chartered Accountants of Nigeria

Pakistan   Pakistan Institute of Industrial Accountants

The Institute of Chartered Accountants of Pakistan

Philippines   Philippine Institute of Certified Public Accountants

Rhodesia   The Rhodesia Society of Chartered Accountants

Sierra Leone	The Association of Accountants in Sierra Leone
Singapore	Singapore Society of Accountants
South Africa	The National Council of Chartered Accountants (S.A.)
Sri Lanka	The Institute of Chartered Accountants of Sri Lanka
Trinidad and Tobago	The Institute of Chartered Accountants of Trinidad and Tobago
Yugoslavia	Yugoslav Association of Accountant and Financial Experts Social Accounting Service of Yugoslavia
Zambia	Zambia Association of Accountants

International Accounting Standard 1

Disclosure of Accounting Policies

International Accounting Standard I comprises paragraphs 16–23 of this Statement. The Standard should be read in the context of paragraphs 1–15 of this Statement and of the Preface to Statements of International Accounting Standards.

16. Going concern, consistency, and accrual are fundamental accounting assumptions. Where fundamental accounting assumptions are following financial statements, disclosure of such assumptions is not required. If a fundamental accounting assumption is not followed, that fact should be disclosed together with the reasons.

17. Prudence, substance over form, and materiality should govern the selection and application of accounting policies.

18. Financial statements should include clear and concise disclosure of all significant accounting policies which have been used.

19. The disclosure of the significant accounting policies used should be an integral part of the financial statements. The policies should normally be disclosed in one place.

20. Wrong or inappropriate treatment of items in balance sheets, income statements or profit and loss accounts, or other statements is not rectified either by disclosure of accounting policies used or by notes or explanatory material.

21. Financial statements should show corresponding figures for the preceding period.

22. A change in an accounting policy that has a material effect in the current period or may have a material effect in subsequent periods should be disclosed together with the reasons. The effect of the change should, if material, be disclosed and quantified.

23. This International Accounting Standard becomes operative for financial statements covering periods beginning on or after 1 January 1975.

International Accounting Standard 2

Valuation and Presentation of Inventories in the Context of the Historical Cost System

International Accounting Standard 2 comprises paragraphs 20–36 of this Statement. The Standard should be read in the context of paragraphs 1–19 of this Statement and of the Preface to Statements of International Accounting Standards.

20. Inventories should be valued at the lower of historical cost and net realisable value.

ASCERTAINMENT OF HISTORICAL COST

21. The historical cost of manufactured inventories should include a systematic allocation of those production overhead costs that relate to putting the inventories in their present location and condition. Allocation of fixed production overhead to the costs of conversion should be based on the capacity of the facilities. If fixed production overhead has been entirely or substantially excluded from the valuation of inventories on the grounds that it does not directly relate to putting the inventories in their present location and condition, that fact should be disclosed.

22. Overheads other than production overhead should be included as part of inventory cost only to the extent that they clearly relate to putting the inventories in their present location and condition.

23. Exceptional amounts of wasted material, labour, or other expenses should be included as part of inventory cost.

24. Except as set out in paragraphs 25 and 26, the historical cost of inventories should be accounted for using the FIFO formula or a weighted average cost formula.

25. Inventories of items that are not ordinarily interchangeable or goods manufactured and segregated for specific projects should be accounted for by using specific identification of their individual costs.

26. The LIFO or base stock formulas may be used provided that there is disclosure of the difference between the amount of the inventories as shown in the balance sheet and either (a) the lower of the amount arrived at in accordance with paragraph 24 and net realisable value or (b) the lower of current cost at the balance sheet date and net realisable value.

27. Techniques such as the standard cost method of valuing products or the retail method of valuing merchandise may be used for convenience if they approximate consistently the results that would be obtained in accordance with paragraph 20.

ASCERTAINMENT OF NET REALISABLE VALUE

28. Estimates of net realisable value should be based not on temporary fluctuations of price or cost but on the most reliable evidence available at the time the estimates are made as to what the inventories are expected to realise.

29. Inventories should be written down to net realisable value item by item or by groups of similar items; whichever method is used should be consistently applied.

30. The net realisable value of the quantity of inventory held to satisfy firm sales contracts should be based on the contract price. If the sales contracts are for less than the inventory quantities held, net realisable value for the excess should be based on general market prices.[2]

31. Normal quantities of materials and other supplies held for incorporation in the production of goods should not be written down below historical cost if the finished products in which they will be incorporated are expected to be realised at or above historical cost. Nevertheless, a decline in the price of materials may indicate that the historical cost of finished products to be produced will exceed net realisable value in which event a writedown of the materials inventories should be made; in this event, replacement cost may be the best available measure of the net realisable value of those materials.

PRESENTATION IN THE FINANCIAL STATEMENTS

32. The profit and loss of the period should be charged with the amount of inventories sold or used (unless allocated to other asset accounts) and with the amount of any writedown in the period to net realisable value.

[2]Firm sales contracts beyond inventory quantities held, and firm purchase contracts are beyond the scope of this Statement.

33. Inventories should be sub-classified in balance sheets or in notes to the financial statements in a manner which is appropriate to the business and so as to indicate the amounts held in each of the main categories.

34. The accounting policies adopted for the purpose of valuation of inventories, including the cost formula used, should be disclosed. A change in an accounting policy related to inventories that has a material effect in the current period or may have a material effect in subsequent periods should be disclosed together with the reasons. The effect of the change should, if material, be disclosed and quantified. (See International Accounting Standard 1, Disclosure of Accounting Policies.)

35. If items are shown under the caption "Inventories" other than those comprehended by the definition in paragraph 4, their nature, amounts and basis of valuation should be disclosed.

EFFECTIVE DATE

36. This International Accounting Standard becomes operative for financial statements covering periods beginning on or after 1 January 1976.

International Accounting Standard 3

Consolidated Financial Statements

International Accounting Standard 3 comprises paragraphs 34–52 of this Statement. The Standard should be read in the context of paragraphs 1–33 of this Statement and of the Preface to Statements of International Accounting Standards.

CONSOLIDATED FINANCIAL STATEMENTS

34. A parent company should issue consolidated financial statements, except that it need not do so when it is a wholly-owned subsidiary.

35. A parent company which issues consolidated financial statements should consolidate all subsidiaries, foreign and domestic, as defined in paragraph 4, other than those referred to in paragraphs 36 and 37.

36. A subsidiary should be excluded from consolidation if:

(a) control is to be temporary, or

(b) the subsidiary operates under conditions in which severe long-term restrictions on the transfer of funds impair control by the parent company over the subsidiary's assets and operations.

37. A subsidiary may be excluded from consolidation if its activities are so dissimilar from those of the other companies in the group that better information for the parent company shareholders and other users of the statements would be provided by presenting separate financial statements in respect of such subsidiary with the consolidated financial statements.

38. A company in which a group does not have control, but in which a group:

(a) owns more than half the equity capital, but less than half the voting power, or

(b) has the power to control, by statute or agreement, the financial and operating policies of the management of the company, with or without more than one half of the equity interest.

may be treated as a subsidiary and consolidated in the consolidated financial statements. In such circumstances, the reasons for consolidating the company should be disclosed.

39. Uniform accounting policies should preferably be followed by companies in the consolidated financial statements. There should be disclosure of different accounting policies used, and of the proportion of assets and liabilities to which different accounting policies have been applied if they are included in a single balance sheet classification.

THE EQUITY METHOD OF ACCOUNTING FOR INVESTMENTS

40. Investments in associated companies as defined in paragraph 4 and in subsidiaries which are not consolidated for the reasons stated in paragraph 37 should be included in the consolidated financial statements under the equity method of accounting.

41. As from the date that

(a) a subsidiary ceases to be consolidated for the reason stated in paragraph 36(b), or

(b) an investee ceases to fall within the definition of a subsidiary and does not become an associated company, or an investee ceases to fall within the definition of an associated company.

the investment should be stated in the consolidated balance sheet at the carrying amount under the equity method at that date. From that date, the investor should discontinue accruing its share of the subsequent profits or losses of the investee.

42. If the carrying amount of an investment dealt with under the equity method, and of investments referred to in paragraph 41, exceeds the value of the investment and that difference is other than temporary, there should be appropriate recognition of the decline in value. Provision should be made for a decline in value of each such investment; individual investments should not be aggregated for evaluation in total.

FINANCIAL STATEMENT PRESENTATION

43. The minority interest in the equity of consolidated companies should be classified in the consolidated balance sheet as a separate item and should not be shown as part of shareholders' equity. The minority interest in the profits or losses of such companies should be shown separately in the consolidated income statement.

44. Investments accounted for under the equity method of accounting should be appropriately classified in the consolidated balance sheet and the investor's share of profits or losses should be disclosed as a separate item in the consolidated income statement. If the profits or losses for the period include unusual items, the investor's share of the unusual items should be shown separately in accordance with the accounting policies applicable to the investor.

45. A gain or loss on a sale of shares in an investee by an investor should be recognised in the consolidated income statement. The amount recognised should be the difference at the time of sale between the proceeds of sale and the carrying amoung in the consolidated financial statements of the shares sold.

DISCLOSURE

46. The disclosure of accounting policies—see International Accounting Standard 1, Disclosure of Accounting Policies—should include a description of the bases on which subsidiaries and associated companies have been dealt with.

47. The following disclosures should be made in the consolidated financial statements:

    (a) An appropriate listing and description of significant subsidiaries and associated companies and, in respect of such companies, differences in reporting dates from that of the parent company, unless disclosed in statements accompanying the consolidated financial statements.

    (b) The reasons for not consolidating a subsidiary.

    (c) The nature of the relationship between the parent company and a company that is not a subsidiary but is treated as a subsidiary in consolidation, as described in paragraph 38.

(d) The amounts relating to any signficant unadjusted transactions occuring between the dates of investors' and investees' financial statements.

(e) An analysis of the amounts under each significant balance sheet and income statement caption if necessary to provide a fair disclosure of the exposure to exceptional risks of operating in other countries, including the risk of foreign currency exchange rate fluctuations.

(f) The extent to which there are statutory or contractual restrictions on the distribution of the acccumulated retained income of the group.

48. When a subsidiary is excluded from consolidation in accordance with paragraph 37, separate financial statements in respect of that subsidiary should supplement the consolidated financial statements. The supplementary statements may be presented in condensed form provided they give adequate disclosure, including particulars of intra-group balances and the nature of transactions with the remainder of the group. There should be a reconciliation of the amount at which the results of operations of the excluded subsidiary are stated in the supplementary financial statements, and the amount included in the consolidated income statement in respect of that subsidiary. For the purposes of this supplementary disclosure the financial statements of two or more subsidiaries with similar operations may be combined.

49. If a subsidiary is excluded from consolidation because of the restriction described in paragraph 36(b), the following disclosures should be made with respect to such investment:

(a) the name of the investee and the group's share in the net assets of the investee,

(b) the carrying value of the investment in the consolidated financial statements,

(c) the dividends received by the group during the period,

(d) the profits or losses for the period, with unusual items separately stated, and

(e) the amounts of any write-downs or adjustments to consolidated net income in the current period.

TRANSITIONAL PROVISIONS

50. On the first occasion that consolidated financial statements are presented, comparative figures should be shown in respect of the consolidated income statement if it is not practicable to do so. In all subsequent years full comparative figures should be shown—see International Accounting Standard 1, disclosure of Accounting Policies.

51. On the first occasion of the application of the equity method, there should be disclosure of the investee's income of earlier periods which is attributable to the investor,

and of any write-down of the investment at that time to recognize a decline in its value.

EFFECTIVE DATE

52. The provisions of this International Accounting Standard become operative for financial statements covering periods beginning on or after 1 January 1977.

International Accounting Standard 4

Depreciation Accounting

International Accounting Standard 4 comprises paragraphs 13–19 of this Statement. The Standard should be read in the context of paragraphs 1–12 of this Statement and of the Preface to Statements of International Accounting Standards.

13. The depreciable amount of a depreciable asset should be allocated on a systematic basis to each accounting period during the useful life of the asset.

14. The depreciation method selected should be applied consistently from period to period unless altered circumstances justify a change. In an accounting period in which the method is changed, the effect should be quantified and disclosed and the reason for the change should be stated.

15. The useful life of a depreciable asset should be estimated after considering the following factors:

(a) expected physical wear and tear
(b) obsolescence
(c) legal or other limits on the use of the asset.

16. The useful lives of major depreciable assets or classes of depreciable assets should be reviewed periodically and depreciation rates adjusted for the current and future periods if expectations are significantly different from the previous estimates. The effect of the change should be disclosed in the accounting period in which the change takes place.

17. The valuation bases used for determining the amounts at which depreciable assets are stated should be included with the disclosure of other accounting policies—see International Accounting Standard 1, Disclosure of Accounting Policies.

18. The following should be disclosed for each major class of depreciable asset:

(a) the depreciation methods used

(b) the useful lives or the depreciation rates used

(c) total depreciation allocated for the period

(d) the gross amount of depreciable assets and the related accumulated depreciation.

EFFECTIVE DATE

19. This International Accounting Standard becomes operative for financial statements covering periods beginning on or after 1 January 1977.

International Accounting Standard 5

Information to be Disclosed in Financial Statements

International Accounting Standard 5 comprises paragraphs 6–19 of this Statement. The Standard should be read in the context of paragraphs 1–5 of this Statement and of the Preface to Statements of International Accounting Standards.

GENERAL DISCLOSURES

6. All material information should be disclosed that is necessary to make the financial statements clear and understandable.

7. The name of the enterprise, the country of incorporation, the balance sheet date, and the period covered by the financial statements should be stated. A brief description of the nature of the activities of the enterprise, the legal form of the enterprise, and the currency in terms of which the financial statements are expressed should be given if they are not otherwise apparent.

8. The amounts and classifications of items should be supplemented if necessary by additional information to make their meanings clear. Significant items should not be included with, or offset against, other items, without separate identification.

9. Financial statements should show corresponding figures for the preceding period.

SPECIFIC DISCLOSURES—BALANCE SHEET

General

10. The following disclosures should be made:
    (a) Restrictions on the title to assets
    (b) Security given in respect of liabilities
    (c) The methods of providing for pension and retirement plans
    (d) Contingent assets and contingent liabilities, quantified if possible
    (e) Amounts committed for future capital expenditure.

LONG-TERM ASSETS

11. *Property, plant and equipment*—The following items should be disclosed:
    (a) Land and buildings
    (b) Plant and equipment
    (c) Other categories of assets, suitably identified
    (d) Accumulated depreciation.
Separate disclosure should be made of leaseholds and of assets being acquired on instalment purchase plans.

12. *Other long-term assets*—The following items should be disclosed separately, including, if applicable, the method and period of depreciation and any unusual write-offs during the period:
    (a) Long-term investments
        Investments in subsidiaries
        Investments in associated companies
        Other investments, stating the market value of listed investments, if different from the carrying amount in the financial statements
    (b) Long-term receivables
        Accounts and notes receivable—trade
        Receivables from directors
        Intercompany[1] receivables
        Associated company receivables
        Other

[1]The term "intercompany" used in this Statement refers to the presentation in the financial statements of balances or transactions between:
    (a) A parent company and its subsidiaries
    (b) A subsidiary and its parent company or other subsidiaries in the group.

(c) Goodwill

(d) Patents, trademarks, and similar assets

(e) Expenditures carried forward, for example, preliminary expenses, re-organisation expenses, and deferred taxes.

CURRENT ASSETS

13. The following items should be disclosed separately:
   (a) Cash

   Cash includes cash on hand and current and other accounts with banks. Cash which is not immediately available for use, for example, balances frozen in foreign banks by exchange restrictions, should be disclosed.

   (b) Marketable securities, other than long-term investments

   The market value should be disclosed if different from the carrying amount in the financial statements.

   (c) Receivables

   Accounts and notes receivable—trade

   Receivables from directors

   Intercompany receivables

   Associated company receivables

   Other receivables and prepaid expenses

   (d) Inventories

LONG-TERM LIABILITIES

14. The following items should be disclosed separately, excluding the portion repayable within one year:
   (a) Secured loans
   (b) Unsecured loans
   (c) Intercompany loans
   (d) Loans from associated companies.

A summary of the interest rates, repayment terms, covenants, subordinations, conversion features and amounts of unamortised premium or discount should be shown.

15. The following items should be disclosed separately:
   (a) Bank loans and overdrafts
   (b) Current portions of long-term liabilities
   (c) Payables

   Accounts and notes payable—trade

   Payables to directors

Intercompany payables
Associated company payables
Taxes on income
Dividends payable
Other payables and accrued expenses

OTHER LIABILITIES AND PROVISIONS

16. The significant items included in other liabilities and in provisions and accruals should be separately disclosed. Examples of such items are deferred taxes, deferred income and provisions for pensions.

SHAREHOLDERS' INTERESTS

17. The following disclosures should be made separately:
   (a) Share capital
       For each class of share capital:
           The number or amount of shares authorised, issued and outstanding.[2]
           The capital not yet paid in
           The par or legal value per share
           The movement in share capital accounts during the period
           The rights, preferences, and restrictions with respect to the distribution of
               dividends and to the repayment of capital
           Cumulative preferred dividends in arrears
           Reacquired shares
           Shares reserved for future issuance under options and sales contracts, in-
               cluding the terms and amounts.
   (b) Other equity, indicating the movement for the period and any restrictions on
       distribution
           Capital paid in excess of par value (share premium)
           Revaluation surplus
           Reserves
           Retained earnings.

[2]Shares outstanding refers to shares other than those held as "treasury stock." Treasury stock are a company's shares which have been acquired by the issuing company or a consolidated subsidiary company and are legally available for reissue or resale. This practice is not permitted in some countries.

SPECIFIC DISCLOSURES—INCOME STATEMENT

18. The following information should be disclosed:
    (a) Sales or other operating revenues
    (b) Depreciation
    (c) Interest income
    (d) Income from investments
    (e) Interest expense
    (f) Taxes on income
    (g) Unusual charges
    (h) Unusual credits
    (i) Significant intercompany transactions
    (j) Net income.

EFFECTIVE DATE

19. This International Accounting Standard becomes operative for financial statements covering periods beginning on or after 1 January 1977.

EXPOSURE DRAFT 6

International Accounting Standard

Accounting Treatment of Changing Prices

> *International Accounting Standard comprises paragraphs 15–20 of this Statement. The Standard should be read in the context of paragraphs 1–14 of this Statement and of the Preface to Statements of International Accounting Standards.*

15. Enterprises should present in their financial statements information that represents a systematic response to specific price changes or to changes in the general level of prices, or to both. The response which has been adopted should be explained.

16. Information that represents a systematic response to specific price changes should consist of financial statements in which the balance sheet and the income statement reflect current prices.

17. Information that represents a systematic response to changes in the general level

of prices should consist of financial statements in which all amounts are stated in a unit defined in terms of the general purchasing power of money at the balance sheet date.

18. Information that represents a systematic response to both specific price changes and changes in the general level of prices should consist of financial statements combining features of each of the systems referred to in paragraphs 16 and 17.

19. The information referred to in paragraphs 16, 17 and 18 may be presented as supplementary information, in which event, it may be in a condensed form.

20. This International Accounting Standard becomes operative for financial statements covering periods beginning on or after
(Note: See headnote to the Introduction.)

EXPOSURE DRAFT 7

International Accounting Standard

Statement of Source and Application of Funds

International Accounting Standard comprises paragraphs 15–19 of this Statement. The Standard should be read in the context of paragraphs 1–14 of this Statement and of the Preface to Statements of International Accounting Standards.

15. A statement summarising the financing and investing activites of an enterprise during the period, including those that do not directly affect working capital, should be included as part of the financial statements. The period covered by the funds statement should be the same as for the income statement. Corresponding figures for the preceding period should be shown.

16. If a consolidated balance sheet and a consolidated income statement are presented, a funds statement should be prepared on a consolidated basis.

17. The net amount of funds provided from or used in the operations of the enterprise should be presented in the funds statement separately from other sources or uses of funds. Unusual items should be separately disclosed.

18. Each enterprise should adopt the format for the presentation of the funds statement which is most informative in its circumstances but in all cases, the changes in individual working capital items, for example, inventories, accounts receivable, ac-

counts payable and cash and cash equivalents, should be disclosed in the funds statement.

EFFECTIVE DATE

19. This International Accounting Standard becomes operative for financial statements covering periods beginning on or after—

This Appendix does not form part of the International Accounting Standard. The examples are illustrative only.

Example 1

OPERATING COMPANY LIMITED AND SUBSIDIARIES
STATEMENT OF SOURCE AND APPLICATION OF FUNDS
FOR THE YEARS ENDED DECEMBER 31

	This Year	Last Year
SOURCE OF FUNDS		
From operations:		
Net income before unusual items	1,000	900
Adjustments for items not involving funds:		
Depreciation	300	275
Minority interest in consolidated income	100	75
Income from associated companies reported on the equity method 200 less dividends received of 50	(150)	—
Total funds from operations	1250	1250
Unusual item (appropriately described)	450	—
Shares issued in part consideration of the acquisition of subsidiary*	250	—
Long-term debt issued	100	—
Reduction in accounts receivable	200	(400)
Increase in accounts payable	100	(50)
TOTAL	2350	800
APPLICATION OF FUNDS		
Dividends paid to minority interest	25	20
Dividends paid to shareholders	400	350
Purchase of property, plant and equipment	600	300
Acquisition of subsidiary company limited*	300	—
Long-term debt redeemed	800	—
Increase in inventory	100	30
TOTAL	2,225	700
NET INCREASE IN CASH AND CASH EQUIVALENTS**	125	100

*SUMMARY OF THE NET ASSETS ACQUIRED AND CONSIDERATION GIVEN IN THE ACQUISITION OF SUBSIDIARY COMPANY LIMITED

NET ASSETS ACQUIRED		CONSIDERATION GIVEN	
Fixed assets	275		
Inventories	100		
Long-term payables	(75)		
	300	Shares issued	250
Cash acquired	50	Cash paid	100
Total	350	Total	350

**This comprises cash at hand and in bank and short-term bank deposits, less bank borrowings.

Example 2

OPERATING COMPANY LIMITED AND SUBSIDIARIES
STATEMENT OF SOURCE AND APPLICATION OF FUNDS
FOR THE YEARS ENDED DECEMBER 31

	This Year	Last Year
SOURCE OF FUNDS		
FROM OPERATIONS:		
Net income before unusual items	1,000	900
Adjustments for items not involving funds:		
Depreciation	300	275
Minority interest in consolidated income 100 (last year —75) less dividends to minority interest of 25 (last year —20)	75	55
Income from associated companies reported on the equity method 200 less dividends received of 50	(150)	—
Total funds from operations	1,225	1,230
Unusual item (appropriately described)	450	—
Shares issued in part consideration of the acquisition of subsidiary*	250	—
Long-term debt issued*	175	—
TOTAL	2,100	1,230
APPLICATION OF FUNDS		
Dividends paid to shareholders	400	350
Purchase of property, plant and equipment*	875	300
Long-term debt redeemed	800	—
Net increase in working	25	580
TOTAL	2,100	1,230

*SUMMARY OF THE NET ASSETS ACQUIRED AND CONSIDERATION GIVEN IN
THE ACQUISITION OF SUBSIDIARY COMPANY LIMITED

NET ASSETS ACQUIRED		CONSIDERATION GIVEN	
Fixed assets	275		
Inventories	100		
Long-term payables	(75)		
	300	Shares issued	250
Cash Acquired	50	Cash paid	100
Total	350	Total	350

**ANALYSIS OF CHANGES IN WORKING CAPITAL ITEMS:		*This Year*		*Last Year*	
Increases in working capital					
Cash		125		100	
Inventory (including 100 from acquired subsidiary)		200	325	30	130
Decreases in working capital					
Accounts receivable		200		(400)	
Accounts payable		100	300	(50)	(450)
Net increase in working capital			25		580

EXPOSURE DRAFT 8

International Accounting Standard

The Treatment in the Income Statement of Unusual Items and Changes in Accounting Estimates and Accounting Policies

International Accounting Standard comprises paragraphs 24–30 of this Statement. The Standard should be read in the context of paragraphs 1–23 of this Statement and of the Preface to Statements of International Accounting Standards.

24. Income from the ordinary activities of the enterprise during the period should be disclosed in the income statement as part of net income. Each unusual item which is included in net income should be separately disclosed together with an explanation of its nature.

25. A change in accounting estimate does not bring an item within the definition of an unusual item or a prior period item. Any such change should be accounted for as part of income from the ordinary activities of the enterprise in (a) the period of change if the change affects the period only, or (b) the period of change and future periods if the change affects both.

26. A change in an accounting policy should be made only if the adoption of a different accounting policy is required by statute or by an accounting standard setting body or because the management of the enterprise believes that the change would result in a fairer presentation of the financial statements of an enterprise.

27. The cumulative adjustments, if any, resulting from changes in accounting policies should be either (a) separately disclosed in the current income statement as part of net

income, or (b) reported by adjusting opening retained income in financial statements for the current period and amending the comparative information in respect of prior years which is included in the financial statements. In either case the disclosure relating to these items should be adequate to facilitate comparisons of the figures for the periods presented.

28. If there is a change in an accounting estimate or a change in an accounting policy that has a material effect in the current period, or may have a material effect in subsequent periods, the effect of the change should be disclosed and quantified together with the reasons for the change.

29. If a change in the nature or composition of a reporting entity has the effect of making it a new reporting entity, all comparative figures presented should be amended to the basis used in the new reporting entity.

EFFECTIVE DATE

30. This International Accounting Standard becomes operative for financial statements covering periods beginning on or after 1 January 1978. (Note: This date is provisional.)

APPENDIX III

Amended Proposal for a Fourth Directive

on

"The Annual Accounts of Limited Liability Companies"

The Council of the European Communities,

Having regard to the Treaty establishing the European Economic Community, and in particular Article 54(3)(g) thereof:

Having regard to the proposal from the Commission;

Having regard to the Opinion of the European Parliament;

Having regard to the Opinion of the Economic and Social Committee;

Whereas coordination of the national provisions concerning the presentation and contents of the annual accounts and report, methods of valuation and publication of those documents in respect of the société anonyme, the Aktiengesellschaft, the società per azioni and the naamloze vennootschap and in respect of the société à responsabilité limitée, the Gesellschaft mit beschränkter Haftung, the società à responsabilità

Supplement 6/1974, Bulletin of the European Communities, Commission of the EC, Brussels, Belgium. Proposal presented to the Commission to the Council on 26 February 1974.

[1] The amendments have been printed in italics.

limitata and the vennootschap met beperkte aansprakelijkheid is of special importance for the protection of members and third parties;

Whereas simultaneous coordination is requisite in these fields for these forms of company because, on the one hand, the activities of those companies frequently extend beyond the frontiers of their national territory and, on the other hand, they offer no safeguards to third parties beyond the amount of their net assets; whereas moreover the necessity and urgency of such coordination have been recognized and confirmed in Article 2 (1)(f) of Directive No 68/151/EEC of 9 March 1968;

Whereas it is also necessary to establish in the Community equivalent legal requirements as regards the extent of the financial information that should be made available to the public by companies that are in competition with one another and have the same legal form;

Whereas the annual accounts must *give a true and fair view* of the company's assets and liabilities, financial position and results; whereas to this end a lay-out comprising items that in principle are obligatory must be prescribed for drawing up the balance sheet and profit and loss account; and whereas on the other hand the different methods permitted in the Member States for valuation of assets and liabilities must be coordinated to ensure that annual accounts present equivalent information;

Whereas the annual accounts of sociétés anonymes, Aktiengesellschaften, società per azioni and naamloze vennootschappen must be available in the fullest possible measure to shareholders and third parties; and whereas to that end it is essential that they be published in full in a national gazette;

Whereas so far as regards sociétés à responsabilité limitée, Gesellschaften mit beschränkter Haftung, società à responsabilità limitata and vennootschappen met beperkte aansprakelijkheid a distinction may be made between the information to be given to the members and that to be given to third parties; whereas the members thereof should be given the same information as the shareholders in a société anonyme, Aktiengesellschaft, società per azioni and naamloze vennootschap; whereas for the information of third parties the same particulars should as a general rule be disclosed as in the case of these latter types of company by reason of the fact that the liability of the members is limited, but some relief can nevertheless be allowed in the case of the smaller companies;

Whereas when a company belongs to a group, only the presentation of consolidated accounts of the group can give a true and fair, as well as a complete view of the situation of the companies concerned; whereas in anticipation of the coordination of national rules in this field and in view of the fact that the Commission has committed itself to submit a proposal as soon as possible,

Member States will take care that consolidated accounts provided for by the legislation are established in in conformity with the principles of this directive;

Has adopted this Directive:

Article 1

1. (a) The coordination measures prescribed by Articles 2 to 47 of this Directive apply to the laws, regulations and administrative provisions of the Member States relating to the following types of company:

—in Germany:
die Aktiengesellschaft, die Kommanditgesellschaft auf Aktien;

—in Belgium:
la société anonyme, de naamloze vennootschap, la société en commandite par actions, de commanditaire vennootschap op aandelen;

— in Denmark:
Aktieselskab, Kommardit-Aktieselskab;

—in France:
la société anonyme, la société en commandite par actions;

—in Ireland:
companies incorporated with limited liability, with the exception of those referred to in Article 6 (II)(1) of Directive No ... of ...,[1]

—in Italy:
la società per azioni, la società in accomandita per azioni;

—in Luxembourg:
la société anonyme, la société en commandite par actions;

—in the Netherlands:
de naamloze vennootschap, de commanditaire vennootschap op aandelen;

—in the United Kingdom:
companies incorporated with limited liability, with the exception as regards Northern Ireland, of these referred to in Article 6 (II)(1) of Directive No ... of ...[1]

(b) The coordination measures prescribed by Articles 48 to 50 of this Directive apply to the laws, regulations and administrative provisions of the Member States relating to the following types of company:

—in Germany:
die Gesellschaft mit beschränkter Haftung;

—in Belgium:
la société de personnes à responsabilité limitée, de personenvennootschap met beperkte aansprakelijkheid;

—in Denmark:
anpartsselskaber;

—in France:
la société à responsabilité limitée;

—in Ireland:
companies incorporated with limited liability, as referred to in Article 6 (II)(1) of Directive No ... of ...;[1]

—in Italy:
la società a responsabilità limitata;

—in Luxembourg:
la société à responsabilité limitée;

—in the Netherlands:
de besloten vennootschap met beperkte aansprakelijkheid;

—in the United Kingdom:
as regards Northern Ireland, companies incorporated with limited liability, as referred to in Article 6 (II)(1) of Directive No ... of ....[1]

2. Until the safeguards required of credit institutions and insurance companies are in due course coordinated, it shall be permissible for the Member States not to apply the provisions of this Directive to those undertakings.

SECTION 1

General requirements

Article 2

---

[1] *Amendment to the Proposal for a Second Council Directive, submitted to the Council by the Commission pursuant to the second paragraph of Article 149.*

1. The annual accounts shall comprise the balance sheet, the profit and loss account and the notes on the accounts. These documents shall constitute a composite whole.

2. *The annual accounts shall give a true and fair view of the company's assets, liabilities, financial position and results.*

3. They shall be drawn up clearly *and in conformity with the provisions of this Directive.*

SECTION 2

Lay-out of the annual accounts

Article 3

The lay-out of the balance sheet and of the profit and loss account, particularly as regards the form adopted for their presentation, may not be changed from one year to the next. Departures from this principle shall be permitted in exceptional cases. Where it is departed from, an indication thereof shall be given in the notes on the accounts together with an explanation of the reasons therefore.

Article 4

1. In the balance sheet, and also in the profit and loss account, the items referred to in Articles 8, 9 and 20 to 23 of this Directive shall be shown separately. A more detailed sub-division of the items that are preceded by Arabic numerals is authorized.

2. *No different lay-out shall be permitted for the balance sheet and profit and loss account items that are preceded by Arabic numerals unless the special nature of the undertaking so requires.* Any such different lay-out shall, however, present an equivalent view and be explained in the notes on the accounts.

3. *The balance sheet and profit and loss account items that are preceded by Arabic numerals may be regrouped where:*
(a) they are of secondary interest only in relation to the object of Article 2(2) of this Directive; or
(b) such regrouping makes for greater clarity, provided that the regrouped items are dealt with separately in the notes to the accounts.

4. In respect of each balance sheet and profit and loss account item the figures for the preceding financial year shall be shown.

Article 5

The Member States may authorize adaptation of the lay-out of the balance sheet and profit and loss account in order to bring out the allocation of the results.

Article 6

Any set-off between assets and liabilities, or between expenditure and income, is prohibited.

SECTION 3

Balance sheet lay-out

Article 7

For the presentation of the balance sheet, the Member States shall introduce into their legislation the lay-outs prescribed by Articles 8 and 9 of this Directive, and shall leave the companies to choose between them.

Article 8

ASSETS
A—Subscribed capital unpaid
—of which there has been called.

B—Formation expenses in so far as the national law permits them to be recorded as assets.

C—Fixed assets:

I. Intangible assets:
1. Cost of research and development in so far as the national law permits them to be recorded as assets,
2. Concessions, patents, licences, trade marks, and similar rights and values, if they were:
(a) acquired for valuable consideration and are not to be shown under C I.(3),
(b) created by the undertaking itself, in so far as the national law permits them to be recorded as assets,

3. Goodwill, to the extent that it was acquired for valuable consideration,

4. Payments on account.

II. Tangible assets:

1. Land and buildings,

2. Plant and machinery,

3. Other fixtures, tools and equipment,

4. Payments on account and tangible assets in process of construction.

III. Participating interests and other financial assets:

1. Holdings in associated undertakings,

2. Claims on associated undertakings,

3. Particpating interests,

4. Claims on undertakings with which the company is associated by virtue of a participating interest,

5. Securities ranking as fixed assets,

6. Other claims,

7. Own shares (indicating their nominal value or proportionate value) to the extent that the national law permits them to be included in the balance sheet.

D—Current assets:

I. Stocks:

1. Raw and auxiliary materials,

2. Goods in course of production and waste products,

3. Finished products and stock in hand,

4. Payments on account.

II. Debtors (amounts becoming due and payable within one year shall be shown separately for each item):

1. Claims in respect of sales and services rendered,

2. Claims on associated undertakings,

3. Claims on undertakings in which the company has a participating interest,

4. Other claims.

III. Securities forming part of the current assets, and liquid assets:

1. Holdings in associated undertakings,

2. Bills of exchange,

3. Bank balances, postal cheque account balances, cheques and cash in hand,

4. Own shares (indicating their nominal value or proportionate value) to the extent that the national law permits them to be included in the balance sheet,

5. Other securities.

E—Pre-payments.

F—Loss *(in so far as the losses are not shown under liabilities):*

I. For the year,

II. Brought forward.

LIABILITIES
A—Subscribed capital (the shares must be shown by classes, indicating their nominal value or proportionate value).

B—Reserves:

1. Legal reserve,
2. Share premium account,
3. Revaluation reserve,
4. Reserve for own shares,
5. Statutory reserves,
6. Optional reserves.

C— *Total of subscribed capital and reserves, less losses, in so far as these are not shown under assets (the result for the year and results brought forward must be shown as separate items).*

D—Provisions for contingencies and charges:
1. Provisions for pensions and similar obligations,
2. Provisions for taxation including future taxation,
3. Other provisions.

E—Creditors (amounts becoming due and payable within one year, amounts becoming due and payable after more than five years, and amounts covered by valuable security furnished by the company, must be shown separately for each item):

1. Debenture loans, showing convertible loans separately,
2. Debts to credit institutions,
3. Payments received on account of orders,
4. Debts in respect of purchases and services received,
5. Debts represented by bills of exchange,
6. Debts to associated undertakings,
7. Debts to undertakings with which the company is associated by virtue of a participating interest,
8. Other creditors.

F—Accruals.

G—Profit:

I. For the year.

II. Brought forward.

Article 9

A—Subscribed capital Unpaid
—of which there has been called.

B—Formation expenses in so far as the national law permits them to be recorded as assets.

C—Fixed assets:

I. Intangible assets:
1. Cost of research and development, in so far as the national law permits them to be recorded as assets,
2. Concessions, patents, licences, trade marks, and similar rights and values, if they were:
(a) acquired for valuable consideration and are not to be shown under C I.(e),
(b) created by the undertaking itself, in so far as the national law permits them to be recorded as assets,
3. Goodwill, to the extent that it was acquired for valuable consideration,
4. Payments on account.

II. Tangible assets:
1. Land and buildings,
2. Plant and machinery,
3. Other fixtures, tools and equipment,
4. Payments on account and tangible assets in process of construction.

III. Participating interests and other financial assets:
1. Holdings in associated undertakings,
2. Claims on associated undertakings,
3. Participating interests,
4. Claims on undertakings with which the company is associated by virtue of a participating interest,
5. Securities ranking as fixed assets,
6. Other claims,
7. Own shares (indicating their nominal value of proportionate value) to the extent that the national law permits them to be included in the balance sheet.

D—Current assets:

I. Stocks:
1. Raw and auxiliary materials,
2. Goods in course of production and waste products,
3. Finished products and stock in hand,
4. Payments on account.

II. Debtors (amounts becoming due and payable within one year must be shown separately in each case):
1. Claims in respect of sales and services rendered,
2. Claims on associated undertakings,
3. Claims on undertakings with which the company is associated by virtue of a participating interest,
4. Other claims.

III. Securities forming part of the current assets, and liquid assets:
1. Holdings in associated undertakings,
2. Bills of exchange,
3. Bank balances, postal cheque account balances, cheques and cash in hand,
4. Own shares (indicating their nominal value or proportionate value) to the extent that the national law permits them to be included in the balanace sheet,
5. Other securities.

E—Pre-payments.

F—Debts becoming due and payable within one year (amounts covered by valuable security furnished by the company must be shown separately for each item):
1. Debenture loans, showing convertible loans separately,
2. Debts to credit institutions,
3. Payments received on account of orders,
4. Debts in respect of purchases and services received,
5. Debts represented by bills of exchange,
6. Debts to associated undertakings,
7. Debts to undertakings with which the company is associated by virtue of a participating interest,
8. Other debts.

G—Current assets in excess of the debts becoming due and payable within one year.

H—Total amount of asset items after deduction of the debts becoming due and payable within one year.

I—Creditors for amounts becoming due and payable after more than one year (amounts becoming due and payable after more than five years and amounts covered by valuable security furnished by the company must be shown separately for each item):

1. Debenture loans, showing convertible loans separately,
2. Debts to credit institutions,
3. Payments received on account of orders,
4. Debts in respect of purchases and services received,
5. Debts represented by bills of exchange,
6. Debts to associated undertakings,
7. Debts to undertakings with which the company is associated by virtue of a participating interest,
8. Other creditors.

J—Provisions for contingencies and charges:
1. Provisions for pensions and similar obligations,
2. Provisions for taxation, including future taxation,
3. Other provisions.

K—Accruals.

L—Subscribed capital (The shares must be shown by classes, indicating their nominal value or proportionate value).

M—Reserves:
1. Legal reserve,
2. Share premium account,
3. Revaluation reserve,
4. Reserve for own shares,
5. Statutory reserves,
6. Optional reserves.

N—Result for the year.

O—Results brought forward.

Article 10

1. Where a component of the assets or liabilities pertains to several items in the balance sheet, its relationship to other items shall be indicated either under the item where it appears or in the notes on the accounts, unless such indication is not essential to the comprehension of the annual accounts.

2. Own shares and holdings in associated undertakings shall be shown only under the item respectively that relates thereto.

Article 11

All commitments by way of guarantee of any kind entered into for account of third parties shall, if there is no obligation to show them under liabilities, be clearly set out below the balance sheet or in the notes on the accounts, distinguishing between the various types of guarantee which the national law recognizes, and specifying what valuable security, if any, has been provided. Commitments of this kind existing in respect of associated undertakings shall be shown separately.

SECTION 4

Special provisions relating to certain items in the balanace sheet

Article 12

1. Whether particular assets are to be classified as fixed assets or current assets shall depend upon the purpose for which they are intended.

2. Fixed assets shall comprise those elements which are intended to be used on a continuing basis to enable the undertaking to operate.

3. (a) Movements in the various items of fixed assets shall be shown in the balance sheet or in the notes on the accounts. To this end there shall be shown, starting with the purchase price or production cost, separately for each of the items of fixed assets, on the one hand the additions, disposals, transfers and upward corrections during the year, and on the other hand the cumulative value adjustments as at the date of the balance sheet. *Value adjustments shall be shown either in the balance sheet, as a clear deduction from the relevant item, or in the notes on the accounts.*

(b) Where at the time the first annual accounts are drawn up in accordance with this Directive, the purchase price or production cost of an element of fixed assets cannot be determined without untoward expense or delay, the residual value at the beginning of the year may be treated as the purchase price or production cost. Any use made of this provision must be mentioned in the notes on the accounts.

(c) In the case of application of Articles 30 and 31 of this Directive, the presentation of the movements in the various items of fixed assets referred to under (a) shall be supplemented by separate mention, for each of the various items, of the cumulative amounts at the date of the balance sheet, on the one hand of the differences referred to in Article 30 (2) and in Article 31(2), and on the other hand of the additional value adjustments.

4. (a) Movements in the various items of current assets shall be presented in the balance sheet or the notes on the accounts. To this end there shall be shown, separately for each of the items of current assets, on the one hand the purchase price or production cost of the elements shown in the balance sheet, and on the other hand the value adjustments. *Value adjustments shall be shown either in the balance sheet, as a clear deduction from the relevant item, or in the notes on the accounts.*

(b) The provisions of paragraph 3(c) shall apply to the presentation of the item relating to stocks.

5. The provisions of paragraph 3(a) and (b) shall apply to the presentation of the item 'formation expenses'.

Article 13

Under the item 'land and buildings' shall be show land not built on as well as the land built on and the buildings thereon, together with fixtures and fittings.

Where national law authorizes the inclusion under assets of rights in real estate which are of like nature to rights of ownership, they shall be included under the item 'land and buildings'.

Article 14

The term 'participating interests' is used in this Directive to mean rights in the capital of other undertakings, whether or not represented by certificates which by creating a durable link with them, are intended to contribute to the activities of the company. A holding of 10% of the subscribed capital of another undertaking shall be presumed to constitute a participating interest.

Article 15

Under 'Pre-payments' on the assets side shall be shown expenditure incurred during the year but relating to a subsequent year, together with the earnings relating to the year to the extent that they will not be received until after the close of the year. The latter, however, may also be shown under debtors. *Where the amount involved is considerable, an explanation must be given in the notes on the accounts.*

Article 16

The value adjustments are adjustment items relating to elements of assets and are intended to take account of depreciation established in respect of these elements at the date of the balance sheet, whether that depreciation is definitive or not.

Article 17

The provisions for contingencies and charges are intended to cover either the certain cost of major maintenance work or of major repairs which will be incurred in the course of subsequent years, or losses or charges the nature of which is clearly defined but which at the date of the balance sheet are either likely to be incurred, or are certain to be incurred but are indeterminate as to amount or as to the date on which they will arise.
The provisions for contingencies and charges shall not be used to adjust the value of elements of assets.

Article 18

Under 'Accruals' on the liabilities side shall be shown income received before the date of the balance sheet but attributable to a subsequent year, together with charges which, though relating to the year in question, will only be paid in the course of a subsequent year. The latter, however, may also be shown under creditors. *Where the amount involved is considerable, an explanation must be given in the notes on the accounts.*

SECTION 5

Lay-out of the profit and loss account

Article 19

For the presentation of the profit and loss account, the Member States shall adopt into their laws the lay-outs appearing in Articles 20 to 23 of this Directive, and shall leave the companies to choose between them.

Article 20

I. Operating result (excluding any earnings and charges shown under II):
1. Net turnover,

2. Changes in stocks of finished and semifinished products,

3. Work effected by the undertaking for its own account and shown under assets,

4. Other operating receipts,

5. Cost of raw and auxiliary materials,

6. Staff costs:

(a) Wages and salaries,

(b) Compulsory social security costs,

(c) Other social security costs, showing as a separate item those relating to old age pensions.

7. (a) Value adjustments in respect of formation expenses and of tangible and intangible fixed assets,

(b) Value adjustments in respect of elements of current assets,

8. Other operating expenses,

9. Operating result.

II. Financial result:

10. Earnings from participating interests, showing separately those derived from associated undertakings,

11. Earnings from other securities and from claims forming part of the fixed assets, showing separately those derived from associated undertakings,

12. Other interest and similar earnings, showing separately those derived from associated undertakings,

13. Value adjustments in respect of participating interests and other financial assets and of securities forming part of the current assets,

14. Interest and similar charges, showing separately those concerning associated undertakings,

15. Financial results.

III. Exceptional result:

16. Exceptional earnings,

17. Exceptional charges,

18. Exceptional result.

IV. Sub-total.

V. Taxes:

19. Taxes on the result:

—actual,

—future,

20. Other taxes not shown under I, II or III above.

VI. Result for the year.

Article 21

A—Charges:

I. Operating expenses (excluding any shown under II):

1. Reduction in the stock of finished and semifinished products,

2. Cost of raw and auxiliary materials,

3. Staff costs:

(a) Wages and salaries,

(b) Compulsory social security costs,

(c) Other social security costs, showing as a separate item those relating to old age pensions,

4. (a) Value adjustments in respect of formation expenses and of tangible and intangible fixed assets,

(b) Value adjustments in respect of elements of current assets,

5. Other operating expenses.

II. Financial charges:

1. Value adjustments in respect of participating interests and other financial assets and of securities forming part of the current assets,

2. Interest and similar charges, showing separately those concerning associated undertakings.

III. Exceptional charges.

IV. Taxes:

1. Taxes on the result:

—actual,

—future,

2. Other taxes not shown under I, II and III above.

V. Result for the year.

B—Receipts

I. Operating receipts (excluding any shown under II):

1. Net turnover,

2. Increase in stocks of finished and semifinished products,

3. Work effected by the undertaking for its own account and shown under assets,

4. Other operating receipts.

II. Financial earnings:

1. Earnings from participating interests, showing separately those derived from associated undertakings,

2. Earnings from other securities and from claims forming part of the fixed assets, showing separately those derived from associated undertakings,

3. Other interest and similar earnings, showing separately those derived from associated undertakings.

III. Exceptional earnings.

IV. Result for the year.

Article 22

I. Operating result (excluding any earnings and charges shown under II):

1. Net turnover,

2. Production costs of output supplied and making-up the turnover (including value adjustments),

3. Gross result achieved from turnover,

4. Distribution expenses (including value adjustments),

5. Administrative expenses (including value adjustments),

6. Other operating receipts,

7. Operating result.

II. Financial result:

8. Earnings from participating interests, showing separately those derived from associated undertakings,

9. Earnings from other securities and from claims forming part of the fixed assets, showing separately those derived from associated undertakings,

10. Other interest and similar earnings, showing separately those derived from associated undertakings,

11. Value adjustments in respect of participating interests and other financial fixed assets and of securities forming part of the current assets,

12. Interest and similar charges, showing separately those concerning associated undertakings,

13. Financial result.

III. Exceptional result:

14. Exceptional earnings,

15. Exceptional charges,

16. Exceptional result.

IV. Sub-total.

V. Taxes:

17. Taxes on the result:

—actual,

—future,

18. Other taxes not shown under I, II or III above.

VI. Result for the year.

Article 23

A—Charges:

I. Operating expenses (excluding any shown under II):

1. Production costs of output supplied and making-up the turnover (including value adjustments),

2. Distribution expenses (including value adjustments),

3. Administrative expenses (including value adjustments).

II. Financial charges:

1. Value adjustments in respect of participating interests and other financial fixed assets and of securities forming part of the current assets,

2. Interest and similar charges, showing separately those concerning associated undertakings.

III. Exceptional charges.

IV. Taxes:

1. Taxes on the result:

—actual,

—future,

2. Other taxes not shown under I, II or III above.

V. Result for the year.

B—Receipts:

I. Operating receipts (excluding any shown under II):

1. Net turnover,

2. Other operating receipts.

II. Financial earnings:

1. Earnings from participating interests, showing separately those derived from associated undertakings,

2. Earnings from other securities and from claims forming part of the fixed assets, showing separately those derived from associated undertakings,

3. Other interest and similar earnings, showing separately those derived from associated undertakings.

III. Exceptional earnings.

IV. Result for the year.

Article 24

The Member States may authorize companies for which at the date of the balance sheet:
— *the balance sheet total does not exceed one million units of account,*
— the net turnover does not exceed two million units of account,
— the average number of employees during the year did not exceed one hundred,
to adopt lay-outs different from those appearing in Articles 20 to 23 of the Directive within the following limits:
(a) in Article 20, under I, items 1 to 5 inclusive may be grouped together under one item called Gross result;
(b) in Article 21, items A I, 1 and 2, and B I, 1 to 4 inclusive may be grouped together under one item called Gross earnings or Gross charges as the case may be;
(c) in Article 22, under I, items 1, 2, 3 and 6 may be be grouped together under one item called Gross result;
(d) in Article 23, items A I, 1 and B I, 1 and 2, may be grouped together under one item called Gross earnings or Gross charges as the case may be.
If subsequently any of the numerical limits set out above is exceeded, the exemptions provided for in this provision may again be applied only if all the conditions specified above are satisfied for two consecutive years.
The amounts in units of account specified in this provision may vary by not more than 10% up or down for purposes of conversion into national currencies.

SECTION 6

Special provisions relating to certain items in the profit and loss account

Article 25

The net amount of turnover includes receipts from sales of products, goods and services falling within the usual operations of the company, after allowing for any price-reduction in respect of those sales, and for value added tax and other taxes directly tied to the turnover.

Article 26

1. Under the items Exceptional earnings and Exceptional charges, shall be shown earnings and charges that are attributable to another year, together with any earnings and charges that do not arise out of the usual operations of the undertaking.

2. Unless such earnings and charges are of no importance in the assessment of the results, explanations of their amount and nature shall be given in the notes on the accounts.

Article 27

Under the item Taxes on the Result shall be shown the actual amount of taxes payable for the year, and separately, the amount of the future liability to tax.

SECTION 7

Valuation rules

Article 28

1. The Member States shall ensure that the valuation of the items shown in the annual accounts is made in accordance with the following general principles:

(a) *The company shall be presumed to continue its business as a going concern.*

(b) The methods of valuation may not be changed from one year to another.

(c) *Valuation must be made on a conservative basis, and in particular:*

(aa) Only the profits earned at the date of the balance sheet may be included in it; account shall nevertheless be taken of all contingencies foreseeable at that date.

(bb) Account shall be taken of any deficiencies that do not become apparent until after the date of the balance sheet, but which do become apparent before it is drawn up, if they arise in the course of the year to which the annual accounts relate.

(cc) Account shall be taken of any depreciation, whether the year closes with a loss or with a profit.

(d) *Account shall be taken of earnings and charges arising during the year to which the accounts relate, irrespective of the date of or receipt of payment of such earnings or changes.*

(e) The components of the asset and liability items shall be valued separately.

(f) The *opening* balance sheet for each year shall correspond to the *closing* balance sheet for the *preceding* year.

2. Departures from these general principles shall be permitted in exceptional cases. Where they are departed from, an indication thereof shall be given in the notes on the accounts together with an explanation of the reasons and an assessment of the effect on the assets, liabilities, financial position and result.

Article 29

The valuation of the items shown in the annual accounts shall be made in accordance with Articles 32 to 39 of this Directive, based on purchase price or production cost.

Article 30

1. Notwithstanding the provisions of Article 29 of this Directive, the Member States may authorize:

(a) for tangible fixed assets with a limited useful life and for stocks, valuation by the replacement value method; and

(b) for tangible fixed assets, for participating interests and other financial assets and for stocks, valuation by methods other than that mentioned in paragraph (a) and which take into account current values.

Where such authorization is given and is implemented, an indication thereof shall be given in the notes on the acccounts, specifying the balance sheet or profit and loss account items concerned, and the method by which the value shown is calculated.

2. Where paragraph 1 is applied, the amount of the difference *between valuation by* the replacement value method *or other method as aforesaid* and valuation in accordance with the general rule contained in Article 29 shall be shown under liabilities in the item Revaluation Reserve, *with any future taxation being shown clearly as a deduction.* This item shall be sub-divided into:

—Reserve for tangible fixed assets,

—Reserve for participating interests and other financial assets,

—Reserve for stocks.

3. The Revaluation reserve may be capitalized at any time.

4. The Revaluation reserve shall be reduced to the extent that the amounts transferred thereto are no longer *necessary to maintain the potential of the undertaking.* The amounts in question shall be added to the result for the year. They shall be shown separately in the profit and loss account.

5. Save as provided in paragraphs 3 and 4 the Revaluation reserve shall not be reduced.

6. Value adjustments shall be calculated each year on the basis of the *value* shown for the year in question.

Article 31

1. Notwithstanding *the provisions of* Article 29 of this Directive, the Member States may authorize revaluation of the tangible fixed assets, participating interests and other financial assets.
Where such authorization is given and is implemented, an indication thereof shall be given in the notes on the accounts specifying the balance sheet or profit and loss account items concerned, and the method by which the value shown is calculated.
2. In the event of paragraph 1 being applied, the amount of the difference in valuation made in accordance with paragraph 1 above and the valuation made in accordance with the general rule contained in Article 29 shall be shown under liabilities in the Revaluation Reserve. This item shall be sub-divided into:
—Reserve for tangible fixed assets,
—Reserve for participating interests and other financial assets.
3. The Revaluation reserve may be capitalized at any time.
4. The Revaluation reserve shall be reduced to the extent that the increases in value concerned have been actually realized. The amounts in question shall be added to the result for the year. They shall be down separately in the profit and loss account.
5. Save as provided in paragraphs 3 and 4 the Revaluation reserve shall not be reduced.

Article 32

1. (a) Where the national law authorizes the inclusion of formation expenses under assets, they shall be written off over a maximum period of five years.
(b) In so far as the formation expenses have not been completely written off, no distribution of profits shall take place unless the amount of the optional reserves is at least equal to the amount of the expenses not written off.
2. The amounts entered under this item shall be explained in the notes on the accounts.

Article 33

1. (a) The items of fixed assets shall, without prejudice to the provisions of (b) and (c) below, be valued at purchase price or production cost.
(b) The purchase price or production cost of the items of fixed assets which have a

limited useful life shall be reduced by value adjustments calculated according to a method that satisfies the requirements of good management.

(c) (aa) Value adjustments may be made in respect of the *participating interests and other financial interests,* so that they are valued at the lowest figure to be attributed to them at the date of the balance sheet.

(bb) *Value adjustments shall be made in respect of the items of fixed assets, whether or not their useful life is limited, so that they are valued at the lowest figure to be attributed to them at the date of the balance sheet, if it is expected that the depreciation in value will be permanent.*

(cc) The value adjustments referred to in (aa) and (bb) shall be shown separately in the profit and loss account or in the notes on the accounts.

(dd) Valuation at the lowest value provided for in (aa) and (bb) shall be discontinued if the reasons for which the value adjustments were made have ceased to apply.

(d) If the items of fixed assets are the subject of exceptional value adjustments *solely for the purpose of* fiscal law, the amount of the adjustments *and the reasons for making them, together with the relevant future taxation,* shall be indicated in the notes on the accounts.

2. The purchase price shall be calculated by adding to the price paid the expenses incidental thereto.

3. (a) The production cost shall be calculated by adding to the purchase price of the raw and auxiliary materials the manufacturing costs directly attributable to the product in question.

(b) A reasonable proportion of the manufacturing costs which are only indirectly attributable to the product in question *shall* be added to the production costs to the extent that they relate to the period of manufacture.

(c) Costs of distribution shall not be included in production cost.

4. *Interest on capital borrowed to finance the manufacture* of fixed assets may be included in production cost to the extent that it relates to the period of manufacture. In that event, *an indication shall be given* in the notes on the accounts that such interest is included under assets.

Article 34

1. Article 32 of this directive shall apply to the item 'Cost of research and development'.

2. Article 32(1) (a) shall apply to item C I 3 under Articles 8 and 9.

Article 35

Tangible fixed assets, raw and auxiliary materials, which are constantly being replaced and of which the overall value is of secondary importance to the undertaking may be shown under assets at a fixed quantity and value, if the quantity, value and composition thereof do not vary appreciably.

Article 36

1. (a) The items of current assets shall be valued at purchase price or production cost, without prejudice to the provisions of (b) and (c) below.

(b) Value adjustments shall be made in respect of the items of current assets so that they are valued at the lowest figure attributable to them at the date of the balance sheet.

(c) The Member States may authorize exceptional value adjustments if, on the basis of a reasonable commercial assessment, these are necessary so that the valuation of these items does not have to be modified in the near future because of flucuations in value. The amount of these value adjustments shall be shown separately in the profit and loss account or in the notes on the accounts.

(d) Valuation at the lowest value provided for in (b) and (c) shall be discontinued if the reasons for which the value adjustments were made have ceased to apply.

(e) If the items of current assets are the subject of exceptional value adjustments *solely for the purpose of* fiscal law, the amount of the adjustments *and the reasons for making them, together with the relevant future taxation,* shall be indicated in the notes on the account.

2. The definitions of purchase price and of production cost contained in Article 33(2) to (4) shall apply.

Article 37

1. The purchase price or production cost of stocks of goods in the same category may also be calculated either on the basis of weighted average prices or by the 'First in— First out' (Fifo) method or 'Last in—First out (Lifo) method, or some similar method.

2. *Where the value shown in the balance sheet as a result of the method used differs considerably from the value on the basis of the actual purchase price, the difference shall be indicated in the notes on the accounts.*

Article 38

1. Where the amount of any debt repayable is greater than the amount received, the difference may be shown as an asset. It shall be shown separately in the balance sheet or in the notes on the accounts.

2. The amount of such difference shall be written off not later than the time when repayment of the debt is made.

Article 39

Provisions for contingencies and charges shall not exceed in amount the sums which a reasonable businessman would consider necessary.

The provisions shown in the balance sheet under the item 'Other provisions' shall be specified in the notes on the accounts if they are at all substantial.

SECTION 8

Contents of the notes on the accounts

Article 40

The notes on the accounts shall contain commentary on the balance sheet and profit and loss account in such manner as to give a true and fair view of the company's assets, liabilities, financial position and results.

Article 41

In addition to the information required under other provisions of this Directive, the notes on the accounts shall set out information in respect of the following matters in any event:

1. The valuation methods applied to the various items in the annual accounts, and the methods employed in calculating the value adjustments. *For foreign currency debtors and creditors, the method used for calculating the rate of exchange must be shown;*

2. The name and head office address of each of the undertakings in which the company holds at least 10% of the capital, showing the proportion of the capital held and the amount of the subscribed capital, the amount of the reserves and the results for the latest business year of the undertaking concerned;

3. The way in which the authorized capital has been employed, if any such capital has been created;

4. Whether there are any entitlements carrying the right to a share of profits, and whether there are any convertible debentures or similar securities or rights, specifying the number thereof and what rights they confer;

5. The overall amount of the financial commitments that are not shown in the balance

sheet, in so far as this information is of assistance in assessing the financial position. Commitments existing with regard to associated undertakings shall be shown separately;

6. *The net amount of turnover within the meaning of Article 25 of this Directive, broken down by categories of products and activities and by geographical markets. The amount contributed by each category and market to the result for the year must be indicated;*

7. *The number of persons employed during the year, broken down by categories and, if they are not shown separately in the profit and loss account, the whole of the personnel costs relating to the accounting period, broken down as provided by Article 20.I.6;*

8. The taxes included in the operating result, the financial result or exceptional result;

9. The amount of the changes in the result for the year due to the application of fiscal laws;

10. The amount of the emoluments granted during the year to the members of the administrative, managerial and supervisory bodies by reason of their responsibilities, *and any commitments arising or entered into in respect of retirement pensions for ex-members of those bodies,* showing the total for each category;

11. The amount of advances and credits granted to the members of administrative, managerial and supervisory bodies, and commitments entered into on their account by way of guarantees of any kind, showing the total for each category.

Article 42

1. The Member States may allow the particulars prescribed by Article 41(2):

(a) to take the form of a statement deposited in accordance with Article 3, paragraphs 1 and 2 of Directive 68/151/EEC of 9 March 1968. This shall be mentioned in the notes on the accounts;

(b) to be omitted when their nature is such that, in the view of a reasonable business man, they would be seriously prejudicial to any of the undertakings to which this provision relates. The omission of the particulars shall be mentioned in the notes on the accounts.

2. *Subject to the provisions of the second paragraph of Article 24 of this Directive, the Member States may authorize the omission by companies to which that Article applies of the information required under Article 41(6).*

SECTION 9

Contents of the annual report

Article 43

1. The annual report shall contain a detailed review of the development of the company's business and of its position.
2. The report shall also give particulars of:
(a) any important events that have occurred since the close of the business year;
(b) the company's likely future development;
(c) *the activities in the field of research and development and the costs thereof.*

SECTION 10

Publication

Article 44

1. The annual accounts duly approved and the annual report, together with the report submitted by the person responsible for auditing the accounts, *as referred to in Article 60 of Directive No ... of ...,*[1] shall be deposited without delay in accordance with Article 3(1) and (2) of Directive 68/151/EEC of 9 March 1968.
2. In derogation from Article 3(4) of that Directive, the annual accounts shall be published in full in a national gazette designated by the Member State. The report submitted by the person responsible for auditing the accounts, *as referred to in paragraph 1,* shall be published therein at the same time.

3. The annual report shall be published in accordance with the requirements of Article 3(4) of the Directive referred to in paragraph 1.

Article 45

On any other occasion when publication is made in full, the annual accounts and report shall be reproduced in the form and text on the basis of which the person responsible for auditing the accounts drew up his report. They shall be accompanied by the full text of the certificate. If the person responsible for auditing the accounts made any qualifications or refused to certify the accounts, the fact shall be stated and the reasons given.

[1] *Proposal for a fifth Directive under Article 54 (3) (g), submitted to the Council by the Commission on 9 October 1972: OJ C131 of 13.12.1972 and Supplement 10/72 — Bull. EC.*

Article 46

If the annual accounts are not published in full, it shall be pointed out that the version published is abridged, and reference shall be made to the national gazette in which they were published. The certificate of the person responsible for auditing the accounts shall not accompany this publication, but it shall be stated whether the certificate was made with or without qualification, or was refused.

Article 47

There shall be published along with the annual accounts, and in like manner:
—the proposed allocation of the result,
—the allocation of the results in cases where these items do not appear in the annual accounts.

SECTION 11

Special provisions relating to the société à responsabilité limitée, the Gesellschaft mit beschränkter Haftung, the società a responsabilità limitata and the vennootschap met beperkte aansprakelijkheid

Article 48

The companies referred to in Article 1(1) (b) shall draw up their annual accounts and report for the information of their members in accordance with the requirements of Articles 2 to 23 and 25 to 43 of this Directive, subject to the following qualifications:
(a) In Article 8 a separate item, 'Claims on members', shall be included under assets at C III and D II and a further separate item, 'Debts to members', under liabilities at E;
(b) In Article 9 a separate item, 'Claims on members', shall be included at C III and D II and a further separate item, 'Debts to members' at F and I.

Article 49

1. *(a)* The companies referred to in Article 1, (1) (b) shall cause their annual accounts to be audited by one or more persons authorized by the national law to audit accounts.
(b) The person or persons responsible for auditing the accounts shall also verify that the annual report is consistent with the annual accounts of the year to which it refers.
2. The Member States may exempt from the obligation imposed under paragraph 1

companies 'of which at the date of their balance sheet:

—the balance sheet total does not exceed one hundred thousand units of account,

—the net turnover as defined in Article 25 of this Directive does not exceed two hundred thousand units of account,

—the average number of employees during the year did not exceed twenty.

In that case they shall introduce appropriate sanctions into their law for cases in which the annual accounts and reports of such companies are now drawn up in accordance with the requirements of this Directive.

If subsequently any of the numerical limits set out above is exceeded, the exemption provided for in this provision may again be applied only if all the conditions specified above are satisfied for two consecutive years.

The amounts in units of accounts specified in this provision may vary by not more than 10% up or down for purposes of conversion into national currencies.

Article 50

1. (a) The companies referred to in Article 1(1) (b) shall publish their annual accounts and report, and the report drawn up by the person responsible for auditing the accounts, in accordance with Article 44 of this Directive.

(b) Articles 45 to 47 of this Directive shall equally apply to the companies referred to in paragraph 1(a).

2. Notwithstanding paragraph 1(1), the Member States may permit:

(a) companies other than those referred to in Article 49(2), in the case of which at the date of their balance sheet:

—the balance sheet total does not exceed one million units of account;

—the net turnover as defined in Article 25 of this Directive does not exceed two million units of account;

—the average number of employees during the year did not exceed one hundred;

to publish their profit and loss account in the abridged form provided for in Article 24 of this Directive. If subsequently any one of the numerical limits set out above is exceeded, the exemption provided for in this provision may again be applied only if all the conditions specified above are satisfied for two consecutive years.

The amounts in units of account specified in this provision may vary by not more than 10% up or down for purposes of conversion into national currencies.

(b) the companies referred to in Article 49(2) of this Directive to publish merely an abridged balance sheet showing only the items preceded by letters and Roman numerals set out in Articles 8 and 9 with separate particulars of:

—the information required by the provisions in brackets under Items D II of the assets and E of

the liabilities in Article 8 and under items D II, F and I in Article 9, but showing the total for the items concerned;

—claims on and debts to members, and notes on the accounts but not necessarily including the explanations required under Article 41(4) to (11);

(c) the publication requirements laid down for the companies referred to in (a) and (b) to be effected in manner prescribed by Article 3 of Directive 68/151/EEC of 9 March 1968.

SECTION 12

Final provisions

Article 51

1. (a) The Member States shall, within eighteen months of notification of this Directive, make all the necessary amendments to their laws, regulations and administrative provisions so as to comply with the provisions of this Directive, and shall inform the Commission thereof immediately. They shall bring the amendments into force within thirty months of notification of this Directive.

(b) The Governments of the Member States shall communicate to the Commission for information the draft tests of the laws and regulations together with the statements of grounds, relating to the matter covered by this Directive. These shall be communicated at least six months before the date envisaged for final adoption of the texts.

2. The obligation to show in the annual accounts the items prescribed by Articles 8, 9 and 20 to 23 which relate to associated undertakings, and the obligation to provide infdrmation concerning these undertakings in accordance with Articles 10(2), 11 or 41(5) of this Directive shall enter into force simultaneously with a Council Directive relating to consolidated accounts.

Article 52

This Directive is addressed to the Member States.

APPENDIX IV

Excerpts from the Amended Proposal

for a Council Regulation on the

"Statute for European Companies"

SECTION SIX

Preparation of group accounts

Article 196

[Group accounts and part-group accounts]

1. If the SE is the controlling undertaking within a group of undertakings, it shall, in respect of the group, draw up a consolidated balance sheet, a consolidated profit and loss account, notes on the group accounts, a statement of source and application of funds for the group (group accounts) and a group annual report.

The group accounts, prepared as at the same date as the annual accounts of the SE, shall relate to every undertaking which, in accordance with Article 223, is a member of the group.

Supplement 4/1975, Bulletin of the European Communities, Commission of the EC, Brussels, Belgium. Articles 148-195 are omitted, because these are similar to details shown in Appendix III. Amended Proposal presented by the Commission to the Council on 13 May 1975.

2. If the SE is a dependent undertaking and if other undertakings within a group are controlled through it, it shall, in respect of its own part of the group, draw up a part-consolidated balance sheet, part-consolidated profit and loss account, notes on the part-group accounts, a part-group statement of source and application of funds (part-group accounts) and a part-group annual report, unless the controlling undertaking within the group prepares group accounts in accordance with the provisions of this Title. Such accounts, which shall be prepared as at the same date as the annual accounts of the SE, shall relate to the undertakings controlled through the SE. Articles 197 to 202 shall apply to part-group accounts and reports.

Article 197

[Non-consolidation of accounts of an undertaking within group]

1. *(a)* Consolidated accounts shall not relate to undertakings within the group where the effect would be to make the information contained in the consolidated accounts less meaningful;
(b) consolidated accounts need not relate to undertakings within the group which are so small that the view reflected of the assets, liabilities, financial position and results of the group is not affected by omitting them.
2. *(a)* The reason for non consolidation of the accounts of any undertaking within the group shall be stated in the notes on the accounts;
(b) the annual accounts of undertakings such as are referred to in paragraph 1(a) shall be drawn up as at the date of the consolidated accounts and shall be annexed to the notes thereon.

Article 198

[Drawing up of group accounts]

1. The group accounts shall comprise the consolidated balance sheet, the consolidated profit and loss account, the notes on the group accounts and a statement of source and application of funds for the group. These documents shall constitute a composite whole.
2. The group accounts shall give a true and fair view of the group's assets, liabilities, financial position and results.
3. They shall be drawn up clearly, accurately and in accordance with the following provisions regarding the valuation of assets and the lay-out of accounts.

Article 199

[Presentation of group accounts]

The provisions of Section Two of this Title shall apply to the presentation of consolidated accounts, subject to the following exceptions:

1. In the group balance sheet:

(a) the amount of any differences as between the book value at the date of first consolidation of investment holdings in the capital of undertakings in the group, and the value thereof including reserves and profits, on subsequent valuation, shall be shown separately under one item entitled 'Consolidation equalization account';

(b) interests held by companies outside the group in the capital, reserves and profits of undertakings within the group shall be shown as a separate item;

(c) stocks may be grouped together under one global item.

2. In the group profit and loss account the following items may be lumped together;

(a) Article 168, items I-2 to 9,

(b) Article 169, items A-I-1 to 5 and B-I-2 to 4,

(c) Article 170, items I-2 to 6,

(d) Article 171, items A-I-1 to 3 and B-I-2.

Article 200

[Valuation]

1. As the undertakings in a group constitute one economic unit, all assets and liabilities shall be incorporated in the group consolidated balance sheet at the values shown in the balance sheets of the undertakings within the group.

2. The annual accounts of undertakings to which consolidated accounts relate shall be prepared so far as possible in accordance with the sames rules of valuation.

Article 201

[Information contained in noted on consolidated accounts]

1. In so far as the information contained in the notes on the consolidated accounts is important for the purpose of assessment thereof, Articles 191 to 193 shall apply.

2. The methods of consolidation and, in particular, the sources and composition of the consolidation equalization account and the non-elimination, if any, of profits on transactions between undertakings within the group shall be explained.

Article 202

Article 195 shall apply to the consolidated annual report.

SECTION SEVEN

Audit

Article 203

[Audit by auditors]

1. The annual accounts and, in so far as it reviews developments in the company's business and position during the past financial year, the annual report shall be audited by an independent auditor acting on his own responsibility.

2. Only persons who are suitably qualified and experienced may be appointed auditors. They shall have obtained their professional qualifications by satisfying the requirements for admission and by passing an examination, both of which must be legally established or recognized and shall be persons authorized in a Member State to act as auditors of the annual accounts of companies limited by shares whose shares are quoted on a stock exchange.

Article 203a

[Independence of auditor]

1. The audit may not be carried out by persons who are, or who within the last three years prior to their appointment have been, members of the Board of Management or of the Supervisory Board or employees of the SE or of an undertaking dependent on it or controlling it.

2. Further, the audit may not be carried out by:

(a) companies, whose members, whose members of the management or supervisory body, or whose duly authorized representatives are or, in the last three years prior to their appointment were, members of the Board of Management or of the Supervisory Board or employees of the SE or of an undertaking dependent on it or controlling it;

(b) a firm of auditors which is dependent on or which controls the SE, or which is dependent on the undertaking controlling the SE.

Article 203b

[Independence of auditor]

1. Persons who have carried out the audit may not become members of the Board of Management or of the Supervisory Board or employees of the SE or of an undertaking dependent on it or controlling it for at least three years after expiry of their term of office.

2. Further, members of the management or supervisory bodies, or duly authorized representatives or members of companies which have carried out the audit, may not for at least 3 years after completion of their duties, become members of the Board of Management or of the Supervisory Board or employees of the SE or of an undertaking dependent on it or controlling it.

Article 204

[Appointment and removal of auditor]

1. The auditor shall be appointed annually by the General Meeting. In respect of the first financial year, the auditor may be appointed by the General Meetings of the founder companies.

2. If the appointment is not made by the General Meeting in due time or should an appointed person be unable to carry out his task, the court within whose jurisdiction the registered office is situated shall, upon application by the Board of Management, the Supervisory Board or a shareholder, appoint an auditor.

3. Upon application by the Board of Management, the Supervisory Board or one or more shareholders whose shares represent in total at least 5% of the share capital or a nominal value of at least 100,000 u.a., the court within whose jurisdiction the registered office is situated may remove an auditor appointed by the General Meeting and appoint another person in his place if there are serious grounds for so doing. Such application shall be made within 2 weeks of the appointment by the General Meeting.

4. Notwithstanding paragraph 3, the auditor may not be removed by the General Meeting before expiry of his term of office save where there are serious grounds for so doing. He shall be entitled to take part in any discussions concerning his removal.

5. The auditor shall be entitled to withdraw from his contract where there are serious grounds for so doing.

Article 204a

[Remuneration]

1. The auditor's remuneration shall be fixed by the General Meeting or, if he is appointed by the court, by the latter, before commencement of his duties.
2. No remuneration or benefits may be granted to him for auditing the accounts other than the remuneration fixed in pursuance of paragraph 1.

Article 205

[Object of audit]

The auditor shall ascertain whether the accounting system, the annual accounts and the annual report, insofar as the latter reviews developments in the company's business and position during the previous financial year, comply with this Statute, the Statutes of the company and the principles of regular and proper accounting.

Article 206

[Auditor's right to examine and check documents and assets]

1. In carrying out his duties, the auditor shall be completely free to examine and check any documents and assets of the SE.
2. He shall be entitled to require any explanation or information that he may consider necessary for the proper execution of his duties.
3. If the carrying out of his duties shall so require, he shall have the like rights in respect of associated undertakings.
4. The auditor may be assisted in his work by colleagues or specialists. They shall have the same rights as the auditor himself and shall act under his responsibility. The auditor and those who assist him shall keep secret all matters of professional confidence.

Article 207

[Auditor's certificate]

1. If, on completion of his audit, the auditor has no objection to make in respect of the annual accounts or annual report, he shall issue a written certificate to this effect.

2. If he has any objection to make in respect of the annual accounts, he shall qualify his certificate as appropriate or withhold it altogether.

Article 208

[Auditor's report]

The auditor shall, within three months following the end of the financial year, draw up a written report on the results of his audit. The report must contain at least the following information:

(a) whether he has carried out the audit in accordance with Article 205;

(b) any infringements of this Statute, the Statutes of the company or the principles of regular and proper accounting which he has discovered in the accounting system, the annual accounts or the annual report;

(c) any matters which he has discovered which might jeopardize the financial position of the SE, or substantially impair its future prospects or which indicate serious infringements by the Board of Management otherwise than in respect of preparation of the accounts, of any of the provisions of this Statute or of the Statutes of the company;

(d) the complete text of the certificate issued under Article 207. If the certificate is qualified or a certificate has been withheld, the reasons therefor shall be given.

Article 209

[Liability of auditor]

1. An auditor shall be fully liable to the SE, to its shareholders and to third parties for all loss or damage resulting from his failure to observe the provisions of this Statute or from any other breach of the obligations imposed on him in carrying out his duties. If more than one auditor shall have been appointed, all auditors shall be liable jointly and severally. An auditor shall not, however, be liable if he can prove that no fault is attributable to him.

Such liability shall continue for a period of three years as from the day of publication in the Official Journal of the European Communities pursuant to Article 219, or, in the event of harmful acts or omissions having been concealed, as from the time of their discovery.

2. As regards any action brought by the SE in respect of such liability Article 72 shall be of corresponding application.

Article 210

[Audit of consolidated accounts]

The provisions of this section shall apply to the audit of the consolidated accounts and report of a group of companies or of part of a group of companies.